Understanding China

If the West wishes to understand China better, it needs to appreciate the depth of thought and range of debate that is taking place within the Chinese political system. China is entering a new and complicated phase in its development. From a minnow in the 1970s it has become a mighty player on the global stage. It is likely that its role in the global economy and international relations will continue to expand. Today, despite its vast size, China is still a developing country. The country's leaders in the Communist Party of China face innumerable policy challenges. Two key issues facing the Party are its role in the Asia-Pacific region and the ideological legacy from Karl Marx. The CPC is engaged in deep research, debate and reflection on both of these questions. This study provides a unique, in-depth insight into these critically important issues for the evolution of China's political economy.

Peter Nolan is Professor of Chinese Development and Director of the Centre of Development Studies, University of Cambridge, UK.

Routledge Studies on the Chinese Economy

Series Editor: Peter Nolan
Director, Centre of Development Studies; Chong Hua Professor in Chinese Development; and Director of the Chinese Executive Leadership Programme (CELP), University of Cambridge

Founding Series Editors: Peter Nolan, University of Cambridge and Dong Fureng, Beijing University

The aim of this series is to publish original, high-quality, research-level work by both new and established scholars in the West and the East, on all aspects of the Chinese economy, including studies of business and economic history.

Routledge Studies on the Chinese Economy – Chinese Economists on Economic Reform

Understanding China

The Silk Road and the Communist Manifesto

Peter Nolan

Routledge
Taylor & Francis Group

LONDON AND NEW YORK

First published 2016
by Routledge
2 Park Square, Milton Park, Abingdon, Oxon OX14 4RN

and by Routledge
711 Third Avenue, New York, NY 10017

Routledge is an imprint of the Taylor & Francis Group, an informa business

British Library Cataloguing in Publication Data
A catalogue record for this book is available from the British Library

Library of Congress Cataloging in Publication Data

Nolan, Peter, 1949-
Understanding China: the Silk Road and the Communist manifesto / Peter Nolan.
    pages cm. — (Routledge studies on the Chinese economy; 60)
Includes bibliographical references and index.
    1. China—Economic conditions—2000– 2. Economic development—China. 3. China—
    Foreign economic relations. 4. China—Commerce—History. I. Title.
HC427.95.N653 2016
330.951—dc23   2015019540

ISBN: 978-1-138-94356-8 (hbk)
ISBN: 978-1-138-64464-9 (pbk)
ISBN: 978-1-315-67238-0 (ebk)

Typeset in Times New Roman
by codeMantra

MIX
Paper from
responsible sources
FSC
www.fsc.org   FSC® C013056

Printed and bound in Great Britain by
TJ International Ltd, Padstow, Cornwall

For Siobain, Dermot and Maeve.

I am most grateful to Elizabeth Briggs for her expert editing.

Contents

List of Tables

Introduction

China is entering a new and complicated phase in its development. From a minnow in the 1970s, it has become a mighty player on the global stage. It is likely that its role in the global economy and international relations will continue to expand. Today, despite its vast size, China is still a developing country. The country's leaders in the Communist Party of China (CPC) face innumerable policy challenges. Two key issues facing the Party are its role in the Asia-Pacific region and its ideological legacy from Karl Marx. The CPC is engaged in deep research into and reflection on both of these questions. If the West wishes to understand China better, it needs to appreciate the depth of thought and range of debate that is taking place within the Chinese political system about these issues.

The four chapters in this book each relate to a different aspect of these core issues facing the Chinese leadership. Chapter One examines China's long-term relationship with Central and Southeast Asia in the 2,000 years prior to the Industrial Revolution. Up until the eighteenth century China was by far the world's largest and most vibrant economy. Many of the key technologies that led to the British Industrial Revolution found their way from China to Europe via merchants along the Silk Road by land and sea. Chapter Two concerns the penetration of the Asia-Pacific region by countries from the industrialized West in the nineteenth and twentieth centuries, after the Industrial Revolution gave the West unrivalled global economic and military power. The West's violent conquest has left a legacy of property rights over the West's distant territories across the world, including, especially, the Asia-Pacific, in China's own 'backyard'. These rights are enshrined in the United Nation's Convention on the Law of the Sea (UNCLOS), which provides legal protection for the 'Exclusive Economic Zones' (EEZs) around the distant possessions of Western countries. Chapter Three addresses the core ideological issue for the Communist Party of China, namely the way in which to interpret and make use of the intellectual legacy of Karl Marx in analyzing the policy challenges facing China in the era ahead. The question of what 'communism' means for China is of great ideological and practical importance for China today. Chapter Four examines the issue of class struggle. During the Cultural Revolution, China experienced widespread 'class struggle', which was essentially violent inter-factional fighting among political groups. The deep impact of the market economy since the 1980s has produced wide socio-economic differences within China. The way in which class struggle took place in Britain is of great interest for China's leaders, who are trying to understand how Britain avoided 'class warfare' during the Industrial Revolution and instead took the 'Parliamentary Road to Socialism'.

When Chairman Mao died in 1976 China was mired in deep poverty and was minuscule in terms of the global economy. In December 1978 the Third Plenum of the Eleventh Central Committee of the Communist Party of China set out the broad guidelines for 'reform and opening up' of the Chinese economy under the leadership of the CPC. Few people outside China believed this project would succeed. When President Gorbachev visited China in May 1989 the demonstration in Tian An Men Square prevented him from leaving the building by the front door. The demonstration was suppressed violently on June 4th in the full spotlight of the global media. By the end of 1989 communist party rule had collapsed throughout Eastern Europe. In February 1990 the communist party formally ended its seventy-year rule in the Soviet Union, and in December 1991 the Soviet Union ceased to exist, breaking up into different countries. The widely held consensus in the West following the events in China in 1989 and those in Eastern Europe and the Soviet Union in 1989–91 was that communist party rule would not survive for long in China. Moreover, in the consensus view the history of the communist bloc, from East Germany to Vietnam, demonstrated the impossibility of a communist party leading a 'transition' to a market economy. In this widely repeated view, 'regime change' was a necessary condition for a market economy to operate. Almost the entire apparatus of Western scholarship, with policy advice from the international 'Washington Consensus' institutions, from Western politicians and in the Western media, was united in its belief that communist party rule in China would not survive, and in the unlikely event that it did so, it would be unable to build a successful market economy.[1]

It is now a quarter of a century on from 1989–90 and the picture looks very different from the one that was widely expected and hoped for in the West. The collapse of the 'Evil Empire' in the Soviet Union was not followed by the collapse of communist party rule in China. The 'regime change' in China that many people still hope for and work towards has not happened. The CPC has eighty-seven million members, and in 2021 it will celebrate the centenary of the founding of the party. Under communist party rule, China has experienced the most remarkable era of growth and development in modern history. Under the protective umbrella of political and social stability, China achieved three decades of high-speed growth. The Chinese government orchestrated a massive, sustained programme of infrastructure construction, including roads, railways, ports, airports, dams, electricity generation and distribution facilities, telecommunications, water and sewage systems, and housing, on a proportional scale far exceeding that of comparable developing countries, such as India, Indonesia, Pakistan and Bangladesh.

China's reforms permitted the gradual extension of market competition into most segments of the economy. By following a path of cautious, experimental reforms, 'groping for stones to cross the river', system change took place gradually, which allowed the population to become slowly accustomed to the transition from the state-administered economy to a market-driven one. The gradual, experimental process also permitted policy-makers to solve problems in a sequential fashion, while keeping control over the overall path of system change. The reforms released the productive energies of indigenous firms, attracted investment from most of the leading international firms, and permitted the rapid absorption of advanced technologies, which enabled China to enjoy on a massive scale the 'advantages of the latecomer'. China today has the world's largest economy. It is the world's largest country in terms of its international trade. It is the largest country also in terms of its manufacturing output, surpassing that of the United States by one-third and exceeding that of France, Germany, Japan and the UK combined. Since the 1980s, levels of poverty have fallen remarkably, and the real standard of living of almost every social group has improved significantly.

Despite the remarkable progress, China confronts large and well-documented policy challenges as it attempts to move from a low-middle-income to a high-income country. The challenges include an ageing population, exhaustion of the rural labour surplus, corruption, heavy environmental pollution, a low level of indigenous innovation, the weak global competitive position of indigenous firms, wide disparities in income and wealth and a hostile international environment. The Decision of the Third Plenum of the Eighteenth Central Committee of the CPC held in November 2013 identified the comprehensive nature of the challenges and outlined the roadmap for system reform in the coming era (Central Committee, 2013). The Decision reiterated the need to conceive of reform in a 'systematic, integrated and coordinated fashion', which promoted the 'development of the socialist market economy, democratic politics, advanced culture, a harmonious society and ecological progress'. It emphasized that the market should play 'the decisive role in allocating resources' and that the government should 'greatly reduce' its role in allocating resources. There should be continued investigation of how to 'strike the balance between the role of the government and that of the market'. The Decision stressed that building a 'socialist market economy with Chinese characteristics' required 'putting the promotion of social fairness, justice and improvement of people's lives as the starting point and ultimate goal'. In order to achieve these goals the Decision emphasized that China needed to 'reform the income distribution system, promote common prosperity' and ensure 'equal access to basic public services'. It stressed the need to 'deepen political system reform' while 'upholding the leadership of the Party': 'We should build a socialist country with the rule of law and develop people's democracy with wider, more adequate and sound participation'. The Decision characterized China as entering a 'new phase' in which the reforms were in a 'deep water zone'. In this phase China 'faces tough choices' and will need to 'ford dangerous rapids'. In order to surmount these multiple challenges the Party needed to 'shatter the fetters of outdated concepts', 'emancipate the mind', and 'seek the truth from the facts'. It needed to be 'realistic and pragmatic' and 'base itself on reality'. It needed to 'summarize useful domestic experience and learn from useful experience from other countries'.

China's gradual return towards the position of relative global economic importance that it held prior to the Industrial Revolution raises profound issues for its international relations. For over 2,000 years from the Han Dynasty (206 BC-220 AD) through to the late eighteenth century, China was the most economically and technologically advanced part of the world. Throughout most of this period China had deep commercial and cultural interaction with Central Asia and the lands around the Eastern and Southern Seas. The 'tributary system' constituted the diplomatic symbol of these relationships. Chapter One explores the historical evidence on these relationships. Through its deep commercial interaction with the region around it, Chinese technology spread not only to these regions, but also to Europe. Many of the key technologies of the Industrial Revolution had their origin in China. After the Industrial Revolution the West's relationship with the Asia-Pacific region altered dramatically. Within half a century Britain had supplanted China as the 'workshop of the world'. The economic revolution laid the foundation for a military and naval revolution, which enabled the countries of the West to establish their far-flung colonial empires. The Central Committee's Decision (Central Committee, 2013) identifies the Silk Road by Land and Sea as a core aspect of China's international relations in the period ahead. China is in a position to make use of its rich experience in domestic infrastructure construction in order to make a major contribution to the development of the Silk Road in Central and Southeast Asia. This holds out enormous promise for stimulating harmonious relations between the countries along the Silk Road by Land and Sea. Indeed, it holds out the prospect for European renewal, using its rich reservoir of financial and human capital to participate in and contribute to the development of the vast territories along the Silk Road.

Chapter Two analyses the legacy of Western colonial history in the shape of the United Nations' Convention on the Law of the Sea (UNCLOS). This treaty permits each country to establish an 'exclusive economic zone' (EEZ) of 200 nautical miles from its territory within which it has exclusive rights over the resources in and under the sea. China has around 0.9 million square kilometres of undisputed EEZ and is in dispute with several countries about the EEZ in the South China Sea. Even if China won all of these disputes, it would still have an EEZ of less than three million sq. km. This is less than one-tenth of the area of EEZs legally controlled under UNCLOS by countries from the West (Russia, the United States, France, Britain, Australia and New Zealand) in and around the Pacific Ocean, which they possess as a consequence of their colonial rule in China's own 'backyard'. In December 2014 Denmark claimed 0.9 million sq. km of the North Pole as part of its EEZ, which includes 149,000 sq. km around Denmark, a further 262,000 sq. km around the Faroe Islands and no less than 4.4 million sq. km around Denmark's huge 'autonomous' overseas territory of Greenland, far from the Danish mainland. Denmark's claim to the North Pole Territory rests mainly on the fact that the 1,800 km-long Lomonosov Ridge, which extends from Canada to the waters above Siberia, is connected to Greenland (*Financial Times,* 16 December 2014). Consideration of the West's vast overseas territories legally held under UNCLOS, in defence of which Western countries are willing to go to war,[2] puts China's claims in the South China Sea in a different perspective, especially when considered in relation to China's 2,000 year-long relationship with the region.

Since 1949 China has been led by the Communist Party of China. There is every likelihood that it will continue to lead the country for the foreseeable future. The Central Committee's Decision of November 2013 expresses the intention to 'build the Party into an innovative, service-oriented and learning Marxist govern-ing Party', and to 'improve the Party's art of leadership and governance'. As part of the endeavour to 'shatter the fetters of outdated concepts' and 'emancipate the mind', communist party members have been engaged in deep study of the original texts of Karl Marx and Friedrich Engels in order to consider their relevance to negotiating the 'deep water zone' that China is entering. No text is more impor-tant in this exercise than the *Manifesto of the Communist Party*, written by Marx and Engels in 1848. Chapter Three is devoted to a re-examination of this text in the light of conditions of the early twenty-first century. Engels welcomed the prospect of violent class warfare in Britain, which never came about. For Marx, the 'communist revolution' was an evolutionary process in which capitalism pro-duced the class that would take control of the very system that had produced it. The violent seizure of power through a *coup d'état* idea by a minority 'vanguard' party indicated that the working class had not yet reached maturity through the development of capitalism. The process through which the working class took control politically and the degree of conflict involved could not be predicted. In the case of Britain, the classic example of capitalism and the country with which Marx was the most familiar, he believed that a peaceful evolutionary path towards the working class becoming the dominant political power was feasible. By the time of his death in 1883 Britain had already advanced along this path, includ-ing the development of trade unionism, extension of the franchise, and a wide array of Parliamentary Acts to ameliorate the living and working conditions of the working class. The fact that the process was peaceful did not make it any less 'revolutionary' or any less 'communist'.

In attempting to ensure a stable and harmonious development in the era ahead, China's leadership is acutely aware of the immense damage experienced as a result of so-called 'class struggles' (*jieji douzheng*) during the Cultural Revolution. As market forces have increasingly deeply penetrated the economy, inequalities of income, wealth and social status have widened alarmingly. Marx and Engels emphasized the potential for class inequality to turn into violent 'class warfare'. A large part of the Central Committee's Decision (Central Committee, 2013) is focused on ways in which to achieve a fairer and more just society, with 'common prosperity' and 'equal access to public services regardless of income'.

Large sections of the Decision are concerned with reform of the systems of government, law, income distribution and social welfare. The planned reforms are directed towards 'expanding citizens' orderly political participation' at all lev-els of the system of people's congresses, from the grass roots to provincial and central levels. The foundation of the legal system is the Constitution, which has 'supreme authority' and 'guarantees the long-term peace and stability of the coun-try'. The Decision promises: 'We will uphold the principle that everyone is equal before the law, and no organization or individual has the privilege of overstepping the Constitution and laws'. The ambitious objective is to ensure that 'the people are satisfied with the equality and justice in every court verdict'. The Decision includes major reforms in the education system, including 'abolition of the prac-tice of establishing key schools or classes' and putting into practice a system in which students 'stay in the same school within their respective district throughout their nine-year compulsory education without taking any examinations'. The distribution of income will be mainly regulated through taxation, social security and transfer payments. The goal is to establish 'an individual income and property information system, protect legitimate incomes, regulate excessively high incomes, redefine and clear away hidden incomes, outlaw illegal incomes, increase the incomes of low-income groups, and increase the proportion of the middle-income groups in society as a whole'. Reform of the social security system aims to achieve a 'balanced development of the minimum living allowance in both urban and rural areas' and to 'place the basic old-age pension under unified national planning'. The government plans to undertake a 'comprehensive reform in medical security, medical care, public health and the medicine supply and regulatory system', and to 'extend the medical insurance system to all the people'.

Britain was the country in which the First Industrial Revolution took place and in which 'the proletariat can be studied in all its relations and from all sides' (Engels, 1845: 50). It is also the country in which Marx and Engels spent most of their adult lives and in which they both died. 'Class struggle' was central to their understanding of the propulsive force of historical change. Translating this term into Chinese is fraught with difficulty. The standard Chinese translation is '*jieji douzheng*'. This term was used to describe the violent, destructive political fighting in China during the Cultural Revolution. In fact, as Chapter Four demonstrates, the history of class struggle in Britain rarely approached the violent 'class warfare' that Engels in *The Condition of the English Working Class* predicted would take place in Britain and 'in comparison with which the French Revolution and the year 1794 [The Great Terror] will prove to have been child's play' (Engels, 1845: 233). In fact, Britain experienced a long, slow, evolutionary path towards resolving 'class struggle' through trade union organization and following the 'Parliamentary Road to Socialism'. China's leaders are studying this experience closely.

Notes

1. See Nolan, 1995, for a detailed analysis of these issues.
2. The Falklands War was fought by the UK in defence of its distant territories of the Falkland Islands, South Georgia and South Sandwich Islands, which have a combined EEZ of 1.8 million sq. km., which is twice the size of China's undisputed EEZ.

Bibliography

Communist Party of China, Third Plenary Session of the Eighteenth Central Committee (2013) 'Decision of the Central Committee of the CPC on some major issues concerning comprehensively deepening the reform', Beijing.

Engels, F. (1969) Preface to the first English edition of *The Condition of the Working Class in England*, Panther edition, with Foreword by E. Hobsbawm, originally published in German 1845 and in English 1892.

Nolan, P. (1995) *China's Rise, Russia's Fall*, London: Macmillan.

1 The Silk Road by Land and Sea[1]
Yi Dai Yi Lu （一带一路）

In 1987, twenty exquisite pieces of colored glaze were excavated at the under-ground chamber of Famen Temple in Shaanxi, China. These East Roman Islamic relics were brought into China during the Tang Dynasty. Marveling at these exotic relics, I thought hard and concluded that as we approach the world's different civilizations, we should not limit ourselves to just admiring the exquisiteness of the objects involved. Rather, we should try to learn and appreciate the cultural significance behind them. Instead of only satisfying ourselves with their artistic presentation of people's life in the past, we should do our best to breathe new life into their inherent spirit.

(President Xi Jinping, Speech at the UNESCO headquarters, 28 March 2014)

Introduction

In 2011–12 the United States announced a major shift of strategic direction towards an emphasis on the Asia-Pacific region:

> US economic and security interests are inextricably linked to developments in the arc extending from the Western Pacific and East Asia into the Indian Ocean region and South Asia, creating a mix of evolving challenges and opportunities. Accordingly, while the US military will continue to contribute to security globally, *we will of necessity rebalance toward the Asia-Pacific region.*
>
> (US Department of Defense, 2012: 2)(emphasis added)

US Secretary of State Hillary Clinton affirmed that 'the twenty-first century will be America's Pacific century, just like previous centuries have been' (Clinton, 2012). She expanded on the shift in US strategic direction:

> The future of politics will be decided in Asia, not Afghanistan or Iraq and the United States will be right at the centre of the action … One of the most important tasks of American statecraft over the next decade will therefore be to lock in substantially increased investment – diplomatic, economic, strategic, and otherwise – in the Asia Pacific region.
>
> (Clinton, 2011)

Constructing a network of Asian political and military alliances is a critically important part of US international relations strategy in the decades ahead. The United States believes that its renewed involvement in Asia is vital to the region's future:

> The region is eager for our leadership and our business – perhaps more than at any time in modern history. We are the only power with a network of strong alliances in the region, no territorial ambitions and a long record of providing for the common good ... Our challenge now is to build a web of relationships across the Pacific that is as durable and as consistent with American interests and values as the web we have built across the Atlantic.
>
> (Clinton, 2011)

Until around 200 years ago Europe's knowledge of Central and Southeast Asia, as well as China itself, was extremely limited and mainly acquired second-hand through the intermediary of trade with East Asia via the Silk Road by Land and Sea. When Captain Cook made his famous voyages of exploration between 1768 and 1779 the Asia-Pacific region was hardly known to Europeans. When Britain's North American colonies announced their independence from Britain in 1776, the United States consisted of a small group of colonial settlers huddled together in the eastern fringes of the vast continent of North America.[2] The west coast state of California, which looks out on the Pacific Ocean, only became part of the 'United States' in 1850.

China's President Xi Jinping has made the policy of 'The New Silk Road by Land and Sea', which connects China with the West, a key part of China's international relations. On 7 September 2013, President Xi proposed to build a 'Silk Road Economic Belt' during his speech at Kazakhstan's Nazarbayev University. On 3 October 2013, he proposed to build a 'Twenty-first Century Maritime Silk Road' during his speech at the Indonesian House of Representatives. For over 2,000 years China has had a deep inter-relationship with the surrounding regions of Asia. China has had extensive long-term trade and cultural interactions with Central Asia through Xinjiang and with Southeast Asia through the Southern Sea (Nan Hai). Xinjiang and the Southern Sea constitute China's 'doorway' into Central and Southeast Asia, respectively.

In 2013 President Xi visited Central Asia, including Uzbekistan, Turkmenistan, Kyrgyzstan and Kazakhstan. The visit was especially significant, as no US president has visited the post-Soviet states of Central Asia. President Xi also visited Southeast Asia, including Malaysia and Indonesia. In spring 2014 he visited Europe. In a sequence of speeches during these visits he clarified China's conception of the bridge between China and Europe along the New Silk Road by Land and Sea. He paid close attention to the importance of infrastructure development, including ports, airports, roads, rail, water, electricity and telecommunications. These are vital in order to stimulate commercial relations, which are the foundation of enhanced mutual understanding.

In each of his visits President Xi Jinping stressed the importance of an appreciation of history for mutual understanding:

> For any country in the world, the past always holds the key to the present and the present is always rooted in the past. Only when we know where a country has come from, could we possibly understand why the country is what it is today, and only then could we realize in which direction it is heading.
>
> (Xi Jinping, 2014b)

He emphasized the contribution that commercial relations make to cultural interaction and peaceful development. He repeatedly drew attention to the importance of enhanced mutual understanding of culture for peaceful development:

> History tells us that only by interacting with and learning from others can a civilization enjoy full vitality. If all civilizations can uphold inclusiveness, the so-called 'clash of civilizations' will be out of the question and the harmony of civilizations will become reality.
>
> (Xi Jinping, 2014a)

China and Europe stand at either end of the New Silk Road. His speeches drew attention to the long connections between China and Europe from ancient times along both the land and the sea routes: 'We need to build a bridge of common cultural prosperity linking the two major civilizations of China and Europe. China represents in an important way the Eastern civilization, while Europe is the birthplace of the Western civilization' (Xi Jinping, 2014a). In his visit he emphasized the contribution that the spread of ideas from China along the Silk Road had made to European development:

> China's Four Great Inventions, namely, papermaking, gunpowder, movable-type printing and compass, led to changes in the world, including the European Renaissance. China's philosophy, literature, medicine, silk, porcelain and tea reached the West and became part of people's daily life. *The Travels of Marco Polo* generated a widespread interest in China.
>
> (Xi Jinping, 2014a)

President Xi stressed the importance of Central Asia and Southeast Asia as bridges to link China and Europe: 'A bridge not only makes life more convenient; it could also be a symbol of communication, understanding and friendship. I have come to Europe to build, together with our European friends, a bridge of friendship and cooperation across the Eurasian continent' (Xi Jinping, 2014b).

The Land Route: Xi Yu, the Western Region

In the second century BC, China began working on the Silk Road leading to the Western Regions. In 138 BC and 119 BC, Envoy Zhang Qian of the

Han Dynasty made two trips to those regions, spreading the Chinese culture there and bringing into China grape, alfalfa, pomegranate, flax, sesame and other products. The Tang Dynasty saw dynamic interactions between China and other countries. According to historical documents, the dynasty exchanged envoys with over seventy countries, and Chang'An, the capital of Tang, bustled with envoys, merchants and students from other countries. Exchanges of such a magnitude helped the spread of the Chinese culture to the rest of the world and the introduction into China of the cultures and products from other countries.

(Xi Jinping, Speech at the UNESCO Headquarters, 2014)

Economic Geography

The 'Western Region' (Xi Yu), or 'Greater Turkestan', is the heartland of the Silk Road by Land. It spans a territory that stretches for around 1,000 miles from Yu Men Guan ('Jade Gate') in China's Gansu province to the Oxus River (Amu Darya) in western Uzbekistan. The source of true jade stone (nephrite) is in the mountain slopes and river beds around Khotan, in the heart of Xinjiang. The Western Region is divided in two by the Tian Shan-Kun Lun Mountain Ranges. 'Inner Turkestan' in Xinjiang and 'Outer Turkestan' in Central Asia have been intimately inter-connected for over 2,000 years through trade and inter-mingling of the diverse people who live in the 'Greater Turkestan' region. The key vehicle of trade for over 2,000 years was the Bactrian two-humped camel. Large camel caravans typically had 2–3,000 camels in each.

Xinjiang forms the main part of 'Inner Turkestan'. Owen Lattimore called it 'China's front door to the heart of Asia' (Lattimore, 1950: ix), at its core is the Tak-lamakan Desert in the Tarim Basin. Water from the surrounding mountain chains feeds a series of oases around the perimeter of the Basin. China's first systematic knowledge of Central Asia came through the Emperor Wu Di's envoy, Zhang Qian, who made a thirteen-year journey (from 138–126 BC) through Xinjiang into Central Asia in order to report on the 'Western Regions'. The First Great Wall was constructed in 221–206 BC, in order partly to protect the trade routes through Xinjiang to Central Asia. China's entrance to the 'Western Region' was made through the 'Jade Gate' that was erected under the Han Dynasty emperor Wu Di, who ruled from 141–87 BC. The Jade Gate is located at the terminus of the Great Wall, at the western end of the Hexi Corridor, which is squeezed between the Gobi Desert to the north and the Tibetan massif to the south.

Although Xinjiang has 'lain within China's political horizon for more than two thousand years', China's control over Xinjiang has been intermittent (Lattimore, 1950: 5). During the Han (206 BC–220 AD), Tang (618–907 AD), Yuan (1271–1368) and Qing (1644–1911) dynasties, there were periods of direct Chinese control over Xinjiang, in which there was a 'Pax Sinica' in the relationship between Xinjiang and Central Asia. China only once made a serious effort to establish control over territories to the west of Xinjiang. In 751 AD the army of the Muslim Abbasid caliphate defeated the Chinese army in the battle of Talas, which is in today's Kyrgyzstan. Thereafter, China did not attempt to expand its frontiers beyond the Tian Shan mountain range into Central Asia.

The Western Region has been linked by trade for millennia with the Middle East, Russia and India:

> The pre-history of Inner Asia can now be traced all the way back to the Stone Age migrations and trade over the whole territory between Europe and China … Between the Black Sea and the Yellow River a very ancient line of travel, trade and culture diffusion traversed Inner Asia.
>
> (Lattimore, 1950: 6)

The ancient trade routes survived successive political and religious upheavals. The inter-connected regions of Xinjiang and Central Asia constituted a 'valve' between China, India, the Middle East and Europe, 'through which pulsated the movements of trade, migration and conquest' (Lattimore, 1950: 7).

Transoxiana (ancient Sogdiana) is the core of Central Asia. It lies between the Amur Darya (Oxus) and Sri Darya (Jaxartes) Rivers, which contain the cities of Samarkand and Bukhara, which are at the heart of the Silk Road. A wider definition of the 'broad cultural zone' of Central Asia includes Afghanistan, northern Pakistan and Xinjiang. At an early point in its history the region developed a complex irrigation system and urban settlements. In the first century BC, the Greek geographer Strabo described Central Asia as a 'land of 1,000 cities', including great urban trading and manufacturing centres surrounded by rich agricultural regions, such as Balkh, Merv and Afrasaib (Samarkand) (Starr, 2013: 29). The trade links of these cities reached India, the Middle East and China:

> The distinctive achievement of Central Asia cities [in late antiquity] was to have combined the organizational sophistication required by large-scale irrigation systems with export-oriented agriculture and manufactures and to have nurtured large cadres of traders who travelled the world and businessmen who managed their trade.
>
> (Starr, 2013: 35)

There were prosperous kingdoms around Transoxiana, which included Chorasmia (to the west), Bactria (to the south) and Ferghana (to the east). The region was open to invasion from all directions and has only intermittently been united under a single ruler. However, powerful common influences affected the whole region, mainly spread through trade. The most important of these were Buddhism and Islam, but they included also Zoroastrianism and Sufism.

The Buddhist Era

Trade. In a series of military campaigns in 73–49 BC China established complete control over the Tarim Basin, occupying the main cities around the Taklamakan

Desert. Through the conquest of Xinjiang China became the 'undisputed master of the Tarim', which allowed the caravan route linking China to the West to be brought into regular use (Talbot-Rice, 1965: 175). The introduction of Chinese agricultural technology and irrigation techniques helped the development of a series of 'oasis kingdoms' on either side of the desert, including Hami, Turfan, Urumqi, Aksu, Kashgar, Yarkand and Khotan. By the first century AD they were already important trading centres. The Silk Road followed routes to the north and south of the Taklamakan Desert, as well as through Dzungaria, to the north of the Tian Shan Mountains.

The Silk Road developed during the Han Dynasty (206 BC–220 AD), when Europe was united under Roman rule.[3] China's imports from Central Asia consisted of a wide variety of goods, including warhorses, spices, fragrances, wine, precious stones (e.g., lapis lazuli), gold and silverware and glassware. Although silk textiles were for a long period China's main export to Central Asia, the region had its own ancient textile industry, much of it for export. It developed its own silk textile industry, learning from Chinese technology. Moreover, Central Asia developed its own paper industry based also on Chinese technology, which Central Asia improved upon, substituting cotton fibre for silk (Starr, 2013: 46–7). The main body of China's exports consisted of silk yarn and silk fabrics. By the end of the Zhou Dynasty (221 BC) the art of glass-making had spread to China from the West (Sullivan, 1964: 187).

In the final centuries of the Roman Empire, much of the trade across Central Asia passed through the Kushan kingdom. At its peak in the first to the third centuries AD, the kingdom united much of Central Asia as well as north-western India. A network of roads linked the Kushan kingdom with India, China and the Middle East: 'By these means the Kushan Empire was brought into contact with the world's great cultural centres. And wherever caravans and, more especially, the silk caravans passed, intellectual and cultural exchanges took place' (Talbot-Rice, 1965: 142). Archaeological excavations of the great treasury in the Kushan summer palace at Kapisi[4] in Afghanistan, revealed a wide variety of exotic wares, including bronze sculptures from the Mediterranean, Indian ivory carvings and lacquer ware from China. It almost certainly contained silk products from China, but these had perished (Liu Xinru, 2010: 48).

Towards the end of its rule the Han Dynasty lost control over Xinjiang and the Kushan Empire collapsed. However, large quantities of Chinese silk continued to pass through Central Asia, 'thanks largely to autonomous trading networks sustained by religious institutions, merchants' organizations and local communities' (Liu Xinru, 2010: 62). Throughout the Buddhist era silk remained the most frequently traded commodity along the Silk Road (Liu Xinru, 2010: 72). While the great empires fell apart, the oasis cities along the Central Asian Silk Road survived and prospered. This section of the Silk Road had developed into a 'relatively stable and viable commercial highway' (Liu Xinru, 2010: 64). Following the collapse of the Roman Empire, silk continued to hold an important place in Byzantium. Although it developed its own weaving industry the silk yarn was imported from China via Central Asia (Liu Xinru, 2010: 74).

Due to the key role occupied by their merchants, Central Asian cities became 'the main international *entrepôts* for the entire Eurasian continent', constituting 'the major centre for banking and finance for trade between China, India and the Middle East' (Starr, 2013: 44). The cities of Central Asia were not only the headquarters of extensive trading networks, they also were centres of manufacturing production, much of it for export, including high-quality steel products such as blades, screws, crankshafts and pumps, glassware, drugs, a wide variety of exotic products (Schafer, 1985) and, even, musical instruments. These were among the numerous products that were exported to China and elsewhere along the Silk Road.

Although China was by far the world's most important producer of silk yarn[5] and textiles, Central Asia became increasingly skilled at producing its own silk textiles. By the fifth and sixth centuries a complex two-way exchange in specialist silk products and technical progress developed between China and Central Asia (Liu Xinru, 2010: 80). By the end of the eighth century the technology and production of silk threads from silkworms had spread all the way from Central Asia to the Middle East, including Byzantium and North Africa. The most important production base developed in the Sogdian trading cities of present-day Uzbekistan.

Silk garments became increasingly gorgeous. The art of 'cut silk' (*ke si*) was developed by the Sogdians, improved upon by the Uighurs and perfected by the Chinese in the eleventh century: 'Before the end of the Middle Ages panels of *ke si* were already reaching Europe and were being incorporated in the cathedral vestments at Danzig, Vienna, Regensburg and elsewhere, while the weavers of Lucca were imitating Chinese phoenixes and dragons, adapting them to the grammar of late medieval ornament' (Sullivan, 1964: 184). The famous Zandaniji silks were produced at Zandan, near Bukhara. The colourful silk brocades with vibrant animal motifs were produced for many centuries and sold all along the Silk Road (Liu Xinru, 2010: 82–3). At one end of the Silk Road, Zandaniji silk textiles adorned medieval European churches and at the other end they adorned the Buddhist caves in Dunhuang (Liu Xinru, 2010: 83).

In the seventh century the Tang Dynasty (618–907 AD) re-established control over the Tarim Basin and the oasis towns around the Taklamakan Desert. Trade with Central Asia reached new heights and 'goods from China were to be found in market towns throughout the Near and Middle East': 'A never-ending stream of camel caravans carried Chinese goods across the highways of Central Asia' (Sickman and Soper, 1956: 143). In the other direction, 'camel caravans carrying exotic commodities arrived in droves at the gates of the Great Wall' (Liu Xinru, 2010: 87). In the seventh and eighth centuries, the Chinese capital, Chang'An (modern Xi'An), was the greatest city in the world:

> The streets were filled with the cosmopolitan populace befitting the capital of such an extensive empire. There were priests from India, officials and merchants from Persia and the kingdoms of Central Asia, Turks, Arabs and traders from Mesopotamia ... There grew up side-by-side the Buddhist and Taoist temples, Muhammedan mosques, Manichean and Nestorian churches.
>
> (Sickman and Soper, 1956: 143)

Culture. As Han military power reached out into Xinjiang and trade relations deepened, Han Dynasty culture was strongly affected by Central Asia. Emperor Wu Di's conquest of Xinjiang permitted Chinese travellers to journey relatively easily to Central Asia. Travellers brought 'tales of the vast deserts and great mountain ranges of Central Asia, of Kun Lun, the axis of the world, of the Huns who fought and hunted over the desert and of India, the home of a strange new religion' (Sullivan, 1964: 217). Han Dynasty art is 'full of Western [i.e., Central Asian] themes ... Evidence of this receptiveness is everywhere in Han art' (Sullivan, 1964: 217). The 'heavenly horses' imported from Uzbekistan became the royal symbol of the Han Empire and they were deeply embedded in the iconography of the Han Dynasty (Liu Xinru, 2010: 18).

A succession of different people and cultures have influenced Central Asia through conquest, trade and missionary activity. Alexander the Great conquered Bactria and Sogdiana in 334–323 BC. The Greeks established numerous walled cities in Central Asia and many Greek settlers remained after the collapse of Alexander's empire in Central Asia. Hellenistic culture had a deep influence on Central Asia, but this became interwoven with Buddhist culture from north India. The deep influence of Buddhism upon Chinese culture, mediated through Central Asia, began during the Han Dynasty: 'It is hard to imagine that Central Asia was for nearly a millennium as deeply Buddhist as it is Muslim today. But from the first or second century BC to the Arab conquest, this was the case' (Starr, 2013: 81).[6]

The historic Buddha lived around 500 BC. He was a prince in the state of Magadha in what is now Nepal. Buddhism spread into Central Asia from northern India under the Kushans. The kingdom's coins bore the image of their rulers on one face and the image of the Buddha on the other. The artistic styles of the Kushan Empire were strongly Hellenistic, brought about largely through the silk trade. These became fused with Indian Buddhist styles to produce the archetypical Buddhist sculptural and painting style, which spread from Gandhara in northern India to Central Asia and from there into China. A vast quantity of Buddhist buildings, art and sculpture were produced in Central Asia in the pre-Muslim era. Buddhist merchants contributed to monasteries along the Silk Road and the monasteries themselves frequently became large commercial enterprises. Before the Islamic conquest of Central Asia in the eighth century 'Buddhist institutions provided the infrastructure all along the eastern Eurasian section of the Silk Road' (Liu Xinru, 2010: 72). Like their later European counterparts, the monasteries produced religious objects of great beauty, often encrusted with jewels and precious stones. Their products included murals, statues, temples and silk paintings, as well as giant Buddhas carved upon of cliff faces: 'From Bamiyan [in Afghanistan] to Yun Gang [in Shanxi province] Buddhist monuments lined the entire length of the Central Asian Silk Road' (Liu Xinru, 2010: 64).

Buddhism reached China around 120 BC by means of both merchants and missionaries along the caravan routes through Central Asia into China. For half a millennium after the fall of the Han Dynasty (220 AD) Buddhism became firmly implanted in China: 'The desert road that linked China with the West ... played a role of ever-increasing importance as a high road for ideas and art forms that poured into China' (Sickman and Soper, 1956: 86). The whole of the era from the fourth to the eighth century can be considered as the 'Buddhist Age', not only in China but across the whole of Asia: '[Buddhism] blanketed the whole of the Asian continent, except for Siberia and the Middle East, giving to this vast area a degree of cultural unity that has never been matched since then' (Reischauer and Fairbank, 1958: 147–8).

During the early centuries of its expansion 'Buddhism was nourished by a constant stream of missionaries and pilgrims flowing back and forth between India and China' (Sullivan, 1964: 221). The names exist of almost 200 Chinese monks who made the long and dangerous trip to India to absorb Buddhist teachings at their source. The most famous of these were Fa Xian and Xuan Zang. Fa Xian left for India in 399 AD and made his way across Central Asia and returned to China by sea in 414 AD (Fa Hsien, 1886). In the seventh and early eighth centuries Tang power was at its peak. Under the 'Pax Sinica' missionaries and pilgrims 'could move freely back and forth across Central Asia' (Sullivan, 1964: 224–5). Xuan Zang made a round trip to northern India between 629 and 645. When he returned to China he wrote a famous account of his journey, the *Great Tang Record of the Western Region* (Beales, 1906) and devoted the rest of his life to translating Buddhist texts into Chinese. Central Asian scholars and monks were crucially important in the translation of Buddhist texts into Chinese.[7]

Buddhist monasteries in China accumulated enormous economic resources. They also expanded their functions as 'havens of refuge for the persecuted, inns for travellers, hospitals, public baths and even as primitive banking institutions' (Reischauer and Fairbank, 1958: 175). An enormous array of Buddhist sculptures and paintings was produced in China. They combined Hellenistic, Indian, Central Asian and Chinese artistic traditions in a rich mixture. They include such remarkable sites as Dunhuang, Yun Gang, Long Men and Kucha. Dunhuang, in western Gansu, was an oasis city that grew into a thriving centre of trade and Buddhist learning, thanks to its position on 'the great highway between China and the countries to the West' (Sickman and Soper, 1956: 135). The caves contain a wealth of Buddhist paintings from the end of the fifth century to the eighth century. A magnificent sequence of Buddhist sculptures were produced at Yun Gang, in Shanxi, in the fifth century AD: '[A]ll the polyglot languages of Buddhism as it reached China – Hellenistic, Gandaharan, Indian, Iranian and Central Asian – were beginning to be fused into a consistent declaration of Chinese faith and zeal' (Sickman and Soper, 1956: 90). Luo Yang was the Chinese capital during the Wei Dynasty (386–556 AD). During the sixth century AD there were said to be three thousand foreign monks living there. The site contains a massive central group of Buddhist sculptures cut into the cliff face, as well as thousands of smaller sculptures. Kucha is in western Xinjiang. The Kizil site contains fourteen Buddhist cave complexes with over eight hundred grottoes, with a large number of Buddhist paintings and sculptures produced between the second and seventh centuries AD. Xuan Xang spent two months at Kucha during his visit in the seventh century. Between the years 258–312 AD at least six monks from Kucha were engaged in translating Buddhist texts, including the Lotus Sutra, into Chinese (Ghose, 2008: 12). By the third century, Buddhist monks at Kucha played an important role as 'cultural brokers' between Indian, Central Asian and Chinese Buddhism (Ghose, 2008: 13). Foremost among them was Kumarajiva (344–413), who is said to have translated around 300 Buddhist texts into Chinese (Ghose, 2008: 15).

The cosmopolitan nature of Tang Dynasty China was not only reflected in monumental Buddhist sculptures and monastic sites. The arts and crafts of the Tang display an astonishing array of influences from Central Asia, influenced by the large number of foreigners who lived and worked in Chinese cities as well as by the flow of exotic goods imported from Central Asia (Schafer, 1985).

> Persian and Sassanian shapes, such as the amphora, rhyton and shell-cup, imported in metal, are turned out in pottery; the repoussé decoration of Western silverware is copied in appliqué relief on the sides of pottery ewers; Arab glass cups are reproduced in white porcelain. The foreigners who crowded the streets of Luoyang and Chang'An, carrying on their own trades and practising their own religions, are often portrayed, or caricatured, in lively manner in the pottery tomb-figurines.
>
> (Sullivan, 1964: 215)

In Central Asia, Buddhism came under attack following the Arab conquests of the seventh century. Many Buddhists retreated to Xinjiang, strengthening the already important role of Buddhism in the region. The influence of Buddhism in China was severely checked by the violent attack of 841–845.[8] Thereafter, it never regained its position as a nationwide organized religion analogous to that of Christianity in Europe. However, Buddhism remained an important part of Chinese cultural life, including the extraordinary paintings associated with Chan ('Zen') Buddhism, which fused the Chinese Daoist tradition with Buddhism from India and Central Asia.[9] The tradition reached a peak in the thirteenth century. It included enormous landscapes, portraits, and, above all, still life paintings such as Mu Qi's 'Six Persimmons', in which 'passion has congealed into stupendous calm' (Arthur Waley, quoted in Sickman and Soper, 1956: 263).[10] Following the collapse of the Mongol Yuan Dynasty in China in 1368, the dynasty returned to Mongolia. Thereafter the Mongols became comprehensively converted to Buddhism. By the sixteenth century the dominant form of Buddhism among the Mongols was Tibetan Lamaism. In the main body of China, Buddhism ceased to be a formal religion and was absorbed into Daoism, whereas in Mongolia and Tibet it remained a formal religion based on monasteries and priests.

The Muslim Era

Following the Arab conquest of Persia and Transoxiana in the seventh and eighth centuries, Islam replaced Buddhism as the belief system across Central Asia. Despite many vicissitudes, it remains at the heart of Central Asian culture and today there is little trace of the millennia-long Buddhist era in the region. Muslim influence extended deep into India from Central Asia with the founding of the Mughal Empire, following Babur's victory at the Battle of Panipat in 1526. In the eighth and ninth centuries Central Asia prospered under the rule of the Persian Samanid conquerors, who made Bokhara their capital city: 'Prosperity based on agriculture, handicrafts and trade made their realm the envy of visitors from other parts of the Islamic world' (Soucek, 2000: 73). At the turn of the millennium, the Persian Sassanids were replaced by the Turkic Qarakhanids, who ruled Central Asia until the twelfth century.

Under both the Umayyad (661–750) and the Abbasid (750–1258) caliphates Muslim merchants dominated trade routes across Central Asia: 'Muslim traders soon took over the bulk of the trade on the Silk Road, while Islamic institutions, like the Buddhist ones before them, established themselves on all the major trade routes … [providing] the infrastructure for a large section of the Silk Road' (Liu Xinru, 2010: 106). All along the Silk Road, following the earlier practice of Arab rulers, Islamic patrons built caravanserai, which provided lodging and security for merchants, their animals and their merchandise. For example, between the eleventh and the fourteenth century Anatolia's Seljuk (1037–1144) and the Ottoman (1453–1922) rulers built a series of monumental caravanserai across the region to facilitate trade, especially with Central Asia (Stierlin, 1998).

The Mongol conquests of the thirteenth century across most of Asia wrought great destruction, including both Islamic and Buddhist artefacts. However, in the thirteenth and fourteenth centuries under the Mongols the vast territory from China to the Middle East was part of a united empire. After the violence of the conquest was over, under Mongol rule Central Asia enjoyed relative peace and prosperity, benefiting from its position at the crossroads of civilizations in the heart of the Mongol empire. When Kublai Khan established the capital city of China at Dadu (today's Beijing) in 1257, he brought weavers from Bukhara in order to produce silk brocades, especially the Zanadaniji-style textiles, for the Mongol court: 'Kublai Khan chose to display the imperial glory of his realm by dressing his entire retinue, including the palace guards, in gold brocade' (Liu Xinru, 2010: 123).

It was the unity achieved under the 'Pax Mongolica' that made Marco Polo's journey across Central Asia possible. Marco Polo encountered a long sequence of vibrant commercial cities, including Baghdad and Basra (in today's Iraq), Tabriz, Yazd and Kerman (in today's Iran). Marco Polo wrote in detail about the colourful oasis cities along the Silk Road in Xinjiang, including Yarkand, Pem, Charchan, Kashgar and Khotan. Of Kashgar he writes:

> [It] was once a kingdom, but now it is subject to the Great Khan. It has villages and towns aplenty. Its inhabitants live by trade and industry. They have very fine orchards and vineyards and flourishing estates. Cotton grows here in plenty, besides flax and hemp. The soil is fruitful and productive of all the means of life. This country is the starting-point from which many merchants set out to market their wares all over the world.
>
> (Marco Polo, 1974: 80)

Of Khotan he writes: '[It] is subject to the Great Khan ... It has cities and towns in plenty ... It is amply stocked with the means of life. Cotton grows here in plenty. It has vineyards, estates and orchards in plenty. The people live by trade and industry' (Marco Polo, 1974: 82).

In 1370, the Muslim Turk, Timur seized power in Central Asia and founded a dynasty that ruled the region from 1370–1507. Although his campaigns extended from Xinjiang to Syria, the core of the Timurid empire was Transoxiana. This period was 'the most glorious chapter' in the history of Central Asia (Soucek, 2000: 123). It witnessed a renewed flourishing of long-distance trade, including trade with the Ming Empire. The great trade routes across Central Asia stimulated an era of great prosperity in Anatolia, at the western terminus of the Silk Road. In the thirteenth and fourteenth centuries, China supplied raw silk to the Middle East and Europe in 'unlimited amounts' (Inalcik, 1994: 218).[11] Under both the Seljuk Empire and in the early years of the Ottoman Empire trade conducted mainly by Muslim merchants continued to prosper across Central Asia: 'The high point in the development of silk and wool tapestries and rugs, from the Middle East to Central Asia, came after the Islamic Turks extended their rule from Central Asia to Baghdad, Egypt and Southern Europe' (Liu Xinru, 2010: 107).

These formed the basis for the flourishing silk textile industry in medieval Europe. Bursa, at the heart of the Ottoman Empire, became a 'world market between East and West not only for raw silk but also for other Asian goods as a result of the revolutionary changes in the network of world trade routes in the fourteenth century' (Inalcik, 1994: 219). As well as silk from China, the goods produced and traded along the caravan routes included silk, woollen and cotton textiles, carpets, tapestries and draperies from India and Central Asia, spices, ivory and cloth from Southeast Asia and furs from Siberia (Stierlin, 1998: 60). Moreover, in this period tea began to be exported from China along the Silk Road (Liu Xinru, 2010: 109).

From the ninth century through to the fifteenth century Central Asia made tremendous scientific and artistic progress. The region produced towering intellectual figures who made fundamental advances in mathematics, astronomy, geography, medicine and philosophy, including al-Khwarizmi (783–847), al-Farghani (798–865), al-Khwarajandi (eleventh century), al-Biruni (973–1048), Ibn Sina (Avicenna) (980–1037) and al-Quschi (1402–1474). The most famous figure in Central Asian astronomy was Ulag Beg (1394–1449), who was the virtual ruler of Transoxiana. Among numerous achievements in the arts and sciences, Ulag Beg is renowned for his remarkable *madrassa* in the Registan square in Samarkand and for the observatory he built just outside Samarkand. He catalogued 1,108 fixed stars. Under the Yuan Dynasty, China's Mongol rulers made extensive use of scientists from Central Asia. Kublai Khan introduced doctors from Central Asia to his court and ordered Ibn Sina's *Canon of Medicine* to be translated into Chinese. The same work was used in Indian medicine as well as being translated into Latin and used as a basic medical text in European universities until the eighteenth century. Both the Yuan and Ming Dynasties made extensive use of astronomers from Central Asia. There was an 'astronomical Silk Road', with Muslims from Central

Asia playing an important role in Chinese astronomy. The first Ming Emperor, Tai Zi, established a Muslim Astronomical Bureau in 1368, headed by Jamal al-Din, from Bukhara (Starr, 2013: 452–3). The Bureau operated alongside the traditional Chinese astronomical bureau. Central Asian studies of astronomy were translated into Chinese and Muslim astronomers built an astrolabe, which was installed in Nanjing in 1385, in order to observe the stars.

With traditional technologies, which mainly used camels, transport costs across the Silk Road routes were high and trade along the sea route gradually outpaced that along the land route. Silk yarn and woven fabrics had a high ratio of value to weight. However, as exports of Chinese porcelain, tea and, eventually, cotton textiles increased over the centuries, the balance of advantage in trade with the West shifted from the overland routes across Central Asia towards the long-established maritime routes through Southeast Asia across the Nan Hai. The fact that trade along the Maritime Silk Road increased rapidly after the sixteenth century does not mean that trade along the Central Asia route declined absolutely.

In Central Asia in the sixteenth century the Timurid Dynasty was replaced by the Shaybanids. In the sixteenth and seventeenth centuries the region 'seems to have experienced a period of prosperity and growth' (Soucek, 2000: 150). In the eighteenth and early nineteenth centuries, Khiva, Bukhara and Khoqand were each ruled by a separate khan. Alongside the growth of trade along the maritime route trade along the land route remained vibrant through to the eighteenth century (Levi, 1999), stimulated by interaction with China, the Mughal Empire and the Russian Empire.[12]

The vast Chinese economy experienced continued commercial development and prosperity in the late Ming (1368–1644) and early Qing (1644–1911) Dynasties, which stimulated continued trade with Central Asia through Xinjiang, which was once again brought under direct Chinese rule in the eighteenth century. In the seventeenth and eighteenth centuries an extensive trade developed between northern India and Central Asia. Mughal India generated great demand for the horses of Central Asia, while Central Asia imported cotton, cotton textiles and dyes from Mughal India (Levi, 1999: 528–530). India's Mughal rulers stimulated the growth of trade with Central Asia 'by constructing hundreds of bridges, caravanserai and securing critical trade routes' (Levi, 1999: 529). The khans of Bukhara in the late seventeenth century regularly exchanged diplomatic letters with the Mughal rulers requesting that efforts be made to ensure that the roads be kept safe for merchants (Levi, 1999: 530).

The eastward expansion of the Russian Empire after the sixteenth century stimulated Russian demand for goods produced in South Asia traded through Central Asia. The Ferghana Valley under the Khoqand Khanate experienced rapid economic development in this period:

> Throughout the eighteenth and nineteenth centuries increasingly large quantities of Russian goods were taken from Orenburg to the Khoqand Khanate (1709–1876)[13] and further transported by thousands of Khoqandi merchants across the Tian Shan to Kashgar, Yarkand and other Xinjiang

cities from where a significant percentage of these goods was transported on to more distant markets in China and India. These Khoqandi merchants returned to the Ferghana Valley with Chinese goods, such as tea bricks, silk textiles, porcelain, silver and rhubarb, which was used for medicinal purposes and as a dye.

(Levi, 1999: 540)

Increasing Russian demand stimulated the development of Tashkent and the Ferghana Valley. The Khoqand Khanate invested in irrigation facilities in order to stimulate development of cotton production for export to Russia's growing markets (Levi, 1999: 541).

The Maritime Silk Road: Nan Hai, the Southern Sea

Southeast Asia has since ancient times been an important hub along the ancient Maritime Silk Road ... Over the centuries, the vast oceans have served as the bond of friendship connecting the two peoples, not a barrier between them. Vessels full of goods and passengers travelled across the sea, exchanging products and fostering friendship. 'A Dream of Red Mansions', *a Chinese classic novel, gives vivid accounts of rare treasures from Java. The National Museum of Indonesia, on the other hand, displays a large number of ancient Chinese porcelains ... As early as the Han Dynasty in China about 2,000 years ago, the people of the two countries opened the door to each other despite the sea between them. In the early fifteenth century, Zheng He, the famous Chinese navigator of the Ming Dynasty, made seven voyages to the Western Seas. He stopped over at the Indonesian archipelago in each of his voyages and toured Java, Sumatra and Kalimantan. His visits left stories of friendly exchanges between the Chinese and Indonesian peoples, many of which are still widely told today.*

(Xi Jinping, Speech to the Indonesian Parliament, 2013)

Economic Geography

China's internal trade and commercialization were highly developed from early in its history and the total value always greatly exceeded the value of international trade. International trade was heavily restricted by the Chinese government during relatively brief periods, most notably during the early Ming Dynasty, while in the Qing Dynasty between 1757 and 1842 European merchants were confined to trade only through Canton (Guangzhou). However, apart from these limitations, international trade from China with and through the Nan Hai continued relatively unimpeded throughout most of China's history. Although dwarfed by domestic trade in terms of its total value, the Nan Hai trade occupies an important place in the history of both China and Southeast Asia. The lands around Nan Hai encompass the area that today includes China's Guangdong, Guangxi and Hainan provinces, Taiwan, the Philippines, Vietnam, Cambodia, Thailand, Malaysia, Singapore and Indonesia. It can be considered historically as a single region: '[The Nan Hai] is remarkable for its near-Mediterranean nature. Its main trade route from one end in the north-east to the other in the south-west lies in the path of the two monsoons and is, therefore, eminently suited for monsoon sailing' (Wang Gungwu, 1998: 3). The South China Sea was the main trade route of what may be called the Asian east-west trade in commodities and ideas: 'It was the second Silk Route. Its waters and islands straits were as the sands and mountain passes of Central Asia; its ports were like the caravanserais. It became to the southern Chinese what the land outside the Jade Gate was to the northern Chinese' (Wang Gungwu, 1998: 3–4).

Ancient and Medieval Era

Trade across the Nan Hai from China to Southeast and South Asia is of great antiquity. During the era of the Roman Empire, the seafaring trade between China and the West connected with the Central Asian route through Indian ports such as Barbaricum and Bargaza. The merchants included both Arabs and Romans. The Romans even established a trading depot at Poduca, on the southeast coast of India. They built warehouses, workshops for processing merchandise and docks for ships (Liu Xinru, 2010: 40). Trade between China and Southeast Asia, as well as to South Asia and the Middle East, was already well developed by the Han Dynasty (206 BC–220 AD). It expanded greatly during the Tang Dynasty (618 AD–907 AD) and continued to grow to even greater heights during the Song Dynasty (960–1271 AD).

Chinese ships were engaged in long-distance trade across the Nan Hai and beyond from an early point in history. Chinese merchants may have reached Ethiopia and East Africa as early as the first century BC (Needham, 1970: 42). Chinese ships were sailing to Penang in Malaya around 350 AD, to Ceylon by around 400 AD and by the fourth century they were probably coming to the mouth of the Euphrates in Iraq and calling at Aden (Needham, 1970: 41). There are large quantities of Chinese coins on the East African coast, with the earliest ones dating from around 620 AD. East Africa also contains hoards of Chinese porcelain sherds. In 1955 a British archaeologist wrote:

> I have never seen so much broken china as in the past fortnight between Dar es Salaam and the Kilwa Islands, literally fragments of Chinese porcelain by the shovelful. I think it is fair to say that as far as the Middle Ages is concerned, from the tenth century AD onwards the buried history of Tanganyika in written in Chinese porcelain.
>
> (Mortimer Wheeler, quoted in Needham, 1970: 51)

China's long tradition of trade on the high seas, especially across the dangerous waters of the Nan Hai, stimulated nautical technical progress. Chinese pilots were the first to use the magnetic compass at sea: 'This great revolution in the sailor's art, which ushered in the great era of quantitative navigation, is solidly attested for Chinese ships by 1090 AD, just about a hundred years before its initial appearance in the West' (Needham, 1970: 44). However, it is certain that the magnetic compass was in use in China for geomantic purposes long before it was used at sea, and the original date of its introduction on Chinese ships may have been as early as 850 AD (Needham, 1970: 48 and 247). The stern post rudder was vitally important for long-distance sailing across the high seas. It was first applied in Europe in the late twelfth century. However, it had been in use in China 'long before its appearance in the West', perhaps as early as the fifth century AD (Needham, 1970: 253–4). It seems likely to have spread to the West through its adoption by Arab merchant ships (Needham, 1970: 258). The use of the magnetic compass and stern-post were vitally important to the Portuguese voyages of discovery (Needham, 1970: 261). The principle of watertight compartments was first used in Chinese ships as early as the second century AD, but was not adopted in Western ships until the end of the eighteenth century (Needham, 1970: 66). The resulting bulkhead construction offered the possibility of free-flooding compartments in the event of penetration of the hull. From at least the third century Chinese ships adopted multiple masts. It was only in the fifteenth century that European ships adopted the system of 'full-rigged' multi-masted ships (Needham, 1970: 67).

As early as the Tang Dynasty there were large numbers of foreign merchants and sailors in the port cities of Southern China. A visitor to Guangzhou in 750 found in the harbour countless numbers of South Asian, Mon-Khmer (Kunlun) and 'Persian' (i.e., from the Middle East) ocean-going ships, some of great size. The drugs, spices and precious goods that they carried were 'piled mountains high'. Merchants and sailors from Ceylon, the Islamic world, Southeast Asia and of many different races either visited or resided in the city (Twitchett and Stargardt, 2002: 47). In 722 it is said that forty of these great foreign ships arrived in Guangzhou annually. When Guangzhou was sacked in 879 by Huang Chao's rebels, Arabic sources recorded that 120,000 foreigners were massacred, including Muslims, Jews, Christians and Manicheans (Twitchett and Stargardt, 2002: 47–8). Although the numbers appear to be greatly exaggerated, they nevertheless demonstrate how large was the presence of foreign merchants in China even at this early date.

From Roman times up until the fourteenth century Arab merchants dominated trade between Southeast Asia across the Indian Ocean (Needham, 1970: 42). As we have seen, they were important also in the trade across the Nan Hai. Indians, Persians and merchants from Southeast Asia itself, also played a role in the trade across the Nan Hai. However, Chinese merchants played a central role in the trade. As early as the thirteenth century Chinese-built ships, manned by Chinese crews and with Chinese traders on board, formed an important part of the Nan Hai trade (Twitchett and Stargardt, 2002: 46). When the first Europeans entered into trade with China in the sixteenth century they encountered a flourishing trade across the Nan Hai, which was 'conducted largely by the Chinese' (Fairbank and Teng, 1941: 202): 'Native Chinese commercial expansion stemming from the Mongol period, or probably much earlier, paved the way for the

European invasion of China by sea' (Fairbank and Teng, 1941: 202). For example, under Spanish rule, Manila prospered chiefly as an *entrepôt* between China and America. Trade between China and Manila was conducted entirely by Chinese ships and merchants (Fairbank and Teng, 1941: 202). There is ample evidence of a vibrant Chinese junk trade with Malaya in the early nineteenth century.

The main Chinese export across the Nan Hai traditionally was silk, but porcelain and tea became increasingly important during the Tang and Song Dynasties. A wide array of products was imported by China from lands beyond the Nan Hai, including goods not only from Southeast Asia, but also from Persia, Syria, Arabia, eastern Africa and north India. The southern Chinese cities of Yangzhou, Guangzhou, Ningbo and Wenzhou, were among the most important ports involved in the Nan Hai trade. Quanzhou (in Fujian province) is considered by many experts to be the terminus of the old Maritime Silk Road[14]. It was arguably the most important port in the Nan Hai trade up until at least the Yuan Dynasty. Indeed, in the view of some scholars it deserves the label of 'emporium of the world' between the tenth and fourteenth centuries (Schottenhammer, 2001).

Recent archaeological research at Satingpra on the Malay peninsula has cast new light on the nature of the trade across the Nan Hai between 1000 and 1400 AD (Stargardt, 2001).[15] Satingpra was an identifiable kingdom from around the fifth century AD. From the eighth or ninth century it came under the influence of the Srivijaya/Sanfoqi kingdom of southeast Sumatra and may even have been conquered by it. Satingpra has a particularly advantageous location in terms of trade across the Nan Hai and *entrepôt* trade to the Indian Ocean. It is located on the eastern side of the Isthmus of Kra on the narrow neck of the Malayan peninsula. At this point the isthmus is only around 70 kilometres wide and a substantial lake extends for around one-third of the width of the isthmus, so that the distance by land from the lake to the Indian Ocean is only around 40 kilometres. Satingpra was engaged in trade across the Gulf of Thailand from at least the seventh century. From the mid-tenth century on, there is a rising density of remains of ceramics from China. From this time until at least the late fourteenth century, Satingpra was at the centre of a growing inter-regional trade network that connected south China, Northeast Asia and Sumatra, as well as the Indian Ocean through trans-shipment across the Isthmus of Kra.

Satingpra provides a remarkable example of early modern public action to provide collective goods. The Satingpra kingdom constructed a network of transport canals, which meant that goods could be transported across most of the isthmus by water, the cheapest form of bulk transport. The final stage in the construction of the canal network was completed in the eleventh century. It appears that Satingpra's rulers even gave priority to the transport canals across the isthmus to the neglect of canals for irrigation and local transport. The trans-shipment of goods across the isthmus reduced by around 2,000 kilometres the distance involved in transporting goods from the Nan Hai to the Indian Ocean (Stargardt, 2001: 338).

Satingpra has by far the largest volume of Chinese porcelain sherds of any archaeological site in Southeast Asia. Although excavations were only possible on a small fraction of the total site, they revealed a total of 50,000 sherds of

Chinese ceramics from the period 1000 to 1400 alone. In addition to the huge volume of ceramics, it is highly likely that a large quantity of silk and tea were traded through Satingpra, although silk and tea do not survive for 1,000 years buried underground, while sherds of ceramics do so. The ceramics were mostly of high quality and relatively valuable in relation to their weight. They came mainly from a small number of kilns in south China. Those from Longquan in Zhejiang province accounted for 45 per cent of the total of Chinese sherds found at the site. They were 'among the most beautiful ceramics of their time' (Stargardt, 2001: 344). Most of the remainder came from Jingdezhen in Jiangxi province and Dehua in Fujian province. The presence of such a huge volume of high quality ceramic exports from China reflects a remarkable level of mercantile organization in China:

> These high quality ceramics reflect specific demands of the Satingpra *entrepôt* and the trading network of which it was a part. The show that the ceramics industry and the domestic trade within China was sufficiently highly organized to be able to assemble the right cargos to meet that demand and to continue to do so over a long period of time.
>
> (Stargardt, 2001: 356)

It is likely that the Chinese merchant communities sustaining this remarkable system existed at both Quanzhou and Guangzhou.

The research at Satingpra can be supplemented by other archaeological sources, including the discovery at Quanzhou of the wreck of a late Song ship engaged in the Nan Hai trade.[16] Due to the unique conditions under which it sank, its cargo of Nan Hai tropical incenses and other trade products survived. The ship was returning from the Nan Hai with a wide array of wood products, including 2,400 kilograms of incense logs. The repairs made to the ship lead to the conclusion that it spent long periods in Southeast Asian waters. By the twelfth century there were already semi-resident or even fully resident communities of Quanzhou merchants in Southeast Asia (Stargardt, 2001: 373). The exports from Satingpra to China are likely to have consisted of four main categories of forest products from different parts of the Malayan peninsula (Stargardt, 2001: 358). These were: firstly, incense products from aromatic woods, wood resins and resinous crystals, including two high-quality frankincenses, two high-quality camphors and one medium-quality incense that was sold in huge volumes in China; secondly, medicinal materials; thirdly, a deadly poison; and fourthly, ship-building wood sealants, rigging and cordage, packing and floats. There were 'huge values involved in the trade in high-grade incenses': 'Enormous sums were involved in the southern exotic goods' and the export of large quantities of high-quality Chinese ceramics was necessary in order to pay for the imports (Stargardt, 2001: 364–5).

The discovery and excavation of a tenth century Chinese wreck at Intan, which is 150 kilometres north of Jakarta, cast further light on the extent of the traditional Nan Hai trade (Twitchett and Stargardt, 2002). The ship appears to have been on a return journey from Guangzhou and contained a wide range of Chinese ceramics.

Their wide geographical spectrum from within China 'provide invaluable insights into the complex internal processes of marketing and transport that were involved, inside China, in assembling the cargo of one ship going on a long distance voyage into the Southern Sea' (Twitchett and Stargardt, 2002). The ship also contained Middle Eastern glassware. Most importantly, the ship contained a huge weight of silver ingots, equivalent to 1.15 per cent of the entire annual revenue of the Song government from the whole of China (Twitchett and Stargardt, 2002: 27). The wreck demonstrates vividly the integrated character and large scale of long-distance trade in Chinese ships across the Nan Hai between China, Java, Sumatra and the Malayan peninsula.

Early Modern Era

In the fifteenth century, between 1405–1433, the Chinese government organized giant fleets to undertake seven diplomatic expeditions, ranging from Borneo to East Africa. They were all under the command of Zheng He, who was born of a Yunnanese Muslim family, with a father who had made the pilgrimage to Mecca. The first expedition contained sixty-two great sailing ships and carried a force of around 30,000 men. The first stop was Malacca. The next stop was Palembang in Sumatra. This city was 'long known to the Chinese'. In 1377, thirty years before Zheng He's arrival, a Chinese pirate leader, Liang Daoming, who was a native of Nan Hai *xian* in Guangdong Province, had seized control of the city: 'This is one of the first indications of large numbers of Chinese in Indonesia or Malaya' (Fitzgerald, 1972: 95). Although Palembang was not a Ming colony, 'it remained under the control of the Chinese for nearly two hundred years' (Fitzgerald, 1972: 96). The fleet then sailed across the Indian Ocean to Calicut, before returning to China. The second expedition in 1405 went to Java, Calicut, Ceylon and Siam. The third expedition in 1409 made a similar journey. The first three expeditions visited places around the Nan Hai and in the Indian Ocean that were 'long familiar to Chinese navigators' (Fitzgerald, 1972: 97). The prosperity of the south Indian cities was 'in part due to the fact that they were the meeting-place for Arab ships coming from the West and Chinese ships coming from the East' (Fitzgerald, 1972: 97). The final four expeditions went much further afield, visiting Hormuz, the Persian Gulf, the Maldives and covered the whole coast of East Africa, including Mogadishu and Mozambique.

The main purpose of the expeditions was to deepen Chinese knowledge of the outside world. They were intended also to 'demonstrate the power and glory of China as the leading political and cultural nation in Asia to the kings and sultans of the Southern and Western Asian regions', to 'induce them to acknowledge the nominal suzerainty of the Chinese emperor and to send tribute missions to the Chinese court' (Needham, 1970: 50). The large fleet of ocean-going junks were far bigger than European ships of that era. Many of the ships in the fleet were of at least 1,500 tons, compared with just 300 tons in the ships in which Bartolomeu Dias rounded the Cape of Good Hope in 1488. Although Zheng He's ships were armed, including gunpowder weapons and the fleet was of great size, no effort was made to establish foreign forts or colonies. The operations were entirely those of 'a navy paying friendly visits to foreign ports': 'Indeed the term navy is hardly applicable to the Chinese fleets, which were more like assemblies of merchant fleets than of a nationalized trading authority' (Needham, 1970: 53).

It is widely thought that China 'turned inwards' after the Zheng He expeditions and that Chinese trade by sea declined drastically. It is also widely thought that a major reason that China did not have its own British-type 'Industrial Revolution' was because China's foreign trade had shrunk significantly after the last Zheng He expedition. However, Zheng He's fleet was an official government expedition, which had no direct relationship to the long-term trade conducted by Chinese and foreign merchant shipping across the Nan Hai. By the middle of the eighteenth century, foreign trade by sea had increased greatly, both with Southeast Asia and with Europeans. Chinese junks compared favourably in size with their European counterparts. The biggest junks might be of 1,000 tons and carry a crew of 180 men:

> Hundreds if not thousands of these sturdy merchantmen plied annually between Amoy or Canton and the Straits of Malacca, south in winter, north in summer. They followed detailed sailing directions through numerous ports of call. The so-called 'western' route led along the coasts of Vietnam, Siam and the Malay Peninsula ... The 'eastern' route took vessels to Manila, the Moluccas and Java ... The trade with Southeast Asia was carried on in Chinese vessels and ... was entirely in Chinese hands.
>
> (Fairbank et al., 1965: 73)

By this time Jiangnan was much the most developed area of China. It comprised the Delta Region of the Yangzi River. In 1815 it had a population of around 26 million (Li Bozhong, 1986), out of a total Chinese population of around 330 million. This compares with a European population in 1820 of around 190 million, including 31 million in France, 25 million in Germany and 14 million in Great Britain (Cipolla, ed., 1973: 747).

By the late sixteenth century textiles had become the largest single part of the Jiangnan industrial economy. By the end of the seventeenth century Jiangnan was the world's biggest exporter of textiles and fibres and was more highly commercialized and urbanized than any other part of the world (Li Bozhong, 1986). Nanjing was the centre of the silk industry. In the 1840s there were nearly 200,000 people engaged in the industry, with more than 35,000 looms (Li Bozhong, 1986: 21). Songjiang prefecture was the most highly developed part of China in terms of the production of cotton cloth for the market and Suzhou, the country's most important commercial centre, 'teemed with cloth merchants and was also a dyeing centre' (Xu Dixin and Wu Chengming, 2000: 171). During the Qing about 90 per cent of the marketed cotton cloth produced in Jiangnan was exported to other parts of China or abroad. In the eighteenth century, the fastest growth rates of exports were to Europe: between 1786 and 1798, the export of 'Nankeens' (cloth woven in Nanjing and other places in Jiangnan) to Western Europe and the Americas increased almost fivefold (Li Bozhong, 1986: 27). In the early eighteenth century around 5,000 seagoing ships were based in Jiangnan, with a tonnage that was 2.8 times that of British ships of all kinds in 1700 (Li Bozhong, 1986: 53). In the late eighteenth century, there were reported to be about 5,000 seagoing ships in the ports of Shanghai and Zhapu alone, with a total weight estimated at around 550,000 tons. Large merchants were reported to each own fleets of more than 100 ships employing over 2,000 people (Xu Dixin and Wu Chengming, 2000: 364).

The famous expeditions of Zheng He in the fifteenth century demonstrated China's technical and cultural superiority over the lands he visited, including those of Southeast Asia. However, although China had deep trade relations with Southeast Asia, it did not attempt to colonize the region around the Nan Hai. China's technical superiority and vast size was such that this would have been entirely feasible. Instead, China's leaders chose to focus on governing their own country.

Over time, communities of Chinese people developed in the lands around the Nan Hai. They mainly travelled there due to trade-related activities. By the time of Zheng He's expeditions in the fifteenth century 'the flow of Chinese sea trade and migration into the ports of Southeast Asia had already assumed important dimensions' (Fairbank et al., 1965: 423). Long before European ships entered the Nan Hai, 'Chinese trading junks were the principal carriers in the international commerce of East Asia' (Fairbank et al., 1965: 29). Unlike the later activities of European merchants, the activities of Chinese merchants in the lands around the Nan Hai were 'seldom aided by naval or political action by the Chinese government' (Fairbank et al., 1965: 29). The community of Chinese overseas traders has been aptly described as 'merchants without an empire' (Wang Gungwu, 1990).

In the sixteenth century the Chinese trade community in Sumatra was far larger than that of the Portuguese. In Jambi, Sumatra's chief pepper port, the Chinese were the principal merchant community, dealing with ship captains from Siam, Java and Melaka as well as Holland, England and China (Curtin, 1984: 171). The port of Banten, at the western end of Java, had a 'substantial community of Chinese middlemen in the pepper trade' (Curtin, 1984: 170). Some were involved in the local seaborne trade, while others offered brokerage and other commercial and financial services. The sultan of Banten used Chinese brokers, interpreters and weighers in the government service (Curtin, 1984: 170).

In the seventeenth century there were reportedly more than 10,000 Chinese residents in Siam, with 3,000 to 4,000 in the capital city, Ayudha (Curtin, 1984: 168). Bangkok had grown into the largest centre anywhere for building Chinese-style junks, due to the easy availability of local teak. In the seventeenth century trade between China and Siam grew rapidly. The ship owners and captains were mainly local Chinese (Curtin, 1984: 169). In the late eighteenth century the Siamese king was half-Chinese, the son of a merchant from Chaozhou (Shantou, in Eastern Guangdong Province). He fostered Chinese immigration, mainly from Chaozhou. When Bangkok became the capital of Siam in 1767, more than half the population were Chinese (Fairbank et al., 1965: 459). Out of a total population of around 30 million Chaozhou people today, around one-half live in the lands around the Nan Hai, mainly in Thailand. They have their own dialect and financial networks, which are hard for outsiders to penetrate.

Since at least the Tang Dynasty the port of Ningbo had deep commercial relationships with Southeast Asia (as well as Northeast Asia). A large part of its manufactured goods involved procurement of materials imported from the Nan Hai as well as from elsewhere within China. The goods manufactured in Ningbo from imported materials included ships, furniture, wood carvings, lacquer ware and paper (Shiba, 1977: 430–1). Ningbo's thriving inter-regional trade within China was heavily reliant on networks of local businessmen working in cooperation with traditional local banks (*qian zhuang*). In the eighteenth and nineteenth century, as well as migrating to other parts of China, colonies of Ningbo people developed overseas in Southeast Asia: 'In the nineteenth century Ningbo businessmen abroad were noted for their "clannishness" and fierce regional loyalty' (Shiba, 1977: 437).

Chinese communities in Southeast Asia were attacked repeatedly, unprotected by the Chinese government. For example, between 1565 and 1815 a thriving trade existed across the Pacific Ocean between Spain's colony in the Philippines and its colonies in Central America. Chinese merchants brought Chinese goods to Manila in their Chinese-owned junks. In return for Chinese silks, porcelain and high-value furniture, they received silver from Spain's mines in Mexico and Peru. A large community of Chinese people grew up in Manila. In addition to merchants and sailors, there was also a wide range of Chinese people working in diverse occupations. By 1586 there were estimated to be 10,000 Chinese people in Manila. In 1603 it is estimated that Spanish forces in combination with indigenous Filipino and Japanese troops massacred around 20,000 Chinese people.[17] The numbers of Chinese quickly increased again, but in 1639 there followed another massacre in which an estimated 23,000 Chinese were killed. Further massacres followed in 1686 and 1763.

From the mid-nineteenth century onwards, under European colonial rule the number of Chinese people in Southeast Asia increased rapidly, including a large body of poor people who migrated in order to work in rubber plantations and mines. Today, there may be as many as 40–50 million people of Chinese origin living in countries around the Nan Hai. In each of these countries a small fraction of the Chinese population occupies an important part of the business structure,[18] alongside a much larger number who occupy a wide array of ordinary occupations.

China's Long Relationship with the Nan Hai[19]

There is a wide perception among Western commentators that China's assertion of its rights over the Southern Sea is of recent origin, related mainly to the fact that there may be a large amount of oil and gas under the Southern Sea. Whatever one's perception of the legal validity of China's claims and however the disputes over the Nan Hai may be resolved, China's views concerning its rights in the Nan Hai are of great antiquity, pre-dating by far the recent energy discoveries under the sea. They are closely related to the long history of Chinese merchant shipping across the Nan Hai from southern Chinese ports to the ports of Southeast Asia. It is widely thought that China is unusual in claiming jurisdiction over an area that is distant from the main body of the country. In fact, it is far from unusual for countries to have jurisdiction over territories that are far from their main territory, in many cases much further away than the Nan Hai is from the man body of China.

Under traditional shipping technologies, without modern maps and navigation aids, the Nan Hai was extremely dangerous. The *Nansha* (Spratley) Islands consist of as many as 400 islands, cays, reefs, atolls, banks and shoals. None of them is permanently habitable. The *Xisha* (Paracel) Islands consist of more than twenty islands, cays, reefs, atolls and shoals. The International Court of Justice has argued that 'even an insignificant display of sovereignty' can establish sovereignty over a 'remote or barely populated territory'.[20] Few territorial features in the world can more adequately be described as 'remote' or 'uninhabited' than the islands in the Nan Hai. Except for a few of the Xisha Islands, the islands of the Nan Hai are mostly uninhabitable.

Chinese ships have crossed the dangerous seas of the Nan Hai for more than 2,000 years. China was already making large ocean-going boats by the Han Dynasty or even earlier. The Western Han (206 BC–8 AD) rulers established and maintained close navigational and commercial ties with Southeast Asia, Ceylon and India. The Chinese envoys of the Western Han used the sea route through the Nansha Islands rather than using the conventional route along the coast. This reduced the journey time by several months, but this was only possible because of detailed knowledge of the obstacles in and under the Nan Hai. Later generations either continued to utilize previously opened sea lanes, or sought to open new sea routes in order to further shorten the voyages between the Chinese mainland and destinations in and beyond the Southern Sea. When Zheng He made his voyages through the Nan Hai the routes he followed had been known and used by Chinese mariners for several centuries. They had been systematized into two major sea lanes since the Song era: the East Sea Route and the West Sea Route and each of these was subdivided into a major and a minor route.

For many centuries Chinese fishermen from Guangdong province, Hainan and other coastal areas used the Nan Hai as their fishing grounds. The fishermen regularly used the islands as shelters or stopping-off points. Some of them even grew farm products on the islands. The *China Sea Directory* published in London in 1868 noted that the footmarks of fishermen from Hainan Island 'could be found on every isle of the [Spratley] Islands and some of the fishermen would even live there for a long period of time' (Shen Jianming, 2002: 130).

China regarded the Nan Hai and its islands as under its authority and control since no later than the Han Dynasty. During the Tang Dynasty the Xisha and Nansha were placed under the jurisdiction of Qiongzhou Prefecture (now Hainan Province). The central Chinese government in both the Ming and the Qing Dynasties 'invariably considered itself to have sovereignty over both the South China Sea Islands and their adjacent areas' (Shen Jianming, 2002: 130–133). Various official records of Guangdong province, Hainan and some of their lower level administrative prefectures and counties in the periods from the Northern Song Dynasty (960–1127 AD) to the Qing Dynasty invariably confirm that China intended to, and did, exercise jurisdiction over the Nansha and Xisha Islands and their adjacent waters.

Chinese naval patrols regularly sailed the Nan Hai during the era when northern Vietnam was a Chinese province (111 BC–938 AD). The Chinese navy continued to patrol in the Nan Hai during the Yuan, Ming and Qing Dynasties. During the Ming Dynasty the official records of Qiongshan *xian* (Hainan Island) record:

> Guangdong [province] is adjacent to the grand [South China] Sea, and the territories beyond the Sea all internally belong [to the Ming Empire] … The General led more than ten thousand soldiers and fifty huge ships to patrol several ten thousand *li* on the Nan Hai.
>
> (quoted in Shen Jianming, 2002: 125)

As early as the Song Dynasty Chinese maps included the islands of the Nan Hai as lying within China's boundaries. Official maps of the Yuan, Ming and Qing Dynasties continued to include the islands of the Nan Hai as part of China. In 1932, 1935 and 1947 the Nationalist Government conducted three large-scale surveys of the Nan Hai. Its 1948 map included standardized names of most of the islands and adopted the famous U-shaped intermittent line to indicate China's sovereignty over the Nan Hai. China's post-1949 government continued to follow this practice in its official maps of the People's Republic of China (Shen Jianming, 2002: 122–9).[21]

In 1951 Premier and Foreign Minister Zhou Enlai stated: 'The Xisha Islands and Nansha Islands, like the Dongsha and Zhongsha Islands,[22] have always been China's territory'. In 1958 the Chinese Government issued the PRC's Declaration on China's Territorial Sea. It stated that the Xisha and Nansha Islands, as well as the Dongsha and Zhongsha Islands, have been China's territory since ancient times. In 1992 China passed its Law on the Territorial Sea and Contiguous Zone. It reiterated that 'the territory of the People's Republic of China includes … the Dongsha Islands, Xisha Islands, Zhongsha Islands, Nansha Islands and all other relevant islands that belong to the People's Republic of China'. In 1996 China's National People's Congress passed the Decision to Ratify the UN Convention on the Law of the Sea. The Decision reiterated China's titles and rights to the various islands referred to in the 1992 Law on Territorial Sea and Contiguous Zone.

Western Colonialism and the Silk Road

Western European Colonialism

For well over one thousand years, trade relations along the Silk Road by Sea were mainly peaceful. Chinese, Arab, Indian and Southeast Asian ships mostly did not carry guns. The ports in which they called, from East Africa to Southern China, were multi-cultural and cosmopolitan. Muslims, Buddhists, Confucians, Zoroastrians and Christians mostly mingled easily in the ports across the Indian Ocean and Nan Hai. The governments of the lands in which merchants traded mostly attempted to nurture trade, which they believed was beneficial for their

societies. The Chinese expeditionary fleets commanded by Zheng He were the highest form of these peaceful relationships. The last of these fleets set out in 1433.

At the time of the Portuguese entry into the Indian Ocean, Europeans produced little that Asians wished to buy. When Vasco da Gama first visited Calicut in 1498, he presented the goods they had brought with them, including striped cloths, scarlet hoods, hats, strings of coral, hand washbasins, sugar, oil and honey. The king laughed at him and advised the Portuguese to offer gold instead. It is estimated that in 1750 the 'West' (i.e., Europe) produced only around 18 per cent of global manufacturing output, compared with 24 per cent in South Asia and 33 per cent in China. Up until the end of the eighteenth century in almost every aspect Chinese technology was at least equal to that of Europe. The one area in which European technology had unquestionable superiority to Asia was the military. In the fifteenth and sixteenth centuries Europe experienced a revolution in military technology on both land and sea. The revolution in military technology was stimulated by the violent internecine rivalry between the emerging European states, which took shape in the Early Modern period, gathered momentum during the Age of Absolutism in the seventeenth and eighteenth centuries and continued during the Industrial Revolution in the nineteenth century.[23]

Within a few years of the last of Zheng He's epic voyages of discovery, the Portuguese had rounded the Cape of Good Hope. The small European state of Portugal was in the vanguard of Europe's violent intrusion into the age-old maritime Silk Road: 'The admitted superiority of the relatively well-armed Portuguese ships over the unarmed Muslim vessels in the Indian Ocean was reinforced by a tenacity of purpose on the part of the European intruders which was largely lacking in their Asian opponents' (C. H. Boxer, quoted in Chaudhuri, 1985: 77–8). The arrival of the Portuguese in the Indian Ocean 'ended abruptly the system of peaceful oceanic navigation that was such a marked feature of the region' (Chaudhuri, 1985: 63). The contrast between the fleets commanded by Zheng He and the Portuguese fleets is 'truly extraordinary': 'The entire Chinese operations were those of a navy paying friendly visits to foreign ports, while on the other hand, the Portuguese east of Suez engaged themselves almost at once in total war' (Needham, 1970: 53). As long as the Portuguese were working their way down the west coast of Africa, their activities were relatively restrained, apart, of course, from slaving: 'It was only after 1500, when they were in a position to carry terrorist warfare against the East African Arabs and then against the Indians and other Asians, that European naval power showed what it could do in earnest' (Needham, 1970: 53). The Portuguese 'perpetuated the Crusader mentality and applied it in attempted naval conquest of all South Asia' (Needham, 1970: 53). Before the end of the sixteenth century the Portuguese were engaged in war against Muslims, Hindus and Buddhists along the length of the Indian Ocean and Southeast Asia. By the end of the sixteenth century Portugal had established a chain of settlements and fortresses along the Silk Road by Sea, including Mozambique, Hormuz, Goa, Colombo, Malacca and Macao. The overseas expansion of Portugal was strongly supported by the king, who styled himself 'Lord of the Conquest, Navigation and Commerce of Ethiopia, Arabia, Persia and India' (Fairbank et al., 1965: 18). The monarch wished to gain financially from the expansion as well as to achieve the religious purpose of converting unbelievers to Catholicism.

Portugal was in turn challenged and defeated by their more powerful European rivals, the Netherlands, France and Britain. In the seventeenth century each of them established state-supported, armed 'East India' trading companies to spear-head expansion in Asia. These in their turn fought each other ferociously to control the sea-borne trade between Asia and the West, replicating overseas their violent rivalry within Europe. By the end of the eighteenth century Britain had established control over much of South Asia, which was formalized in 1858, when the East India Company was dissolved and replaced by direct rule from Westminster. In the final decades of the nineteenth century, following the industrialization of Continental Europe and North America, a new explosive round of rivalry set in among the Western powers. This drastically affected the lands around the Nan Hai. By around 1900 colonial rule had been established by Britain in Malaya, including both Singapore and Sarawak, France in Indo-China, the Netherlands in the Dutch East Indies and the United States in the Philippines. By 1900 also, the main port cities in Southern China that had been at the core of the trade across the Nan Hai had all been forcibly opened up to Western residence and trade under the 'Unequal Treaties'. These included Canton (Guangzhou), Xiamen (Amoy), Fuzhou, Ningbo, Shantou and Shanghai. It also included Hong Kong, which occupies a crucially important position in relation to the Nan Hai and remained a British colony until 1997.

In 1890 the military historian Alfred Mahan published his enormously influential book, *The Influence of Sea Power upon History, 1660–1789*. He argued that sea power was essential to the growth of national strength and prosperity. He believed that Britain's overseas strength depended not only upon its advantageous geographical location off the European mainland, but also on the deliberate acquisition of strategically vital bases abroad. These enabled Britain to control the shipping of the world at its most vulnerable points. Gibraltar, Malta, Suez, Aden, Singapore and the Cape all illustrated this. Mahan's ultimate purpose was to convert his compatriots in the United States. America could become a great naval power, perhaps the greatest, if these lessons were learned and acted upon: 'The overbearing power of command of the sea, which, by controlling the great common, closes the highways by which commerce moves to and fro from the enemies' shores [and] can only be exercised by great navies' (Mahan, 1890: xxxii). It was this belief that underlay the competitive building of great fleets by all the major powers before 1916. Mahan's views were heeded by the US Government. During Theodore Roosevelt's presidency (1901–1909) the United States greatly expanded its navy. Between 1907 and 1909, the 'Great White Fleet', which consisted of a fleet of sixteen giant battleships and supporting ships, made a fourteen-month voyage around the world to demonstrate the United States' newly acquired naval might in Mexico, Brazil, the Philippines, Ceylon, Egypt and the Mediterranean.

The leading Western nations not only colonized the lands around the Nan Hai, but also the wider Pacific Ocean territories. North America was now occupied by a mainly white population that had fought its way across the continent in a long, violent process that involved genocide against the indigenous population. Australia and New Zealand were British colonies in which white colonial rule had been accomplished through virtual extermination of the indigenous population. Most of the significant island territories in the Pacific Ocean were under the jurisdiction of Britain, France and the United States. The United States had annexed the large archipelago of Hawaii and purchased from Russia the vast territory of Alaska, including the Aleutian Island chain, which stretches 1,000 kilometres across the north of the Pacific Ocean. By 1900 also, Japan had seized control of the tiny independent kingdom of Liu Qiu, which had for hundreds of years been a Chinese tributary state and forcibly incorporated it into Japan as 'Okinawa Prefecture'.

Russian Colonialism

Central Asia was changed radically by the expansion of the Russian Empire. In the sixteenth century the Grand Duchy of Moscow annexed Kazan (1552) and Astrakan (1556). The Russian state expanded across Siberia and reached the Pacific Ocean by 1649. In 1783 it annexed the Crimea. From 1730 onwards Russia gradually annexed the northern part of Kazakhstan. In 1864 it commenced the final drive to conquer the core of Central Asia. In succession it conquered Tashkent (1865), Bukhara (1868), Khiva (1873) Khoqand (1876) and Merv (1884). The whole region became a part of the Russian Empire, administered as a single entity of 'Turkestan'. Russia's expansion into Central Asia coincided with the catastrophic decline of the Qing Dynasty in the nineteenth century, including the collapse of Manchu rule in Xinjiang. Under the Russian Empire and the Soviet Union the vast land mass stretching from Europe to the Pacific was unified politically for the first time since the Mongol Empire.

Following the Bolshevik Revolution there was a strong movement within Central Asia to establish an 'autonomous Turkestan' that would have its own army, foreign policy and finances and would unify all the peoples of Central Asia. Between 1920 and 1924 the Soviet leadership rejected the proposal and began a long, drawn-out process to establish separate 'republics' within the Soviet Union (Soucek, 2000: Chapter 16). Soviet anthropologists, linguists and sociologists identified separate cultural and linguistic groups that formed the basis for drawing boundaries around each of the Central Asian 'republics' and reinforcing their separate 'national identities'. This formed the basis of the eventual break up of Central Asia into the separate countries of Kazakhstan, Uzbekistan, Tajikistan, Kyrgyzstan and Turkmenistan.[24]

In the mid-nineteenth century Russia pushed south from Siberia into the Amur Region, which was part of the Qing Empire. Under the Treaty of Peking (1860) Russia took control of the region north of the Amur River as well as the Maritime Provinces between the Ussuri River and the Pacific, which formed the east coast of Manchuria. The main city of the region was Vladivostok, which means 'Rule of the East'. Between 1891 and 1916 the Russian Imperial state constructed the Trans-Siberian Railway across the vast expanse of the steppes and built rail links to Kazakhstan and Uzbekistan. When the Trans-Siberian Railway was completed,

Vladivostok was its eastern terminus. Under the Soviet Union the density of rail links in Central Asia was expanded, which permitted the close integration of the region into the Soviet economy.

UNCLOS and Exclusive Economic Zones

In 1992 the United Nations passed a 'revolutionary' piece of legislation, the UN Convention on the Law of the Sea (UNCLOS). Under this legislation countries are permitted to establish an 'exclusive economic zone' (EEZ) of 200 nautical miles from their shore, which they are entitled to patrol and protect through their coastguard fleet. Under this treaty the West's former colonial powers each have retained jurisdiction over distant possessions, which are often sparsely inhabited or uninhabited. Britain's overseas possessions include the Falkland Islands, South Georgia and South Sandwich Islands, St Helena, Ascension Island and Tristan da Cunha, all of which are in the Atlantic Ocean, the British Indian Ocean Territory and the Pitcairn Islands, as well as various territories in the Caribbean, including the British Virgin Islands and the Cayman Islands. France's overseas possessions include the Crozet Islands, Kerguelen Islands, St Paul and Amsterdam Islands, Reunion and Tromelin Island, which are all in the Indian Ocean and French Polynesia, New Caledonia, Wallis and Futuna and Clipperton Island, which are all in the Pacific Ocean, as well as its Caribbean and South American territories, including French Guiana, Guadeloupe and Martinique. The United States' territories include Hawaii, Guam, American Samoa, Northern Mariana Islands, the Guano Islands and Wake Island, all of which are in the Pacific Ocean. China's undisputed EEZ is only 0.9 million (i.e., 900,000) square kilometres and the total EEZ if it won all its disputes in the Nan Hai would be less than 3 million square kilometres. The total overseas EEZ of France amounts to 10.7 million square kilometres, while that of the United States (including Alaska) is 9.8 million, of Russia is 6.7 million (i.e., its Pacific and Siberian territories), of Britain is 6.0 million, of Australia is 2.6 million and of New Zealand is 3.3 million (Nolan, 2013). In the Pacific Ocean alone, the combined overseas EEZ for the former colonial powers is 30.9 million square kilometres, over thirty times greater than China's undisputed EEZ and ten times greater than the greatest possible extent of China's EEZ if it wins all its disputes with its neighbours around the Nan Hai.

China, the Silk Road and the World

The Silk Road and the Tribute System

The tribute system has existed since ancient times, before even the unification of China under the Qin Dynasty (221–207 BC).[25] It lasted up until the late nineteenth century. The last tribute mission from Liu Qiu (Okinawa) was sent in 1875,[26] from Annam in 1883, from Korea in 1894 and from Nepal in 1908 (Fairbank and Teng, 1941: 197). Under the tribute system representatives of barbarian people formally presented gifts at the Chinese court in recognition of the benefit their country might receive from Chinese civilization. The tributary system was intimately bound up with trade between China and the outside world. Tributary missions were protected by the Emperor during their journey to and from the capital and were allowed to trade in special markets in the city that were supervised by government officials in order to ensure 'just and fair trade':

> If there are any who buy on credit and intentionally delay (payment), cheating or seeking 'squeeze', with the result that the foreigners wait a long time, they, together with those who trade with them in private, will be condemned; and will be put in the cangue for one month in front of their shops.
>
> (Fairbank and Teng, 1941: 167)

Relations between the Son of Heaven and the tributaries were on an ethical basis and hence reciprocal: 'The tributaries were submissive and reverent, the Emperor was compassionate and condescending. These reciprocal relationships required formal expression. Presentation was a ritual performance, balanced by forms of imperial hospitality and bestowal of imperial gifts' (Fairbank and Teng, 1941: 147). All those countries and regions that wished to enter into a relationship with China needed to do so as 'China's vassal, acknowledging the supremacy of the Chinese Emperor and obeying his commands thus ruling out all possibility of intercourse on terms of equality':

> It must not be construed to be a dogma of conquest or universal dominion, for it imposed nothing on foreign peoples who chose to remain outside the Chinese world. It sought peace and security, with both of which international relations were held incompatible. If relations there had to be, they must be of the suzerain-vassal type, acceptance of which meant to the Chinese acceptance of the Chinese ethic on the part of the barbarian ... It must not be assumed that the Chinese court made a profit out of ... tribute. The Imperial gifts bestowed in return were usually more valuable than the tribute ... Chinese statesmen before the latter part of the nineteenth century would have ridiculed the notion that national finance and wealth should be or could be promoted by means of international trade. On China's part the permission to trade was intended to be a mark of imperial bounty and a means of keeping the barbarians in the proper state of submissiveness.
>
> (T. F. Tsiang, quoted in Fairbank and Teng, 1941: 140)

At one time or another, the countries and regions that came to China under the tribute system encompassed a large part of Central Asia, Northeast Asia and Southeast Asia, as well as countries and regions further afield. A detailed list of tributaries from the Ming Dynasty in 1587 includes 'tributes sent to the Court by thirty-eight countries of the Western regions (Xi Yu)', which all 'passes through Hami' (Fairbank and Teng, 1941: 153). The countries and regions sending tribute included Kashgar, Herat, Bukhara, Kashmir, Tabriz, Samarkand, Turfan, Isfahan, Khorasan, as well as the 'Kingdom of Rum' and Mecca (Fairbank and Teng,

1941: 154). The lands around the Nan Hai and those from farther afield along the Maritime Silk Road, sent tribute missions to China's rulers from as early as the Han Dynasty (Wang Gungwu, 1998: 117–121). A detailed list of tributaries compiled in 1587 includes those from Annam, Siam, Champa, Burma, Java, Brunei, Borneo, the Philippines, Malacca, Calicut, Bengal, Ceylon, Syria, Hormuz, [and] the Maldives (Fairbank and Teng, 1941: 151–2).

Trade and Culture

China and Asia. The tributary system was closely connected with trade; however, the main body of China's international trade took place outside the tribute system. In addition to the overseas trade conducted by Chinese merchants, numerous foreign merchants traded in Chinese cities, including ports on the Chinese coast, such as Guangzhou, Quanzhou and Ningbo, as well as inland trading centres in north and western China, such as Xi'an and Lanzhou.

Chinese technologies and their associated culture had a deep impact on the lands along the Silk Road. These included the spread of porcelain-making, silk-producing, silk textile and paper-making technologies into Central Asia. Chinese culture, including the written language and the Confucian bureaucratic system had a deep impact on Japan, Korea, Liu Qiu and northern Vietnam. The Temple of Literature in Hanoi was built in 1070 after Vietnam had achieved independence from China. It functioned as a 'university' for Vietnam's bureaucrats until 1779. The Temple contained many courtyards, all with a long line of giant stone tortoises, each with a stone stele on top, which record in Chinese the names of the successful candidates in the examinations, which were based on the same Confucian principles as those in China. For centuries the written script of Korea and of Japan followed that of China. Confucian ideas deeply permeated Korea, Japan and Vietnam. Japanese 'Zen' Buddhism had its origins in China's 'Chan' Buddhism (Zurcher, 1964).

China's cultural impact on Southeast Asia was smaller than on its immediate neighbours in Northeast Asia. Hindu, Buddhist and Muslim culture spread to the region mainly through trade. In the Philippines, which were under Spanish rule from the sixteenth century until the end of the nineteenth century, Chinese cultural influence was restrained by the wide influence of Catholicism. Islam, Hinduism and Catholicism proved more powerful cultural forces than Chinese Confucianism in most of Southeast Asia. Throughout the region, the large minority Chinese-origin population remained 'sojourners', with increasingly distant connections with their original native place, but retaining their language and culture in relatively closed communities (Wang Gungwu, 2000). A small minority of Chinese in Southeast Asia were extremely successful in business. Several of them established business empires that spanned the whole region. A repeated pattern historically has been attacks on the whole Chinese population, in part due to the perceived business dominance of a segment of the local Chinese population.

In addition to China's impact on the outside world, China's international trade along the Silk Road constituted a powerful mechanism for the spread of culture into China. Buddhism and Islam both spread along the Silk Road, both by land and sea.

China and the West. In the two millennia after China was united under the Qin Dynasty, China was mostly peaceful and it formed a gigantic free trade area in which commerce and 'capitalist sprouts' (*zibenzhuyi mengya*) flourished and expanded over time (Xu Dixin and Wu Chengming, 2000).The state performed critically important functions in areas in which the market failed. Infrastructure was the most important of these. Under this structure, China advanced far beyond Europe in terms of its level of national output, mass living standards, urban prosperity, enlightened culture and level of technical innovation (Needham, 1964).

In numerous areas of technology, China's sophisticated market economy stimulated path breaking innovation long before the West: 'In technological influences before and during the Renaissance China occupies a quite dominating position' (Needham, 1964: 237). Among the innovations which occurred in China before the West were silk textiles, paper, printing, gunpowder, porcelain, steel making, the wheelbarrow, the compass, the sternpost rudder, the segmental arch bridge, watertight compartments on ships, the crank and the double-acting piston bellows, which together constituted 'the complete morphology of the steam engine', the foot-stirrup and the efficient equine harness. The spread of these and other technologies to Europe took place mainly through merchants, both Chinese and foreign, by land and sea along the Silk Road.

Matteo Ricci's journals (1583–1610) from China had an enormous impact in Europe, helping to foster the Enlightenment belief in the possibility of a benevolent despotism, ruling through a rational bureaucratic structure: 'The entire kingdom is administered by the order of the Learned, commonly known as the philosophers. The responsibility for orderly management of the entire realm is wholly committed to their care and charge' (Matteo Ricci, quoted in Dawson, 1964: 10). In his description of the McCartney mission to China in 1793, Sir George Staunton says that:

> ... in respect to its natural and artificial productions, the policy and uniformity of its government, the language, manners and opinions of the people, the moral maxims and civil institutions and the general economy and tranquility of the state, it is the grandest collective object that can be presented for human contemplation or research.
>
> (quoted in Dawson, 1964: 7)

It was not until the British Industrial Revolution in the late eighteenth century that Europe finally caught up and in the following half-century, it raced past China. By the middle of the nineteenth century, Europeans routinely regarded China as a land of 'eternal stagnation' (Dawson, 1964).

Conclusion

The Chinese government's policy of the 'New Silk Road by Land and Sea' has the development of infrastructure and commercial relationships at its core.

Infrastructure building in order to support commerce and foster social stability was a foundation-stone of China's own long-term prosperity over the course of more than 2,000 years. China's newly enunciated policy builds on the history of ancient trade networks and cultural transmission between China and Central and Southeast Asia. Europe is in the Far West at the terminus of these networks. Before the nineteenth century the interaction between China and Europe was mostly indirect, mainly through intermediary trade systems. These trading systems involved not only Chinese people, but also large numbers of inhabitants of the regions that lie between China and the Far West. Although their numbers were tiny compared to the vast Chinese population, substantial trading communities from Central and Southeast Asia, including Buddhists, Arabs, Muslims, Persians and Indians, settled in China's western and southern coastal regions. A significant number of Chinese people settled in regions outside China, especially in the lands around the Nan Hai.

China's traditional international trade was tiny in comparison with the vast volume of internal trade. However, it was highly significant in terms of the deep interconnections between China and the regions immediately around it to the West and the South. Mainly through trade relations, a deep long-term symbiotic, two-way flow of culture took place between China and these regions, which helped to weave them together in a complex cultural tapestry.

From the collapse of the Roman Empire up until the eighteenth-century China's level of commercialization, urbanization, technology and culture was much ahead of that in Europe. The gap only narrowed significantly after the sixteenth century. Through China's trade and cultural interaction with Central and Southeast Asia a long-term flow of technologies took place from China to Europe, which helped to nourish the revolution in military and naval technology in the sixteenth and seventeenth centuries, with which the West achieved its overseas conquests. It contributed greatly also to the Industrial Revolution through which Europe vaulted ahead of China in the space of only half a century after 1800. Through this double revolution the West rapidly rose to dominate the whole global political economy, including that of Central and Southeast Asia; however, the period since the European Industrial Revolution is less than 200 years. The West's massive impact upon the regions between it and China are a thin veneer layered on top of a deep, complex 'lacquer' of interaction between China and these regions. This interaction is of great antiquity, stretching back more than 2,000 years.

Notes

1. A short version of this chapter was delivered at the China Development Forum in March 2014. A longer version was prepared for the conference on 'The historical heritage of scientists and thinkers of the Medieval East, and its role and significance for the modern civilisation' (Samarkand, 15–16 May 2014). I am grateful to Tim Clissold, Stephen Perry and Dr Zhang Jin for their comments on this chapter.
2. In 1780 the United States consisted of just thirteen states on the extreme eastern fringe of the continent. The population was 2.8 million, of whom 2.2 million were white people, mainly from Britain, and 0.6 million were black people, mainly slaves.

3. The first through caravans from China traversed Bactria carrying silk direct from China to Persia in 106 BC (Talbot-Rice, 1965: 140). The western terminus of the Silk Road was in the great trading cities in the Middle East, which included the famous archaeological remains at Petra. Palmyra was the greatest of these cities. It provided financial services to merchant caravans and set up caravanserai in distant lands, with hostels for merchants and their animals, storage buildings for their products, offices and a temple (Liu Xinru, 2010: 31).

4. Kapisi is adjacent to modern-day Bagram, in Afghanistan, the site of the giant US military base during the American occupation of Afghanistan. One interviewee in the *Financial Times* in 2014 commented on the withdrawal of American troops from Bagram: 'Before the foreigners, there was nothing' (*Financial Times*, 10 September 2014).

5. China produces around 80 per cent of the world's raw silk today.

6. Starr (2013: 84) contains a remarkable photograph from 1903 of a perfectly intact statue of Buddha being unearthed at Sahri Bahlol in Pakistan.

7. The Soviet scholar Litvinsky calculated that among known translators of Buddhist writings into Chinese, six were Indians, six or seven were Chinese, but sixteen were Central Asians (Starr, 2013: 86).

8. According to official accounts 4,600 monasteries and 40,000 shrines were destroyed during these years (Reischauer and Fairbank, 1958: 175).

9. Starr has drawn attention to the possible link between Sufism, Zoroastrianism and contemplative Buddhism: 'How different, in the end, is the mental and spiritual discipline of Central Asian Sufism, which seeks obliteration of the ego, emancipation from worldliness and the temporal and an embrace of the eternal from the Buddhist tradition that led to the construction of the huge sculpture of *Buddha Entering Mahaparinirvana,* the highest state of Nirvana in Tajikistan?' (Starr, 2013: 98). One could add to that the link between the contemplative strand in Buddhism and Daoism. There are also strong similarities between the Western Christian mystic tradition and the mystic tradition in the East.

10. Most of Mu Qi's paintings are in Japanese Collections. The spirit of a painting such as 'Six Persimmons' is far removed from the meticulous details of European 'still life' paintings in the seventeenth and eighteenth centuries. Its closest analogy in Western painting may be 'abstract' art in the twentieth century, which also attempts to get close to the Buddhist 'Great Unity'. However, the art historian Michael Sullivan emphasizes the difference between Chinese Zen painters and modern abstract artists: 'Even the most extreme of Chinese expressionists always sought meaning beyond pure form ... Mu Qi and Ying Yujian conveyed their metaphysical excitement not in empty gestures with the brush, but in the shape of a monk tearing up the sutras, or a mountain village emerging out of the mist. For the painter as for the calligrapher, mere form was never enough' (Sullivan, 1964: 199).

11. There is evidence that following the Mongol conquests, supplies of raw silk from China to the Ottoman Empire were supplanted by supplies from Iran, with Tabriz as the base (Inalcik, 1994: 219). However, the evidence is sketchy.

12. Levi's research sheds new light on an under-studied period in the economic history of Central Asia.

13. The Khoqand Khanate was based in Tashkent and the Ferghana Valley.

14. It has been officially designated as such by UNESCO.

15. This remarkable study is a summary of many years of archaeological fieldwork by Dr Janice Stargardt at Satingpra.

16. The wreck is displayed at the Quanzhou Maritime Museum and the relevant information is presented in Green, 1983.

17. See Borao, 1998, for a careful account. Borao's study is especially useful as it makes use of detailed investigations undertaken by the Chinese government itself. The investigation was remarkably objective in seeking to understand why the violence occurred.

It did not absolve the Chinese community itself from blame for the events. The Chinese government's investigation sheds considerable light on the complicated relationship between both rich and poor Overseas Chinese communities and the Southeast Asian societies in which they lived. The repeated pattern of attacks on Chinese communities in Southeast Asia, including those in Indonesia in the 1960s, warrants careful study in order to identify the underlying causes.

18. There is a wide array of estimates of the degree of importance of Overseas Chinese people in the economies around the Nan Hai.

19. This section relies heavily on the meticulous research of Shen Jianming (2002).

20. Advisory Opinion on the Status of Western Sahara, 1975.

21. There is dispute, even within China, about the precise meaning of the 'dotted lines' around the Nan Hai. Some people consider that they apply to China's sovereignty over the whole area within the line, while others argue that China's sovereignty only applies to the islands and island-like features (Sheng Jianming, 2002: 129).

22. The Dongsha (Pratas) Islands are 340 kilometres southeast of Hong Kong. The Zhongsha (Macclesfield Bank) Islands are southwest of the Dongsha Islands and east of the Xisha Islands.

23. A graphic illustration of the long-run revolution in military technology 'achieved' by fiercely competitive European states is provided by Keegan (1976), who compares the incredible technical 'progress' in the science of military killing in three battles, Agincourt (1415), Waterloo (1815) and the Somme (1916).

24. The way in which the Soviet leadership prevented the establishment of a unified republic of Turkestan bears comparison with the way in which Britain and France prevented the establishment of a unified Arab state in the Middle East at the end of the First World War. This arrangement was contained in the notorious 'Sykes-Picot Agreement' involving France, Britain and Russia, which was exposed by Trotsky after the Russian Revolution.

25. 'In the time of King T'ang of Yin (trad. Dates BC 1766–1754), the Ti-ch'iang [an ancient Tibetan tribe in E. Kansu and Kokonor], distant barbarians, came to offer gifts and to visit the king. In the time of (King) T'ai Mou (trad. Dates BC 637–1563) the remote tribes [chung-I, i.e., those so far off as to require repeated interpretations] which came to Court (consisted of) seventy-six countries' (Fairbank and Teng, 1941: 142).

26. In fact, Liu Qiu prepared a tribute mission in 1877, but Japan prevented it from sailing to the Chinese mainland.

Bibliography

Beales, S. (1906) *Si-Yu-Ki: Buddhist Records of the Western World*, London: Kegan Paul, Trench, Trübner & Co.

Borao, J.E. (1998) 'Chinese perceptions of the Spanish in the Philippines', *Itinerario*, vol. 23, no. 1: 22–39.

Chaudhuri, K.N. (1985) *Trade and Civilisation in the Indian Ocean: An Economic History from the Rise of Islam to 1750*, Cambridge: Cambridge University Press.

Cipolla, R., ed. (1973) *The Fontana Economic History of Europe: The Industrial Revolution*, London: Fontana/Collins.

Clinton, H. (2011) 'America's Pacific Century', *Foreign Affairs*, November.

Clinton, H. (2012) 'Forrestal Lecture', Naval Academy, Annapolis, January.

Curtin, P.D. (1984) *Cross-Cultural Trade in World History*, Cambridge: Cambridge University Press.

Dawson, R., ed. (1964) *The Legacy of China*, Oxford: Oxford University Press.

Dawson, R. (1964) 'Western conceptions of Chinese civilisation', in Dawson, ed. 1964.

Fa, Hsien (1886) *A Record of Buddhist Kingdoms,* translated by James Legge, Oxford: Clarendon Press.

Fairbank, J.K. and S.Y.Teng (1941) 'On the Ch'ing tributary System, *Harvard Journal of Asiatic Studies,* vol. 6, no. 2, June.

Fairbank, J.K., E.O. Reischauer and A.M.Craig (1965) *East Asia: The Modern Transformation,* London: Allen and Unwin.

Fitzgerald, C.P. (1972) *The Southward Expansion of the Chinese People,* London: Barrie and Jenkins.

Ghose, R., ed. (2008) *Kizil on the Silk Road: Crossroads of Commerce and Meeting of Minds,* Mumbai: Marg Publications.

Green, J. (1983) 'The Song Dynasty Shipwreck at Quanzhou, Fujian Province, People's Republic of China', *International Journal of Nautical Archaeology and Underwater Exploration,* vol. 12: 253–61.

Inalcik, H. (1994) *An Economic and Social History of the Ottoman Empire, vol. 1: 1300–1600,* Cambridge: Cambridge University Press.

Keegan, J. (1976) *The Face of Battle,* London: Jonathan Cape.

Lattimore, O. (1950) *Pivot of Asia,* Boston: Little Brown.

Levi, S. (1999) 'India, Russia and the eighteenth century transformation of the Central Asian caravan route', *Journal of Economic and Social History of the Orient,* vol. 42, no. 4.

Li, Bozhong (1986) *The development of agriculture and industry in Jiangnan, 1644–1850: Trends and prospects,* Hangzhou: Zhejiang Academy of Social Sciences.

Liu, Xinru (2010) *The Silk Road in History,* Oxford: Oxford University Press.

Mahan, A.T. (1890) *The Influence of Naval Power upon History, 1660–1783,* London: Methuen edition, 1965.

Needham, J. (1970) *Clerks and Craftsmen in China and the West,* Cambridge: Cambridge University Press.

Needham, J. (1964) 'Science and China's influence on the world', in Dawson, ed. 1964.

Nolan, P. (2013) 'Imperial Archipelagos', *New Left Review,* no. 80, Second Series, March-April: 77–98.

Polo, Marco (1974) *The Travels,* Harmondsworth: Penguin Books.

Reischauer, E.O. and J.K. Fairbank (1958) *East Asia: The Great Tradition,* Boston: Houghton Miflin.

Schafer, E.H. (1985) *The Golden Peaches of Samarkand: A Study of T'ang Exotics,* Berkeley: Berkeley University Press.

Schottenhammer, A., ed. (2001) *The Emporium of the World: Maritime Quanzhou, 1000–1400,* Leiden: Brill.

Shen, Jianming (2002) 'China's sovereignty over the South China Sea: A Historical Perspective', *Chinese Journal of International Law,* vol. 1, no. 1: 94–157.

Shiba, Y. (1977) 'Ningpo and its hinterland', in Skinner, ed. 1977.

Sickman, L. and A. Soper (1956) *The Art and Architecture of China,* Harmondsworth: Penguin Books.

Skinner, G.W., ed. (1977) *The City in Late Imperial China,* Stanford: Stanford University Press:.

Soucek, S. (2000) *A History of Inner Asia,* Cambridge: Cambridge University Press.

Starr, F. (2013) *Lost Enlightenment,* Princeton: Princeton University Press.

Stargardt, J. (2001) 'Behind the shadows: Archaeological data on two-way sea trade between Quanzhou and Satingpra, South Thailand, 10th–14th century', in Schottenhammer, ed. 2001.

Stierlin, H. (1998) *Turkey: From the Selcuks to the Ottomans,* London: Taschen.

Sullivan, M. (1964) 'The Heritage of Chinese art', in Dawson, ed. 1964.

Talbot-Rice, T. (1965) *Ancient Arts of Central Asia,* London: Thames and Hudson.

Tracey, J.D., ed. (1990) *The Rise of Merchant Empires: Long-distance Trade in the Early Modern Period, 1350–1750,* Cambridge: Cambridge University Press.

Twitchett, D. and J. Stargardt (2002) 'Chinese silver bullion in a tenth century Indonesian wreck', *Asia Major* (3rd Series), vol. 15, Pt I: 1–49.

US Department of Defense (2012) *Sustaining US Global Leadership: Priorities for 21st Century Defense,* January, Washington DC.

Wang, Gungwu (1990) 'Merchants without empires: The Hokkien sojourning community', in Tracey, ed. 1990.

Wang, Gungwu (1998) *The Nanhai Trade,* Singapore: Times Academic Press.

Wang, Gungwu (2000) *The Chinese Overseas,* Harvard: Harvard University Press.

Xi, Jinping (2013) Speech to Indonesian Parliament, 2 October.

Xi, Jinping (2014a) Speech at the UNESCO headquarters, 28 March.

Xi, Jinping (2014b) Speech at the College of Europe, 1 April.

Xu, Dixin and Wu Chengming (2000) *Capitalism in China, 1522–1840,* translated by Charles Curwen, Basingstoke: Macmillan.

Zurcher, E. (1964) 'Buddhism in China', in Dawson, ed. 1964.

2   Imperial archipelagos[1]

China, Western Colonialism and the Law of the Sea

Since September 2012, the Western media have been filled with reports about China's high-profile dispute with Japan over a group of tiny uninhabited islands, the *Diaoyu* (in Chinese) or *Senkaku* (in Japanese), on the edge of the South China Sea. The media have made frequent reference to Beijing's territorial claims there, widely held to be part of a pattern of 'bullying behaviour' in the region; some commentators have suggested that the dispute may even trigger a new Peloponnesian War in the Pacific.[2] The territory in question is of historical and strategic significance, and it may well possess substantial natural resources, to which the People's Republic of China (PRC) would gain access if its claims were successful. However, the resources of the South China Sea need to be seen in comparative perspective with those obtained by the US and the former European colonial powers through the enactment of the UN Convention on the Law of the Sea (UNCLOS).

The Convention was signed in 1982 after nine years of negotiations and established a legal framework to govern all uses of the world's oceans. International interest in property rights in the oceans had intensified from the 1970s onwards, as concerns mounted over the perceived decline in stocks of exhaustible resources – the most obvious being rapidly falling fish populations.[3] Technical progress had also opened up the possibility for greatly increased extraction of fossil fuels from deep-water and climatically challenging areas. Prior to UNCLOS, maritime states had sovereign authority over their territorial waters, which extended to a distance of twenty-two kilometres (twelve nautical miles) from the shore. Many disputes developed about the extent and nature of rights beyond the twelve-mile limit. UNCLOS effected a revolutionary change in the law of the sea by allowing countries to establish a new resource zone called the 'exclusive economic zone' (EEZ) adjacent to their territorial sea, and which extends 200 nautical miles from the baselines from which the territorial sea is measured.[4] Within the EEZ, coastal states have sovereign rights to explore and exploit the natural resources of the waters immediately above the seabed, as well as those of the seabed itself and its subsoil; they also have rights to other forms of exploitation of the zone, such as producing energy from the water, currents and winds.

By 2011, 161 individual states and the European Union were parties to UNCLOS. Once a state becomes a party to the Convention, it is under an obligation to bring its maritime claims and national laws into conformity with it. The dispute over the South China Sea revolves primarily around the extent of the exclusive economic zone claimed by the PRC compared with that of the countries with which it is in dispute. Five of the parties involved – China, Malaysia, Indonesia, the Philippines and Vietnam – had ratified UNCLOS by 1996. (The other disputant, Taiwan, could not ratify UNCLOS as it is not a member of the United Nations, but it brought its own internal legislation into line with the Convention.) Yet while the complex contention between China and its neighbours over maritime resources has dominated Western discussions, the colossal resource grab by former colonial powers that UNCLOS facilitated has almost entirely escaped international attention.

A critically important part of UNCLOS is the provision that islands are entitled to the same maritime zones as land territory, with each allowed an EEZ of 200 nautical miles (370 kilometres). Although the colonial empires were largely dismantled between the late 1940s and the early 1980s, their former masters have retained administrative control over 'a few scattered remnants' including numerous small islands, either as formal colonies or in other ways. They typically have a small land area – sometimes only a few square kilometres – and generally have tiny or non-existent human populations. Few people in their respective metropoles even know of these far-flung territories: how many Britons could point to 'British Indian Ocean Territory' on a map? How many French citizens could locate the Kerguelen Islands, or Americans identify the North Marianas? Some of these islands are exotic tourist destinations, others are wildlife reserves, others still house scientific research stations; many are regarded as eccentric anachronisms.[5] However, these 'scattered remnants' of the old colonial empires turned out to be far more significant than most people realized. These far-distant territories are often of immense strategic significance, with many of them containing American naval and air force bases, as well as reconnaissance facilities. Under UNCLOS, they have also become important in the allocation of legally enforceable property rights over the world's natural resources. Many of these territories consist of groups of small islands stretching across large expanses of ocean, which allows the powers that control them to claim sole authority over access to the resources within their vast exclusive economic zone. This authority is frequently enforced by their respective armed forces, including the US's huge coast guard and naval fleets.

Thanks to their island holdings, the EEZs of the US, the UK and France dominate enormous stretches of the Pacific, Indian and South Atlantic Oceans; these three, together with Australia, New Zealand and Russia, are the six countries with the largest exclusive economic zones. Each of them is a developed former colonial country, with a mainly white population. Their total population is 604 million, compared with 1.338 billion for China. Each of them established the territorial basis of their vast overseas EEZs during the colonial era, from the fifteenth century to the mid-twentieth century. Their total EEZ amounts to 54 million square kilometres, of which almost three-quarters (39 million square kilometres) is separate from the home territory. Indeed, the overseas EEZs of the United States, France and the UK vastly exceed those of their home territories (see Table 2.1). Moreover, the very existence of the 'home territory' of the United States, Australia and New Zealand is due to settlement by white European colonists, who forcibly and often violently deprived the indigenous people of their resources.

China has only around 900,000 square kilometres of undisputed exclusive economic zone adjacent to the mainland – the size of one of the smaller overseas EEZ areas of the US, France or the UK. There is a further area of probably less than two million square kilometres of EEZ that Beijing claims in the South China Sea.[6] Even if it succeeds in all cases, its total EEZ is unlikely to be more than three million square kilometres. Apart from its South China Sea claims, which are vigorously disputed by countries in the region, and the adjacent island of Taiwan, China has no overseas island territories over which it asserts sovereignty. In sharp contrast to the European powers and their colonial-settler descendants, China did not seek to construct an overseas empire. This difference has had profound consequences for the global distribution of national property rights over the oceans' resources, especially under UNCLOS.

Table 2.1 Exclusive economic zones, selected countries (thousands of sq. km.)

	Mainland	*Overseas Territories*	*Overseas as % of total EEZ*	*Total*
USA	2,450 (a)	9,786	80	12,236
France	335	10,700	97	11,035
Australia	6,633	2,611	29	8,974
Russia	1,400 (b)	6,696 (c)	83	6,805
UK	774	6,031	89	6,805
New Zealand	3,423	3,273	49	6,696
China (d)	ca. 900 (e)	<2,000		<3,000

Source: Pew Trust, 2012.

Notes
a The 48 continental states, excluding Alaska, as well as Hawaii and other offshore islands.
b European Russia.
c Pacific and Siberia.
d These are rough, maximum figures. The precise calculation of China's EEZ is extraordinarily complicated. A large proportion of China's claims in the South China Sea are disputed by the countries that also border the Sea.
e Undisputed EEZ.

Whitehall's Islands

In the case of Britain, the EEZ attached to its overseas territories amounts to over six million square kilometres, which is eight times the total exclusive zone around the UK itself (see Table 2.2). The largest concentration of Britain's overseas EEZs is in the South Atlantic, with a total area of over 3.6 million square kilometres. London first claimed sovereignty over the Falkland Islands/Malvinas in 1765, with Captain Cook commandeering South Georgia and the Sandwich Islands in 1775. When Mrs. Thatcher went to war with Argentina in 1982, far more was at stake than the 16,000 square kilometres of windswept land in these three island groups: the exclusive economic zone of the Falklands, South Georgia and the Sandwich Islands amounts to two million square kilometres, nearly three times that of the UK itself. St Helena, meanwhile, came under the control of the East India Company in 1659 – Cromwell had granted the Company a charter to govern the island two years earlier – and later became a British colony. Ascension Island and Tristan da Cunha were colonized at the end of the Napoleonic Wars. These three South Atlantic territories have a total land area of just 417 square kilometres and a population of 5,400 – the equivalent of a medium-sized English village. However, due to the fact that each of them consists of numerous widely distributed islands, their total EEZ amounts to 1.64 million square kilometres.

Britain also retains several exotic remnants of its eighteenth-century slave empire in the Caribbean and North Atlantic, including Anguilla, Bermuda, the British Virgin Islands, the Cayman Islands, Montserrat and the Turks and Caicos Islands. Their total land area is only 1,093 square kilometres, and their population around 201,000 people. But their EEZ is 903,000 square kilometres, about the same as China's undisputed EEZ. For its part, the British Indian Ocean Territory consists of a group of widely dispersed islands, with a total land area of just sixty square kilometres, but an EEZ of 639,000 square kilometres. The Chagos people originally inhabited the main body of islands, principally Diego Garcia. The islands were charted by Vasco da Gama in the sixteenth century and claimed in the eighteenth by France, which established coconut plantations using African slaves and Indian labourers. In 1810 the islands were ceded to Britain as part of France's Mauritius Territory. In 1965 Britain split the Chagos archipelago from Mauritius to form the British Indian Ocean Territory. The main reason for this was to allow the UK to lease Diego Garcia to the United States, so that it could construct an airbase on the island. The 2,000 or so indigenous inhabitants were forcibly relocated to Mauritius and the Seychelles, and the island was occupied by the US military. Construction of the airbase began in 1971, including a 3,000-metre runway able to accommodate heavy bombers, such as B-52s. The base was used for US operations during the Iraq wars of 1991 and 2003, and the war in Afghanistan that has been going on since 2001. The population at present consists of around 4,000 people, of whom around 2,000 are American military personnel, while another 2,000, mainly from the Philippines, work for contractors.

The main British overseas territory in the Pacific Ocean is the Pitcairn group of islands. In 1790, Pitcairn Island was where the mutineers from the Bounty found refuge. The islands became a British colony in 1838, and were joined in 1902 by the three other groups, the Henderson, Oeno and Ducie Islands. The total land area of the whole Pitcairn group is forty-seven square kilometres, and it has a population of fewer than seventy people – the size of a small English village street. However, due to the wide spatial distribution of the islands, their EEZ is 836,000 square kilometres, around the same size as China's undisputed EEZ.

Table 2.2 The UK's overseas exclusive economic zones

	Land area (thousands of sq. km.)	EEZ (thousands of sq. km.)	Population	Date first occupied by UK
UK	-	774	-	
South Atlantic	*16.5*	*3,643*	*8,580*	
Falkland Islands/Malvinas (a)	12.2	551	3,140	1765
South Georgia & South Sandwich Islands (a)	3.9	1,450	30	1775
St Helena	0.12	445	4,255	1651
Ascension Island	0.09	442	880	1815
Tristan da Cunha	0.2	755	275	1815
Caribbean/ North Atlantic	*1.1*	*903*	*210,429*	
Anguilla	0.09	92	13,500	1650
Bermuda	0.05	450	64,268	1609
British Virgin Islands	0.15	80	27,800	1666
Cayman Islands	0.26	119	54,878	1670
Montserrat	0.1	8	5,164	1632
Turks & Caicos Islands	0.43	154	44,819	
Indian Ocean	*0.06*	*639*	*4,000*	
British Indian Ocean Territory (b)	0.06	639	4,000	1810
Pacific Ocean	*0.05*	*836*	*67*	
Pitcairn Islands	0.05	836	67	1838

Source: Pew Trust, 2012.

Notes
a   disputed with Argentina.
b   disputed with Mauritius.

Outposts Outre-mer

Though the UK's total EEZ is enormous, it pales by comparison with that of France. The latter's overseas EEZ, legacy of its colonial empire, is more than thirty times the size of that of metropolitan France (see Table 2.3). Its former slave-based sugar colonies in the Caribbean and North Atlantic have a combined exclusive zone of 903,000 square kilometres; those in the Indian Ocean total 2.58 million, while France's EEZ in the Pacific Ocean is no less than 6.9 million square kilometres.

French Polynesia contains several groups of islands, with a total land area of 4,167 square kilometres and a population of 260,000 – equivalent to a medium-sized French city. However, its 130 islands are spread across an area of 2.5 million square kilometres of ocean, and its exclusive economic zone totals 4.8 million square kilometres. Until 2007, Clipperton Island was administered together with French Polynesia. It consists of a single uninhabited coral atoll in the Eastern Pacific Ocean, with a total land area of just six square kilometres; France's EEZ on account of this territory, however, is 431,000 square kilometres. New Caledonia, in the southwest Pacific, became a French colony in 1853. The archipelago, which has a population of 252,000, is widely scattered across the ocean; it has a total area of 18,500 square kilometres, but its exclusive economic zone is 1.4 million square kilometres. French territories in the Indian Ocean include the uninhabited sub-Antarctic archipelagos of Crozet and Kerguelen, which together have a land area of 7,500 square kilometres but command an EEZ of 1.1 million square kilometres. Also among the 'Terres Australes et Antarctiques' are the tiny uninhabited islands of Amsterdam and St Paul, which have a total land area of only sixty-one square kilometres; however, their EEZ is 509,000 square kilometres. France's subtropical territory of Réunion, meanwhile, has a land area of 2,512 square kilometres and a population of 800,000; its EEZ is 315,000 square kilometres. In the southern Indian Ocean, Tromelin Island consists entirely of 'one large sandbank', 1.7 km in length and less than a kilometre wide. However, it has an EEZ of 270,000 square kilometres.

Table 2.3 France's overseas exclusive economic zones

	Land area (thousands of sq. km.)	EEZ (thousands of sq. km.)	Population	Date acquired
France	-	335	-	
Pacific Ocean	*22.9*	*6,87*	*527,000*	
French Polynesia	4.2	4,767	260,000	1842
Clipperton Island	568.0	431	0	1711
New Caledonia	18.5	1,423	252,000	1853
Wallis and Futuna	0.26	258	15,000	1837
Indian Ocean	*10.1*	*574*	*800,000*	*1772*
Crozet Islands	0.35	574	0	1772
Kerguelen Islands	7.2	568	0	1772
St Paul & Amsterdam Islands	0.06	509	0	1843
Scattered islands in the Indian Ocean	-	352	-	Various
Réunion	2.5	315	800,000	1638
Tromelin Island	Negl.	270	0	1810
Caribbean	*86.3*	*278*	*1,045,545*	
French Guiana	83.5	134	236,250	1814
Guadeloupe	1.6	96	405,5000	1674
Martinique	1.1	48	403,795	1638

Source: Pew Trust, 2012.

Empire of Bases

The United States chose not to sign the UN Convention on the Law of the Sea, but formally recognized the legality of the EEZ. A year after UNCLOS was enacted, President Reagan duly proclaimed the EEZ of the United States. It is the largest of any country by a wide margin, encompassing more than twelve million square kilometres, larger by a fifth than the land area of the United States; according to one legal scholar, 'Reagan's proclamation can be characterized as the largest territorial acquisition in the history of the United States'.[7]

The forty-eight states of the continental USA have an EEZ of 2.45 million square kilometres in total. The territory was acquired, of course, through the long westward extension of the frontier, primarily through military action. The original thirteen states at Independence came into existence through the expropriation by white colonial settlers of the lands occupied by Native Americans. The Louisiana Purchase of 1803 transferred to US ownership a vast swathe of France's colonial possessions, stretching from Louisiana up to Montana and North Dakota. The Mexican War of 1846–48 concluded with the absorption of the territories of New Mexico, Utah, Arizona, Nevada, part of Colorado, California and Texas. The massacre of Native Americans at Wounded Knee in 1890 brought the construction of the continental nation-state to a conclusion, endowing the US with long coastlines facing on to the Atlantic, the Pacific and the Gulf of Mexico. In that year, the US Bureau of the Census officially declared the frontier complete.

In addition to the EEZ of the forty-eight states, the US has a further 9.6 million square kilometres of EEZ in the Pacific Ocean. This derives from several different sources of territorial acquisition. The largest component consists of the state of Alaska and the Aleutian Island chain, which Imperial Russia colonized in the eighteenth century. In 1867 the US government purchased this vast territory from Russia for $7.2 million. The total EEZ of Alaska is 3.8 million square kilometres – half as much again as that of the forty-eight mainland states. The Aleutian chain is 1,900 kilometres long, stretching out from Alaska's south-western tip across the Pacific Ocean, towards Russia's Kamchatka peninsula. It has a population of just over 4,000, and its EEZ accounts for around one-third of the whole exclusive economic zone of Alaska.

Apart from Alaska and the Aleutian island chain, the total US exclusive economic zone around its Pacific island territories amounts to 5.8 million square kilometres. Within this total, just ninety square kilometres of land area of uninhabited islands accounts for an exclusive economic zone of 1.95 million square kilometres. The majority of this total is contributed by territories annexed in 1856 under the Guano Islands Act. In the late nineteenth and early twentieth centuries, guano was a valuable source of agricultural fertilizer and could also be used to make saltpetre for gunpowder. Washington still possesses most of the groups acquired under the Act, including the Howland and Baker Islands, Jarvis Island, Johnston Atoll, Palmyra Atoll and Kingman Reef. They are little more than rocks and have no permanent human inhabitants. Their combined land area is just eighty-seven square kilometres. However, due to their dispersion across the ocean, they have a total exclusive economic zone of 1.55 million square kilometres, almost as large as that of the entire east and west coast of the US combined and considerably larger than China's undisputed EEZ (see Table 2.4).

By the 1890s, the US was turning its attentions to overseas expansion. An editorial in the *Washington Post* on the eve of the Spanish-American War noted the emergence of:

> ... a new appetite, the yearning to show our strength ... Ambition, interest, land hunger, pride, the mere joy of fighting, whatever it may be, are

animated by a new sensation. The taste of Empire is in the mouth of the
people even as the taste of blood in the jungle.

(Quoted in Howard Zinn, 1999)

As a result of victory over Spain in 1898, the US not only gained effective control
of Cuba and Puerto Rico, but also acquired a string of territories across the Pacific,
including the Philippines, Guam and Wake Island; the latter two remain US territories today. Hawaii was an independent kingdom from 1801 to 1893, when
a group consisting mainly of American businessmen overthrew the monarchy.
After a brief period as a Republic, Hawaii was annexed by the US in 1898, and
admitted to the Union in 1959. Guam and Hawaii are key parts of the US military
command in the Pacific Ocean – which is by far the largest component in the
country's global military structure. Pearl Harbor remains the headquarters of the
Pacific Fleet.

In his November 2011 speech to the Australian Parliament, Obama proclaimed
that 'the United States has been, and always will be, a Pacific nation'; at the same
time, his Secretary of State declared that this would be 'America's Pacific Century'.[8]
The island of Okinawa occupies a particularly prominent place in Washington's
strategic posture in the Pacific. Located 400 miles from the coast of China's Fujian
province and 800 miles from Tokyo, Okinawa is the largest of the Ryukyu/Liuqiu
Islands. These are the most strategically important of all the world's small island
groups, stretching over 700 miles to the southwest of mainland Japan into the East
China Sea, culminating in the Diaoyu/Senkaku Islands. For centuries, Ryukyu/Liu-
qiu was a tiny independent kingdom inhabited by seafaring traders, with a culture
arguably more influenced by Chinese than Japanese tradition. In 1879, it was forcibly incorporated into Japan as 'Okinawa prefecture'. After the Second World War,
American troops occupied Okinawa, and in 1951 the San Francisco Treaty gave
the US 'all powers of administration, legislation and jurisdiction' over the territory,
'including the inhabitants and their territorial waters'. The US constructed massive military facilities on Okinawa, using it as a key base in both the Korean and
the Vietnam wars. In 1972 the Ryukyu/Liuqiu Islands, including Okinawa and the
Diaoyu Islands, were 'returned' to Japan. But the US military presence on Okinawa
continued to grow: today the island has around 25,000 armed-forces personnel,
around half the total number of American troops in Japan.

The island's status as a 'virtual US colony' has been a huge point of contention
in Okinawa as well as in mainland Japan. In 1995, US Defense Secretary Joseph
Nye enunciated a policy of 'deep engagement' in the Asia-Pacific region, deemed
necessary on the grounds that 'rising powers create instability in the international
state system': a 'forward-based troop presence ensures the US a seat at the table
on Asian issues' and 'enables us to respond quickly to protect our interests, not
only in Asia but as far away as the Persian Gulf'. For the foreseeable future, Japan
and the Okinawa base would serve as the 'cornerstones of our security strategy
for the entire region'.[9] The Governor of Okinawa remarked that Nye spoke of
Okinawa as if it were American territory.

The US acquisitions of the Mariana Islands and American Samoa took different forms. The Marianas, running north to south some 1,500 miles east of the Philippines, were annexed by Spain in 1565; Guam is the southernmost island in the chain. The Northern Marianas were sold to Germany in 1899 and then 'awarded' to Japan by the League of Nations after the First World War. After the Japanese defeat in 1945 the islands were placed under American trusteeship, and in 1976 the Commonwealth of the North Mariana Islands (CNMI) was formally integrated in a political union with the US. American Samoa is in the South Pacific, to the northeast of New Zealand. By the late nineteenth century the harbour at Pago Pago had become a regular refuelling station for coal-fired ships. The 1899 Tripartite Convention between Britain, Germany and the United States divided Samoa in two, with Germany taking control of the western islands and the US the eastern, including Pago Pago; it remains an American territory.

Table 2.4 The US's overseas exclusive economic zones

	Land area (thousands of sq. km.)	EEZ (thousands of sq. km.)	Population	Date acquired
48 Continental States	-	*2,450*	-	
East Coast	-	916	-	
Gulf of Mexico	-	708	-	
West Coast	-	826	-	
Alaska	*1,518.0*	*3,770*	*723,000*	*1867*
Puerto Rico	*9.1*	*178*	*3,700,000*	*1898*
Pacific Islands	*29.6*	*5,804*	*5,521,000*	*1898*
Hawaii	28.3	2,475	1,375,000	1898
Guam	0.54	222	159,000	1898
American Samoa	0.2	404	77,000	1904
Northern Marianas	0.46	749	77,000	1944
Islands without permanent inhabitants	0.09	1,954	-	
Including:				
Pacific Guano Islands (a)	0.09	1,1547	0	1856–58
Including:				
Wake Island (b)	0.003	407	0	1899

Source: Pew Trust, 2012.

Notes
a islands claimed under the 1856 Guano Islands Act: Howland and Baker Islands, Jarvis Island, Johnston Atoll, Palmyra Atoll and Kingman Reef.
b Wake Island has no permanent civilian inhabitants, but there are an estimated 150 US military personnel on the island.

Australia, New Zealand, Russia

Australia and New Zealand both benefited greatly from UNCLOS, since their main territories possess a long coastline; each has an exceptionally large EEZ on account of this fact alone. Britain originally staked a claim to Eastern Australia in 1770, and this was extended to the whole landmass in 1829. New Zealand was claimed by James Cook in 1769 and annexed by the UK in 1840. In both cases, there was a relatively large indigenous population, brutally treated by the British authorities and settlers; however, the legacies of colonial Australia and New Zealand extend to their overseas possessions, far removed from their respective main territories. These groups of islands in the southern Indian and Pacific Oceans were acquired by the British in the colonial era; in the case of inhabited islands, the pattern of treatment of the indigenous people was repeated. Each of the island groups in question has a small land area, but each group is spread over a wide area of the ocean, resulting in sizeable EEZs.

Australia has two groups of offshore island territories, one in the Pacific and one in the Indian Ocean; all were annexed by Britain and afterwards transferred to the Commonwealth of Australia (see Table 2.5). The Indian Ocean territories include Christmas Island, the Cocos Islands and the Heard and McDonald Islands in the Antarctic. Their combined land area is 517 square kilometres with a total population of only 2,003 people; their combined EEZ is 1.1 million square kilometres. Australia's Pacific Ocean territories include the Lord Howe Islands, the Macquarie Islands and Norfolk Island. They have a combined land area of 178 square kilometres, and a population of 2,649 people, with an EEZ of 1.5 million square kilometres. Australia's overseas island territories have a total area of 695 square kilometres and a population of 4,652, equivalent to a small town in the Australian outback; however, their combined EEZ is 2.6 million square kilometres.

New Zealand's largest area of EEZ is the Cook Islands, in the South Pacific. They were part of the British Empire, before being transferred to New Zealand. They contain fifteen major islands with a total land area of just 240 square kilometres and a population of 20,000; however, the islands are spread over 2.2 million square miles of ocean, and their total EEZ amounts to two million square kilometres, twice the size of China's undisputed EEZ. Three further South Pacific island groups under New Zealand's jurisdiction, the Kermadec, Tokelau and Niue islands, have a total land area of just 303 square kilometres and a population of only 2,800; however, due to their dispersion over such a wide area, their combined EEZ amounts to 1.3 million square kilometres.

Finally, the vast size of the modern state of Russia is mainly due to its colonial expansion into Siberia in the late sixteenth and early seventeenth centuries. The Russian empire reached the Pacific Ocean in 1639, and between 1742 and 1867 extended to include Alaska. After the collapse of the USSR, Russia lost many of the territorial acquisitions made in the nineteenth century in Central Asia; however, it maintained a firm grip on its vast Siberian territories. Russia's coastline stretches thousands of miles, along the Arctic from Murmansk in the west to the Chukchi Sea in the east, and down the Pacific coast to Vladivostok in the Sea of Japan. At 1.4 million square kilometres, Russia's EEZ in Europe is less than one-fifth of its total EEZ of eight million square kilometres; the main body of its exclusive zone is accounted for by the conquest of Siberia, with the long Arctic and Pacific coasts contributing a total of 6.7 million square kilometres of EEZ.

Table 2.5 Exclusive economic zones of Australia and New Zealand

	Land area (thousands of sq. km.)	EEZ (thousands of sq. km.)	Population	Date acquired (a)
Australia	-	6,363		1770–1829
Indian Ocean	*0.52*	*1,161*	*2,003*	
Christmas Island	0.14	277	1,403	1788
Cocos Islands	0.01	467	600	1888
Heard & McDonald Islands	0.37	417	0	1910
South Pacific	*0.18*	*1,452*	*2,649*	
Lord Howe Island	0.02	543	347	1788
Macquarie Island	0.13	478	0	1810
Norfolk Island	0.04	431	2,302	1788
Overseas Total	*0.7*	*2,613*	*4,652*	
New Zealand (*Main Islands*)	-	3,243	-	1769
South Pacific	*0.54*	*3,273*	*22,800*	
Cook Islands	0.24	1,960	20,000	1888
Kermadec Islands	0.03	678	0	1788
Niue	0.26	316	1,400	1900
Tokelau	0.01	319	1,400	1877
Overseas Total		*6,516*		

Source: Pew Trust, 2012.

Notes

a   Date of acquisition by Britain, later transferred to Australia/New Zealand.

Light Footprints?

An important justification for the UN's establishment of the concept of the 'exclusive economic zone' was the desire to reduce damage to exhaustible natural resources. It was hoped that establishing clear national property rights over those resources would transform the areas in question from open-access 'global commons' into regions of conservation. However, the West's own experience in managing resources within these areas hardly offers an adequate model. The early phases of colonialism, in particular, had a profoundly negative impact on the Pacific Ocean's animal population. The three epic voyages of Captain James Cook between 1768 and 1780, conducted under the orders from the British Admiralty and supported by the Royal Society, were a critically important stimulus to the West's intervention in the region. On each of his expeditions there, Cook was accompanied by scientists who provided a detailed record of the wildlife they encountered. One of the most surprising and striking results of the expeditions was the superabundance of wildlife they discovered in the Great Southern Ocean, including vast numbers of birds, seals and whales.

The detailed accounts in Cook's journals and accompanying maps stimulated a wave of commercial exploitation of the southern seas by European and American ships. Seals were killed mainly for their valuable skin and whales mainly for their oil. By the 1830s fur seals in the Southern Ocean were virtually extinct. The main attack was then directed at the whale population, which came south in the summer breeding season. The US was the leader in this industry. By 1846 New England alone had 735 whalers, each averaging a kill of a hundred whales per voyage. The killing went on until there was virtually nothing left to kill: 'In a period of little more than 50 years – roughly from the 1780s to the 1840s – these little ships with their polyglot crews … combed these vast icy oceans so thoroughly that no large marine animal was to be easily found any more.' By the 1880s commercial whaling had been abandoned over large areas of the Pacific Ocean.[10]

The impact on human populations was on a comparable scale. Prior to the arrival of Western colonists, the combined indigenous population of Australia, New Zealand and the Pacific islands was relatively small; establishing colonial rule thus did not present the same challenge as in India, China or the countries bordering the South China Sea. Nevertheless, numerous conflicts occurred between the Western colonists and the indigenous peoples, particularly over land. The most severe was in New Zealand, between 1843 and 1872, when as many as 20,000 Maoris may have been killed in a series of brutal confrontations with British troops. Colonial forces frequently used 'scorched earth' tactics, laying waste to Maori villages and destroying crops. Although much smaller in scale, the war in New Caledonia between French colonists and indigenous inhabitants was equally bloody. France annexed the territory in 1853, and violent conflicts ensued as French settlers attempted to expropriate land from the native Kanaka inhabitants. A full-scale Kanaka uprising erupted in 1878, and the French authorities responded with attacks on their villages and crops.

Indigenous people in the Pacific were typically treated as sub-human and often killed without compunction. In the case of Tasmania, the settler population – mainly convicts – cleared the indigenous people off their land through a ferocious manhunt. In 1830 Tasmania was put under martial law. Aborigines were 'continually hunted and tracked down like fallow deer, and, once captured, are deported, singly or in parties, to the islands of the Bass Strait'.[11] Within just five years, only 100 to 200 of the aboriginal population survived out of an estimated 5,000.

The spread of disease had an even more serious impact on the demography of the Pacific territories. Sexually transmitted diseases played an especially important role; from the late nineteenth century to the late twentieth, the greatly increased number of sealers, whalers and ordinary commercial shipping brought with it a thriving sex industry, as well as violent sexual attacks on indigenous women. A combination of venereal disease, tuberculosis, smallpox and dysentery was mainly responsible for the large population declines on many Pacific islands, including Hawaii, Tahiti, the Marquesas and Easter Island. Prior to Cook's arrival in 1778, Hawaii's population was around a quarter of a million by conservative estimates, and may have been significantly higher. The impact of infectious diseases produced a demographic catastrophe in which the indigenous population fell to as low as 30,000 by 1900.[12] In the case of Tahiti, annexed by France in 1843, it is estimated that the population dropped from 40,000 in the 1770s to just 9,000 in the 1830s, before falling to 6,000 in the late nineteenth century.[13] In the Marquesas, seized by France in 1842, the population fell from between 70,000 to 80,000 in the late eighteenth century to around 4,000 in 1900. The population of Easter Island is estimated to have fallen from 4,200 in 1860 to just 500 in 1871.[14]

Australia's indigenous population, meanwhile, is estimated to have fallen from around 200,000 in 1800 to just 20,000 in 1900.[15] In Australia, the white settlers also brought new diseases, including venereal disease, to which aborigines had low immunity. But the catastrophic decline was caused to a considerable degree by a deterioration in the health of the indigenous population, resulting from the forcible alienation of their lands. The effect of this was especially serious in the case of hunters and gatherers. When Charles Darwin visited Australia in 1836 he wrote: 'Wherever the European has trod, death seems to pursue the Aboriginal. We may look to the wide extent of the Americas, Polynesia, the Cape of Good Hope and Australia, and we find the same result.'[16]

String of Pearls

It is often alleged in the Western press that Beijing has a long-run 'string of pearls' strategy to build a succession of overseas bases in Southeast Asia and the Indian Ocean. Much of the analysis of the dispute over the Diaoyu/Senkaku Islands has also focused on the possibility that China might gain control over the natural resources in or under the South China Sea. Yet the vast expanse of EEZs derived from the West's colonial expansion in and around the Pacific Ocean, and ratified by UNCLOS, dwarfs by an enormous margin the territories that are in dispute between China and its immediate neighbours in the South China Sea (see Table 2.6).

Table 2.6 Pacific Ocean EEZs of selected countries (thousands of sq. km.)

Country	EEZ
USA	9,574 (a)
France	6,879
UK	836
Australia	3,500 (b)
New Zealand	6,696
Russia	3,419
Total	*30,904*
China	900 (c)

Notes
a   Excluding the US West Coast.
b   Including a rough estimate of the EEZ on Australia's Pacific coastline.
c   Undisputed EEZ.

China has existed as a unified state for many hundreds of years, with the Pacific Ocean forming its 'backyard'. From early in its history China possessed the technological and administrative capability to invade Southeast Asia, as well as the sparsely populated territories of the Pacific, including today's Australia, New Zealand and the other archipelagos. However, it chose not to do so. By the end of the nineteenth century, the Western powers had turned the Pacific Ocean into their own 'backyard' and had colonized most of the territories around the South China Sea, while China itself had been reduced to the status of a beggar. Its drastically altered position was symbolized by the flood of millions of impoverished Chinese migrants to work in the mainly Western-owned mines and plantations around the South China Sea and on the widely scattered Pacific islands.

The West's preoccupation with Beijing's involvement in the South China Sea contrasts sharply with the complete absence of discussion of the West's vast exclusive economic zones in the region, deriving from colonial conquest. The former imperial powers' acquisition of control over vast marine territories and resources through UNCLOS has received negligible attention other than in specialist legal journals, yet it eclipses by some distance the area and resources that are in contention in the South China Sea. The contrast in treatment of the two issues is especially disturbing in view of the talk of a new 'Peloponnesian War' being triggered by disputes over the Diaoyu/Senkaku Islands. It is as though the Western media have succeeded in focusing the minds of their populations on a mouse, when a mighty elephant stands behind them unnoticed.

Notes

1. This chapter first appeared as an article in *New Left Review*, (80) March–April 2013.
2. See, for example, Graham Allison, 'Thucydides' trap has been sprung in the Pacific', *Financial Times*, 21 August 2012.
3. Callum Roberts, *The Unnatural History of the Sea*, Washington, DC: Island Press, 2007.
4. Under certain circumstances a country's EEZ may extend beyond this limit.
5. See, for example, Simon Winchester, *Outposts: Journeys to the Surviving Relics of the British Empire*, London 1985.
6. China's claim to an EEZ in the South China Sea relates to the areas around the 'islands' in the sea rather than to the whole of the sea. The number of them that are simply 'rocks' rather than 'islands' is hotly disputed; only 'islands' are entitled to an exclusive economic zone. The total area of the South China Sea is roughly 3.5 million sq. kms. If the areas of undisputed coastal waters and undisputed high seas are excluded, then the area that China eventually claims as its EEZ in the South China Sea is likely to be substantially less than the total area of the whole sea.
7. Donald Woodworth, 'The Exclusive Economic Zone and the United States Insular Areas: A Case for Shared Sovereignty', *Ocean Development and International Law*, Vol. 25, No. 4, 1994, p. 366.
8. 'Remarks by President Obama to the Australian Parliament', 17 November 2011; Hillary Clinton, 'America's Pacific Century', *Foreign Affairs*, November 2011.
9. Joseph Nye, 'East Asian Security: The case for deep engagement', *Foreign Affairs*, July–August 1995; see also US Department of Defense, *United States Security Strategy in the East Asia–Pacific Region*, 27 February 1995.
10. Alan Moorehead, *The Fatal Impact: An Account of the Invasion of the South Pacific, 1767–1840*, London 1968, pp. 242, 251–2. For a comprehensive account of the destruction of the whale and seal population by the West's commercial whaling and sealing fleets in this period, see Roberts, *Unnatural History of the Sea*, chapters 7 ('Whaling: The First Global Industry') and 8 ('To the Ends of the Earth for Seals').
11. Quoted in Moorehead, *The Fatal Impact*, p. 213.
12. A. O. Bushnell, *Gifts of Civilization: Germs and Genocide in Hawaii*, Hawaii 1993. Cook was killed by Hawaiians on his return to the islands in 1779.
13. Moorehead, *The Fatal Impact*, p. 117.
14. Nicholas Thomas, *Islanders: The Pacific in the Age of Empire*, New Haven, CT: Yale University Press, 2010. Chapter 2 gives a detailed account of the ravages that sexual disease wrought upon the Marquesas in the nineteenth century. Forcible recruitment of Easter Islanders to work in Peru also played a role in the catastrophic population decline.
15. Richard Broome, *Aboriginal Australians: A History since 1788*, Sydney: Allen and Unwin, 1988, p. 172.
16. Quoted in Moorehead, *The Fatal Impact*, p. 212.

3 The Communist Manifesto in the twenty-first century[1]

Introduction

The two most profound analyses of capitalism's contradictory character are those of Adam Smith[2] and Karl Marx. Each of them combines profound philosophical investigation with deep analysis of the economic foundations of social, cultural and political life. Each of them views the socioeconomic structure as a comprehensive system in the process of long-term evolution, extending from the ancient past into the unknown future. Each of them is passionately interested in the long journey of the whole human species in the course of which an individual's own life is but a passing moment.

A crude caricature of Smith's writings provided inspiration for free market, Social Darwinist economists. Marx's writings, especially the *Manifesto of the Communist Party* (Marx and Engels, 1848), inspired revolutionaries in advanced countries who tried and failed to overthrow capitalism through political insurrections, and inspired also revolutionaries in developing countries who overthrew their governments and established regimes led by communist parties. The collapse of communist governments in the USSR and Eastern Europe, the profound changes since the 1970s in China under its communist leadership, and the deep systemic crisis in the advanced countries, require a re-evaluation of Marx's intellectual legacy.

Although China has undertaken enormous system reform since the 1970s, Marx's ideas remain centrally important for the Chinese Communist Party. If the West is to understand China better and cooperate with it to overcome the common challenges of globalization, it is necessary to reconsider the real nature of Marx's rich and complex intellectual legacy, rather than to rely on the crude caricature of his views that dominates the Western media and infuses the outlook of Western politicians.

Growth of Communist Elements within Capitalism

For Marx the 'two-edged sword' is the essence of capitalism. Since its earliest appearance in the ancient world capitalist competition has produced not only immense benefits, but also profound problems:

> Modern bourgeois society with its relations of production, of exchange and of property, a society that has conjured up such gigantic means of production

and exchange, is like the sorcerer, who is no longer able to control the powers of the nether world whom he has called up by his spells.

(Marx and Engels, 1848: 49)

The necessity of regulating the contradictions of capitalism in the interests of the whole human species is the essence of communism, which grows logically out of the character of capitalism itself. Marx used Hegel's term *Aufhebung*, or 'overcoming', to analyze the process by which the dialectic functions through the interaction of thesis and antithesis. Human beings overcome their alienation from their species being, which is the self-conscious exercise of their creativity, by asserting their collective control over the system that they have themselves created: 'As in religion, man is governed by the products of his own brain, so in capitalist production, he is governed by the products of his own hand' (Marx, 1867: 621). For Marx, the emergence of communism within the pores of capitalism takes place through *praxis*, namely man's conscious shaping of the changing historical conditions: 'The revolution expresses the radical need to subject the conditions of life to the conscious power of man who had created them. It integrates man with the circumstances of his life through their conscious direction and mastery' (Avineri, 1968: 149).

For Marx, building communism is a long evolutionary process, in which capitalist development itself creates the conditions for communism, under which the mass of the population incrementally establishes, in its common interest, collective control over the political-economic system. The vast bulk of Marx's writings was about capitalist development, especially in Britain, which was the 'first industrial nation' and 'workshop of the world'. The *Manifesto* (1848) is unique in the detailed examination by Marx and Engels of concrete policies in the future. In the Manifesto they identified a number of measures that a proletarian government might undertake, which were 'generally applicable in the most advanced countries'. They included 'abolition of property in land and application of all rents to public purposes', 'a heavy and progressive or graduated income tax', 'abolition of all rights of inheritance', 'centralization of credit in the hands of the State, by means of a national bank with State capital and an exclusive monopoly', 'centralization of means of communication in the hands of the State', 'extension of factories and instruments of production owned by the State', and 'free education for all children in public schools' (Marx and Engels, 1848: 74–5). The 'most amazing feature' of the list of concrete measures in the *Manifesto* is that 'it does not include nationalization of industry as such' (Avineri, 1968: 206). None of these measures is truly revolutionary. They are 'nothing but a dialectical realization and abolition of the processes already working within capitalist society' (Avineri, 1968: 207).

In the developed countries, from the mid-nineteenth century onward, political rights for the mass of the population expanded steadily and socioeconomic regulation at a national level made halting but significant progress, including the eventual establishment of a welfare state in most developed countries. If we compare capitalism in most developed countries today with that of the mid-nineteenth century, the progress towards communism is obvious. It includes universal suffrage, the advance of which Marx applauded, progressive taxation, free school education, health services free at the point of delivery, extensive government regulation of transport, communications, water services, energy and the environment, government-run central banks to control the financial system, and comprehensive government efforts to control macro-economic fluctuations. Progress has been halting and imperfect, with significant differences between countries, but the mass of the population have groped their way towards increasing control over the system of political economy that is the result of their collective labour. There is a dramatic contrast with the socially unjust, uncontrolled free market in the early phase of modern capitalist development. In Britain this reached its high point in the 1840s with the abolition of the Corn Laws. By the time of Marx's death in 1883 Britain had already advanced far beyond the anarchic free market political economy of the 1840s.[3] In other words, within the developed countries the elements or sprouts (*mengya*) of communism, which were already clearly visible by the time of Marx's death, have grown incrementally within the framework of capitalism itself, emerging from its inner contradictions.

Marx and Engels wrote: '[T]he theory of the Communists may be summed up in a single sentence: abolition of private property' (Marx and Engels, 1848: 63). The rights to own, use and benefit from property ownership can be transformed and regulated in innumerable ways. To identify state ownership as the necessary and defining characteristic of communism does a disservice to the richness of Marx's conception of communism and its evolutionary development within the pores of capitalism. In his 1888 Preface to the English edition of the *Manifesto*, Engels emphasized that 'no special stress' should be laid on the revolutionary measures proposed in the original *Manifesto* of 1848, because 'the practical application of the principles [in the *Manifesto*] will depend everywhere and at all times, on the historical conditions for the time being existing' (Engels, 1888: 21). In other words, communism cannot be equated mechanically with state ownership of the means of production. The concrete form that communism takes depends on the historical conditions and the way in which capitalism resolves its inner contradictions.

The 'social character of property' (Marx and Engels, 1848: 64) in the advanced countries has changed radically since the mid-nineteenth century. During his own lifetime Marx witnessed the rise of the giant family-owned firm. Since then the structure of ownership has evolved from owner-managers into ownership through shares traded on stock markets. Through this mechanism capital has been transformed to a significant extent into 'common property', that is to say, 'the property of all members of society' (Marx and Engels, 1848: 64). By the 1930s the large corporation had evolved into a manager-controlled firm with dispersed share ownership, mainly by individuals (Means, 1930; Berle and Means, 1932). Since the 1960s individual share ownership has declined and ownership of the large corporation is now mainly in the hands of institutions, among which pension funds, which agglomerate the savings of a mass of individuals, are the most important (Minns, 1996). There is a high degree of concentration in the institutions that manage a large part of the assets for both pension funds and the insurance industry. In 2010 the world's 500 largest asset managers had $64,000 billion (i.e., $64 trillion) in funds under management (Towers Watson, 2010). The top fifty firms accounted for 61 per cent of the total funds under management and among the top hundred firms none was from a developing country.

Gordon Clark terms the current system 'pension fund capitalism' (Clark, 2000). Peter Drucker argues that there has been an 'unseen revolution' since the 1950s, which has led to 'pension fund socialism' (Drucker, 1976). Whether directly as individuals or indirectly through institutions, a large proportion of the population of the advanced countries are the owners of large corporations. Ownership of capital is highly unequal and the growth of stock markets has added a large element of instability to financial systems. Marx and Engels noted carefully: 'The distinguishing feature of Communism is not the abolition of property generally, but the abolition of bourgeois property' (Marx and Engels, 1848: 62). The nature of 'bourgeois property' has altered radically since Marx's death in 1883. That would have been unsurprising to Marx, whose whole theoretical foundation was based on the continuous evolution of socioeconomic formations through the resolution of internal contradictions.

The era of capitalist development since the 1970s has witnessed a radical expansion of the international character of capitalism alongside explosive industrial concentration at a global level. Global regulation in the interest of the whole species is a 'choice of no choice' (*mei you xuan ze de xuan ze*) if we are to ensure a sustainable future for the species. However, global regulation is still in its infancy. The necessary global regulation of 'wild capitalism' in order to resolve its profound contradictions presents complex challenges (Nolan, 2009). Global institutions designed to regulate cooperatively the global political economy in mankind's collective interest are crude and deeply flawed. They are handicapped by the differences in national interests and their difficulties are exacerbated by differences between the interests of developed and developing countries as a whole. Although global markets have been established for a wide array of activities, people live mainly in separate countries, with their separate national identities and interests. The relationship between around one billion citizens of the high-income countries (the 'West') and around six billion citizens (rising to around eight or nine billion later this century) of the developing countries will be central to the achievement of the cooperation that is necessary to regulate 'wild capitalism'. China will have a crucially important role in this process.

Industrial Concentration and Oligopolistic Competition

The main body of 'mainstream' economists believes that inter-firm competition is analogous to Alfred Marshall's 'trees in the forest', with large firms constantly being out-competed by small, nimble new entrants (Marshall, 1890). It is widely thought that this process has become even more powerful in the era of modern information technology, which has made the world of industrial competition 'flat', with unprecedented opportunities for small- and medium-sized firms to out-compete large firms (Seabright, 2005; Friedman, 2006). An alternative, non-mainstream view has argued that the inherent tendency of capitalism is towards industrial concentration due to the opportunities for large firms to benefit from economies of scale and scope. Non-mainstream views all to some degree derive from Marx's analysis. In the *Manifesto* Marx and Engels pointed to the replacement of small-scale manufacture with 'giant, Modern Industry' and the replacement of the 'industrial middle class' with 'industrial millionaires, the leaders of whole industrial armies, the modern bourgeois' (Marx and Engels, 1848: 42). In the interval between the first publication of the *Manifesto* in 1848 and the Italian edition of 1893 the growth of large-scale industry had 'everywhere created a numerous, concentrated and powerful proletariat' (Engels, 1893: 37).

In *Capital* Vol. 1 Marx argued that there was a 'law of centralization of capital' or the 'attraction of capital by capital'. The driving force of concentration was competition itself, which pressured firms to cheapen the cost of production by investing ever larger amounts of capital in new means of production and in 'the technological application of science', which in turn create barriers to entry:

> The battle of competition is fought by cheapening commodities. The cheapness of commodities depends, *ceteris paribus*, on the productiveness of labour, and this again on the scale of production. Therefore the larger capital beats the smaller … Everywhere the increased scale of industrial establishments is the starting-point for a more comprehensive organization of the collective work of many, for a wider development of their material motive force – in other words, for the progressive transformation of isolated processes of production, carried on by customary methods, into processes of production socially combined and scientifically arranged.
>
> (Marx, 1867: 626–7)

The recent era of capitalist globalization has provided an opportunity to test the predictive qualities of the contrasting analytical approaches. During this period the brakes on the operation of market forces, which existed for much of the twentieth century, were removed. This period witnessed the most explosive episode of mergers and acquisitions in the history of capitalism. In each industrial sector, a small group of widely recognized companies came to occupy the 'commanding heights' of their respective sectors, accounting for a one-half or more of the total global market (Nolan, 2012). This was the visible part of the 'iceberg' of industrial concentration. However, the pressure from these leading systems integrator firms cascaded down across the supply chain, forcing intense consolidation of their supplier firms, which in turn exercised severe pressure upon their own supply chain (Nolan et al., 2007). Consequently, in the invisible part of the iceberg of industrial concentration, 'below the water level', there also emerged a high degree of global industrial concentration.

The world of industrial competition that has emerged in the period of the global business revolution is not 'flat'. Rather it is profoundly unequal. After more than two decades of the global business revolution, business power is concentrated in the hands of a small number of firms with their headquarters in the high-income countries. Research and development (R&D) is a critical component of long-term competitive capability in the modern sector. The United Kingdom's Department for Business Enterprise and Regulatory Reform (BERR) compiles an annual survey of global R&D spending. Its report for 2008 (*The 2008 R&D Scoreboard*) included the top 1,400 firms in terms of R&D expenditure (the G1400) (BERR, 2008). In 2007, these firms invested a total of $545 billion, which constitutes the main body of global investment in technical progress. The top fifty firms accounted for 45 per cent of the total investment in R&D by the G1400, and the top hundred firms accounted for 60 per cent of the total. The bottom hundred firms accounted for less than 1 per cent of the total. In other words, around a hundred or so firms in a small number of high-technology industries sit at the centre of technical progress in the era of globalization. Intense oligopolistic competition persisted throughout the upper reaches of the supply chain in almost all industries, which was responsible for the most rapid technical progress the world has ever seen. A small group of countries dominates the list of G1400 companies. Firms from the USA, Japan, Germany, France and the UK account for 80 per cent of the total number. Five small European countries (Denmark, Finland, Sweden, Switzerland and the Netherlands), with a total population of 42 million people, have 132 firms in the G1400, while the four 'BRIC' countries, with a total population of 2.6 billion, have 34 firms in the G1400. The developing countries as a whole, which have 84 per cent of the world's population, have a total of just thirty-seven firms in the G1400.

Capitalist Dynamism and Technical Progress

Ferocious global oligopolistic competition has driven innovation and technical progress at an unprecedented rate, bringing to a new highpoint the process analyzed by Marx and Engels in the *Manifesto*:

> The bourgeoisie, during its rule of scarce one hundred years, has created more massive and more colossal productive forces than have all the preceding generations together. Subjection of Nature's forces to man, machinery, application to industry and agriculture, steam-navigation, railways, electric telegraphs, clearing whole continents for cultivation, canalization of rivers, whole populations conjured out of the ground – what earlier century had even a presentiment that such productive forces slumbered in the lap of social labour?
>
> (Marx and Engels, 1848: 48)

In *Capital* Vol. 1 Marx emphasized the critical role of technical progress in the capital goods industries, the 'production of machines by means of machines' (Marx, 1867: Chapter xv). In the recent era of globalization a revolution has taken place in capital goods. These include commercial aircraft, automobiles and trucks, equipment for telecommunications, as well as for mining, oilfields, power generation and distribution, heating, ventilation and cooling. In each of these products technical progress has reduced energy intensity, improved ease of operation and reliability, increased safety, product longevity and ease of maintenance.

The most dramatic innovations have occurred in information technology. In each subsector of information technology (IT), intense oligopolistic rivalry drives innovation forward. In the 2010 list of the world's top 1,000 companies ranked by R&D spending (the G1000), the IT hardware and software sector has the largest R&D spending of any sector, with a total of $135 billion, accounting for 24 per cent of total R&D spending for the G1000 companies (BIS, 2010).[4] There is a total of 226 firms from this sector in the G1000, of which nearly three-fifths (127) are American. The 'software and computers services' subsector in the G1000 has a total of seventy-four firms, of which the top five firms account for 57 per cent of the subsector's R&D spending. Eight of the top ten firms are American, including the industry's super-giants (Microsoft, IBM, Google and Oracle). The 'hardware' subsector has a total of 152 firms, of which the top ten firms account for 45 per cent of the total spending in the subsector. Five of the top ten firms are American (Intel, Cisco, Motorola, Hewlett-Packard and Qualcomm). In each IT market segment, a small group of giant global firms engages in ferocious oligopolistic struggle, with innovation at the core – including IBM and HP in servers, Oracle and SAP in software packages, Google-Android and Apple in smartphone operating systems, ASML and Applied Materials in machines to manufacture semiconductors.

The IT revolution forms the heart of the transformation of global business. It has transformed the nature of the global corporation, making possible centralization of key functions and permitting the transformation of the relationship of core systems integrator firms with the 'external firm' composed of their supply chains. It has permitted the boundaries of the global firm to become blurred, in a new form of separation of ownership and control. The products of the IT revolution are deeply embedded in the manufacturing sector, in everything from automobiles to elevators. It has transformed the service sector, including banking, retail, leisure, entertainment and broadcasting. It has transformed interpersonal relations and political life. It has also powerfully affected international relations[5] and military technology.[6]

Global Character of Capitalism

The international character of capitalism was at the core of Marx's analysis:

> The bourgeoisie, by the rapid improvement of all instruments of production, by the immensely facilitated means of communication, draws all nations into civilization. The cheap prices of its commodities are the heavy artillery with which it batters down all Chinese walls, with which it forces the barbarians' intensely obstinate hatred of foreigners to capitulate. It compels all nations, on pain of extinction, to adopt the bourgeois mode of production; it compels them to introduce what it calls civilization into their midst, i.e., to become bourgeois themselves. In a word it creates a world after its own image.
>
> (Marx and Engels, 1848: 47)

The view is widely held by 'Marxist' economists that colonialism was the basic cause of underdevelopment and was accompanied by 'de-industrialization' in developing countries (e.g., Bagchi, 1982; Baran, 1957; Frank, 1967). In fact, Marx's own view of the impact of colonialism was quite different from this (e.g., Marx and Engels, 1882; Avineri, 1969). It is widely thought by 'Marxists' that Marx opposed colonialism. In fact, although he deplored the hypocrisy and violence of the colonial powers, he argued that colonialism was a progressive force that would permit the development of capitalism in countries ruled by 'Asiatic despotisms', such as China and India. This would, in turn permit industrialization, with the accompanying economic and social progress:

> [The] English cannon in 1840 broke down the authority of the Emperor and forced the Celestial Empire into contact with the terrestrial world. Complete isolation was the prime condition of the preservation of Old China. That isolation having come to an end by the medium of England, dissolution must follow as surely as that of any mummy carefully preserved in a hermetically sealed coffin, whenever it is brought into contact with the open air.
> (Marx and Engels, 1853: 4)

Marx and Engels' view of the benefits of Western colonialism were brutally direct. For example, in the 1840s, the French Army under General Bugeaud carried out the violent conquest of Algeria (e.g., Sessions, 2011), which heralded more than a century of French colonial rule in the country. Engels wrote as follows on the French defeat of the indigenous resistance:

> Upon the whole, it is, in our [i.e., Marx and Engels'] opinion, very fortunate that the Arabian chief has been taken. The struggle of the Bedouins was a hopeless one, and though the manner in which brutal soldiers like Bugeaud have carried on the war is highly blameable, the conquest of Algeria is an important and fortunate fact for the progress of civilization ... After all, the modern bourgeois, with civilization, industry, order, and at least the relative enlightenment following him, is preferable to the feudal lord or to the marauding robber, with the barbarian state of society to which they belong.
> (Engels, 1848)

Although Marx's view of the developing world as mainly ruled by stagnant 'Asiatic Despotisms' is highly problematic, there is an abundance of evidence that colonialism was accompanied by extensive economic progress (e.g., Allen and Donnithorne, 1957; Warren, 1980).

The progressive impact of international capitalism has continued in the post-colonial world. During the recent era of capitalist globalization, firms from the developed countries constructed comprehensive business systems in developing countries. Between 1990 and 2009 the inward stock of FDI in developing countries rose from $525 billion to $4.9 trillion, rising from 14 per cent to 29 per cent of GDP. The inward flow of FDI into developing countries was mainly from firms from the developed countries (UNCTAD, 2010). The average annual GDP growth in low- and middle-income economies accelerated from 3.2 per cent in 1980–1990 to 3.9 per cent in 1990–2000, reaching 6.4 per cent from 2000 to 2010 (World Bank, 2004: 184 and 2012: 216).

The inter-connected, cosmopolitan world has advanced dramatically in the recent era of capitalist globalization. This logical outcome was at the heart of Marx's view of the progressive character of capitalist globalization:

> The need of a constantly expanding market for its products chases the bourgeoisie over the whole surface of the globe. It must nestle everywhere, settle everywhere, establish connections everywhere … The bourgeoisie has, through its exploitation of the world market, given a cosmopolitan character to production and consumption in every country … In place of the old local and national seclusion and self-sufficiency, we have intercourse in every direction, universal inter-dependence of nations. And as in material so in intellectual production. The intellectual creations of individual nations become common property.
>
> (Marx and Engels, 1848: 46)

Class Struggle[7]

Marx regarded class struggle as the central force propelling the transformation of socioeconomic systems:

> The history of hitherto existing society is the history of class struggle … The modern bourgeois society that has sprouted from the ruins of feudal society has not done away with class antagonisms. It has but established new classes, new conditions of oppression, new forms of struggle in place of the old ones.
>
> (Marx and Engels, 1848: 40–41)

Marx and Engels (Engels, 1892) were profoundly affected by the abject poverty in Britain in the mid-nineteenth century. Marx was deeply concerned by the dehumanizing effects of the division of labour under machine production, which 'attacks the individual at the very roots of his life' (Marx, 1867: 363). Class relations are fundamentally important in understanding the evolution of the global political economy today, even if 'new classes, new conditions of oppression and new forms of struggle have replaced old ones'. The main contours of class structure under capitalist globalization are clearly visible.

A distinct global managerial elite has emerged, whose members inhabit the upper reaches of global corporations. They constitute a small fraction of the world's population and earn exceptionally high incomes. Using the purchasing power parity (PPP) exchange rate, and incorporating inter-country measures of income distribution, Milanovic (2007) estimates the Gini coefficient of global income distribution to be 0.64, with the top 10 per cent receiving 50 per cent of global income. This level of inequality is 'perhaps unparalleled in world history': 'If such extreme inequality existed in smaller communities or in a nation-state, governing authorities would find it too destabilizing to leave it alone, or revolutions or riots might break out' (Milanovic, 2007). Using the official exchange rate to convert national income data to a common standard the global Gini coefficient in 1998 was no less than 0.80, with the top 10 per cent accounting for 68 per cent of total global income. Inequality in the distribution of household wealth exceeds that for income. The Gini coefficient for the distribution of global household wealth is 0.89. The high-income countries of North America, Europe and the Asia-Pacific account for 88 per cent of the global total. The top 1 per cent of households accounts for 40 per cent of the global household wealth, the top 5 per cent for 71 per cent and the top 10 per cent for 80 per cent, while the bottom 50 per cent account for 1.1 per cent of the total, and the bottom 80 per cent account for 6.1 per cent (David et al., 2008).

Those who work in the upper reaches of the value chain of global firms share a common culture. The leaders of giant global firms are frequently drawn from nationalities other than those in which the company is headquartered. The global elite is a tiny fraction of the world's population that is made conscious of its special position through many symbols. They share a common language, English. Its members move their main place of residence frequently from country to country. They share common values, read the same newspaper, (the *Financial Times*), and stay in the same hotels. They communicate across their respective companies continuously, connected by ever-advancing information technologies. They buy the same globally branded luxury goods. Their children attend the same international private schools and finish their education at the same elite universities. They own residences in more than one country. Their homes are physically isolated from those of ordinary people. They have less and less attachment to a particular country, both at the level of the company and as a social group.

Global consultancies predict a massive transformation of the global class structure: 'based on current trends the global middle class will soon become the most numerous social group'. However, these predictions are mostly in the realms of wishful thinking rather than careful analysis. The World Bank concludes that by 2030 the world's 'rich and middle class' population[8] will reach 3.0 billion people, compared with 1.1 billion in 2000 (World Bank, 2007: 73). However, they estimate the absolute number of 'poor' people will expand from 5.0 billion in 2000 to 5.2 billion in 2030. In other words, after three decades of capitalist globalization, the combined 'rich and middle-income' group account for less than one-fifth of the world's population today and are likely to constitute less than two-fifths by 2030 (World Bank, 2007: 73). More considered estimates suggest an even smaller proportion of 'global rich and middle class' by 2030. Birdsall estimates that the 'rich and middle-income' population, with incomes of over $10 per day, accounts for less than 5 per cent of the Indian population and around 6 per cent of the Chinese population (Birdsall, 2011). Upper middle-income countries such as Mexico and Turkey have an average per capita GDP twice that of China and four times that of India. The combined share of the middle-income and rich in the total population of Mexico and Turkey amounts to only 20 to 30 per cent of the total population (Birdsall 2011). In other words, it is most unlikely that the share of the global 'rich and middle-income' group in China and India will exceed 30 per cent by 2030.

Within the high-income countries themselves, capitalist globalization has had contradictory results for the class structure. On the one hand, it has helped to raise real incomes due to the falling real prices of imported consumer goods and it has also improved the quality of life immeasurably for most people through technical progress.[9] On the other hand, it has helped to increase inequality. The liberalization of capital and product markets after the 1970s opened up a vast world of low-priced labour across the 'transition' and 'developing' countries. Global labour markets were integrated mainly through the migration of capital to poor countries and through the export of goods and services from poor to rich countries. This placed intense pressure for international equalization of wages and conditions of work through the operation of the 'law of one price'. These pressures added greatly to the impact of technological change, which replaced a wide swathe of secure, full-time, mainly unionized, white-collar office jobs that demanded modest skills, with unskilled, insecure, non-unionized and part-time jobs in the service sector, such as restaurants, entertainment, leisure services, retail and domestic help. In other words, since the 1970s the 'informal' sector has greatly increased its share of employment in the developed countries. The income share of the top 10 per cent of the distribution rose from 33 to 34 per cent between 1950 and 1980 to around 48 to 50 per cent in 2008–10, roughly the same share as in the late 1920s (Piketty and Sasz, 2012). Extrapolation of these trends into the future suggests a grim prospect for the evolution of the class structure of the developed countries. Far from producing a homogenization of class interests, the progressive unification of global labour markets, exacerbated by technical change, has intensified the conflict of interests between workers in rich and poor countries. Workers in poor countries are perceived to undermine conditions of work for people in rich countries, forming a powerful foundation for nationalist, populist, even racist, politics in developed countries, spurred on by a sensationalist mass media.

In developing countries, capitalist globalization has been accompanied by enormous progress for the mass of the population. The proportion of people living in abject poverty on less than $2 per day has fallen from 70 per cent in 1981 to 43 per cent today (World Bank, 2012: 72). Close to half the population of developing countries now lives in cities, with profound implications for social relationships and life opportunities. Literacy, sanitation, electrification and availability of information technology have advanced rapidly. Famine has virtually disappeared. Average life expectancy in developing countries rose from 56 years in the 1970s to around 66 years today.

Alongside immense progress in mass welfare capitalist globalization has been accompanied by increased inequality in developing countries. China has been at the forefront of the process of 'reform and opening up' since the 1970s. The official estimate of the Gini coefficient of inequality in income distribution increased from 0.28 in the early 1980s to 0.50 in 2005 (Nolan, 2009: 140), and unofficial estimates calculate that it has reached around 0.60 today. It is estimated that the top 1 per cent of the Chinese population has 67 per cent of the country's household wealth, while the top 0.1 per of households has 46 per cent (BCG, 2009). In other words, around 1.3 million people out of China's total population of around 1.3 billion people have almost one-half of total household wealth.

Global business schools speak glibly of the 'fortune at the bottom of the pyramid' (Prahalad, 2004). Although the share of the population in poverty in developing countries has fallen, the absolute number of the global abject poor living on less than $2 per day has remained constant since the 1980s, at around 2.5 billion (World Bank, 2010: 92). The share of the Chinese population living on less than $2 per day fell from 98 per cent in 1981 to 36 per cent in 2005, but the absolute number living on less than $2 per day in 2005 was still 474 million. In India, the absolute number living on less than $2 per day rose from 609 million in 1981 to 828 million (76 per cent of the population) in 2005 (World Bank, 2010: 92).

Developing countries contain 83 per cent of the world's workforce (World Bank, 2012: 48). For the foreseeable future the impoverished 'reserve army of labour' (Marx, 1867: 628–40) will powerfully influence labour markets in developing countries. Many millions of workers in developing countries are employed in vast factories performing simple, repetitive tasks assembling products for global customers. Workers are, indeed, 'attacked at the very root of their lives'. A much larger number work in the informal sector in millions of small-scale establishments. The proportion of the non-farm labour force working in the 'informal' sector amounts to around 75 per cent in Africa, 58 per cent in Latin America and 40 to 60 per cent in Asia (ILO, 2002). A large fraction of the world's workforce in developing countries constitutes a 'reserve army of labour' who are employed in the 'informal sector' at a constant real subsistence wage. The sector is characterized by 'casualized and fluctuating employment and piece rates, whether working at home, in sweatshops, or on their own account in the open air; and in the absence of any contractual rights, or collective organization' (Breman, 2009). It is estimated that over 200 million children aged five to fourteen years of age in developing countries are engaged in work, of whom 'at least 111 million are involved in hazardous and exploitative work' (ILO, 2002). Conditions in the 'informal' mining, manufacturing, construction, transport and service sectors and the associated family living conditions are typically little different from those described in Engels' study the *Condition of the Working Class in England*, first published in the 1840s during the early phase of British industrialization (Engels, 1892). Most firms are owner-managed, with a sharply antagonistic relationship between capital and labour, analogous to that in mid-nineteenth century Britain.

Today's high-income countries all experienced severe class struggle during capitalist industrialization.[10] In the early stage the main form of working class struggle consisted of spontaneous and short-lived riots, principally over food prices. In the late eighteenth and early nineteenth century liberals in Europe were deeply fearful of the power of the 'mob'. They regarded a narrowly restricted franchise as essential to social and political stability. In *The Great Transformation* Karl Polanyi observed:

> In England it became the unwritten law of the constitution that the working class must be denied the vote … The Chartists [in 1848] had fought for the right to stop the mill of the market which ground the lives of the people. But the people were only granted rights when the awful adjustment had been made.
> (Polanyi 1957, 226)

It was views such as Edmund Burke's that dominated Britain's political development during the Industrial Revolution. For the European bourgeoisie the French Revolution offered a frightening insight into the possibilities of revolutionary change in Europe. Burke was appalled at the extremism and naivety of the Revolution:

> Hypocrisy, of course, delights in the most sublime speculations ... [With] these professors ... it is a war or a revolution, or it is nothing ... These sorts of people are so taken up with their theories about the rights of man, that they totally forget about his nature.
>
> (Burke, 1790: 155)

He deeply feared the destructive power of the revolutionary clubs in Paris:

> In these meetings of all sorts, every counsel, in proportion as it is daring, and violent, and perfidious, is taken for the mark of superior genius. Humanity and compassion are ridiculed as the fruits of superstition and ignorance. Tenderness to individuals is considered treason to the public.
>
> (Burke, 1790: 160–1)

Burke was acutely aware of defects, not only in the French, but also in the British political system: 'The errors and defects of the old establishments are visible and palpable. It calls for little ability to point them out' (Burke, 1790: 280). However, he argued that political reform is greatly preferable to political revolution:

> [I]t is with infinite caution that any man ought to venture upon pulling down an edifice which has answered in any tolerable degree for ages the common purposes of society, or on building it up again, without having models and patterns of approved utility before its eyes ... Rage and phrenzy, will pull down more in half an hour, than prudence, deliberation and foresight can build in 100 years.
>
> (Burke, 1790: 151–2)

To the criticism that reform might take many years he answered: 'Without question it might; and it ought' (Burke, 1790: 280). He was explicitly conservative in his belief that property owners had a superior right to govern society: '[A]s to the share of power, authority and direction which each individual ought to have in the management of the state, that I must deny to be amongst the direct original rights of man' (Burke, 1790: 150).

In the case of Britain, the 1832 Reform Act only marginally increased the size of the British electorate (from 432,000 to 652,000 electors). It put into place stringent property qualifications for voting, increasing the size of the electorate by only 217,000 voters. Its main result was to 'open the doors of Parliament more widely to representatives of the new industrial bourgeoisie and to bourgeois radicals, but above all it established clearly that their interests would henceforth be decisive' (Engels, 1892: 28). Britain's Industrial Revolution began in the late eighteenth century, and by the 1840s Britain had become the 'workshop of the world'. As industrialization, urbanization, literacy and living standards increased in the nineteenth century, working class collective consciousness advanced, but was still mainly oriented towards reformist demands, which included extension of the franchise, increased rights, better social protection (e.g., restrictions on child labour, restriction of hours of work and safety at work) and social provision for the mass of the working population (e.g., education, health provision). The main struggle was directed towards achieving working class demands through reform of the parliamentary system and through parliamentary legislation. However, extension of the franchise took place slowly in the second half of the nineteenth century. It was not until 1867 that the Second Reform Act was passed, which reduced the property qualification and extended the electorate from 1.3 million to 2.5 million. The Reform Acts of 1884 and 1885 further extended the franchise and introduced secret ballots, increasing the electorate from around 8 per cent to 29 per cent of the adult male population. However, it was not until 1918 that the franchise was extended to the whole adult population, male and female, over the age of thirty.

A democratic system of global governance would be one in which the whole world's adult population voted for a global parliament. One can imagine that many of the policies that were supported by the bottom 80 per cent of the world's wealth distribution, who possess a combined total of only 6 per cent of the world's wealth, might be radically at odds with those of the top 10 per cent of the world's population who possess 85 per cent of the world's wealth.

Finance and the Real Economy

A large part of Volume 3 of *Capital* is devoted to an intense but uncompleted investigation of the nature of money and credit, and the relationship between the financial system and the real economy. This area more than any other demonstrates the way in which human beings, in creating the capitalist system through their collective labour, are like the sorcerer who has 'conjured up forces from the nether world' that are out of his control:

> The credit system accelerates the material development of the productive forces and the establishment of the world market. It is the historical mission of the capitalist system of production to raise these material foundations of the new mode of production to a certain degree of perfection. At the same time credit accelerates the violent eruptions of this contradiction – crises – and thereby the elements of disintegration of the old mode of production. The two characteristics immanent in the credit system are, on the one hand, to develop the incentive of capitalist production, enrichment through exploitation of the labour of others, to the purest and most colossal form of gambling and swindling, and to reduce more and more the number of the few who exploit the social wealth; on the other hand, to constitute the form

of transition to a new mode of production. It is this ambiguous nature which endows the principal spokesmen of credit from Law to Isaac Pereire with the pleasant mixture of swindler and prophet.

(Marx, 1894: 441)

The period of capitalist globalization witnessed an unprecedented global asset bubble, fuelled by the huge increase in money in its myriad forms. The asset bubble was self-reinforcing, with speculation driving up asset prices in a self-reinforcing cycle around the world. The asset bubble affected almost all assets, including equities, property, energy, raw materials, agricultural products, bonds and works of art. In the high-income economies, the asset prices bubble, especially that in property, formed the foundation for an explosive growth of credit, to fund both speculation and current consumption. The level of household debt in the US rose ceaselessly, from 60 per cent of household income in the mid-1980s to over 120 per cent in 2004. The global financial system was now deeply integrated across national boundaries, far more deeply even than the integration of production systems. The massive extent of repackaging and sale of debt meant that debt was far more deeply distributed throughout the economy. This provided a source of stability and enhanced the ability of the financial system to ride out relatively small-scale crises, but it meant that the whole global financial system was far more susceptible to a giant financial crisis should it erupt.

The transition from primarily national to global markets was not accompanied by a strengthening of international regulatory governance. The International Monetary Fund (IMF), the institution that was supposed to guide the global financial system, was aptly described as a 'rudderless ship in a sea of liquidity'. The problem for regulators was exacerbated by the fact that the global financial system developed instruments of such great complexity and at such a high speed, that no one understood how to regulate the whole system, even assuming that the political mechanisms existed to do so. In 2008 the global financial crisis erupted. At the core of the Washington Consensus was the confidence that unregulated financial markets based on privately owned banks were self-correcting. The financial crisis demolished this 'market fundamentalist' view. In May 2008 the former Managing Director of the IMF, Horst Kohler, delivered a devastating verdict on liberalized global financial markets, likening it to Mary Shelley's Frankenstein monster:

> The complexity of financial products and the possibility to carry out huge leveraged trades with little capital have allowed the monster to grow ... The only good thing about this crisis is that has made clear to any thinking, responsible person in the sector that international financial markets have developed into a monster that must be put back in its place.

Marx's comments on financial concentration are wholly applicable to the current era:

> Talk about centralization! The credit system, which has its focus on the so-called national banks and the big money-lenders and usurers surrounding

them, constitutes enormous centralization, and gives to this class of parasites the fabulous power, not only to periodically despoil industrial capitalists, but also to interfere in actual production in a most dangerous manner – and this gang knows nothing about production and has nothing to do with it.

(Marx, 1894: 544–545)

Five years after the global financial crisis erupted global financial regulation had made only slow progress in the face of deep differences among the high-income countries themselves and between the high-income countries and the developing countries. In China, the main body of the 'rescue package' was channelled into real infrastructure assets. In the West, the main consequence of 'quantitative easing' was an asset price bubble, from which the rich benefited disproportionately, with only a small fraction of credit channelled into real investment.[11]

The Environment

Like most nineteenth-century writers, Marx admired the capability of self-conscious *homo faber* to transform nature in accordance with his direction 'subjecting nature's forces to man', 'clearing whole continents for cultivation' with 'whole populations conjured out of the ground' (Marx and Engels, 1848: 48). Rachel Carson's book *The Silent Spring* (1962) warned of the potentially destructive consequences for the natural environment if human beings continued to treat it as a resource to be exploited rather than as a complex living ecology of which they are merely one part:

[Can] any civilization wage relentless war on life without destroying itself, and without losing the right to be called civilized? ... The 'control of nature' is a phrase conceived in arrogance, born of the Neanderthal age of biology and philosophy, when it was supposed that nature exists for the convenience of man. Her fears have come to fruition.

The World Wildlife Fund has constructed a Living Planet Index, which tracks the populations of 1,313 vertebrate species – fish, amphibians, reptiles, birds and mammals – from all around the world. It concluded that between 1970 and 2009 the Index fell by around 30 per cent, a global trend which suggests that we are degrading natural ecosystems at a rate unprecedented in human history. The Harvard ecologist, Edward Wilson, has warned that if present trends in species extinction continue, by the end of the present century humanity will live in an 'Age of Loneliness'.

The high-income economies are locked into a pattern of production and consumption that is profligate in the use of fossil fuels. At its heart is the system of transport of goods and people based on trucks and automobiles. The developing countries have an average of less than fifty motor vehicles per 1,000 people compared with over 800 in the United States. The high-income countries consume 5,400 kilograms (oil equivalent) of primary energy per capita, compared with 1,400 kilograms in the middle-income countries and 500 kilograms in the low-income economies. Prior to 1800 emissions of carbon dioxide are estimated to have been 260 parts per million (ppm). These increased to 397 ppm in 2005, and in the absence of strict controls, are predicted to reach 800 ppm in 2100. If developing countries follow the development path of the high-income countries, even with rapid technical progress there is little chance of avoiding catastrophic global warming.

Communism and the Commune

There is a complex relationship in Marx's writings between the words 'commune' and 'communism'. In his *Critique of Hegel's Doctrine of the State* (1843) Marx argued that 'true democracy' is a society in which the individual is no longer juxtaposed against society. He used the term 'communist essence' for the first time:

> The atomization into which civil society is driven by its political act is necessarily caused by the fact that the commonwealth (*das Gemeinwesen*), the communist essence (*das kommunistische Wesen*) within which the individual exists, civil society, is being divorced from the state, or because the political state is a mere abstraction of it.
>
> (translated in Avineri, 1968: 34)

In the *Critique* Marx originally used the word *Kommune*, which is derived from the French word 'commune'. However, he replaced it with the word G*emeinwesen,* 'a good old German word' (Engels, quoted in Avineri, 1968: 34). The word G*emeinwesen* 'means both commonwealth in the dual sense of *res publica* and republic in the narrower meaning, as well as man's common, universal nature and "commune" … [T]he word forcefully suggests Marx's idea of an integrated human being who has overcome the dichotomy between the public and the private self' (Avineri, 1968: 34–5). The French revolutionaries of 1871 famously described their newly established political structure as the 'Paris Commune' and they themselves as 'communards'.

The idea of the 'commune' (*gongshe*) was centrally important in both the Great Leap Forward and the Cultural Revolution. Chairman Mao enthusiastically supported the 'commune' as a new sociopolitical form to overcome the divorce of the masses from the state. Study of Marx's writings on the Paris Commune of 1871 was centrally important in the Cultural Revolution (Marx and Engels, 1961). The Cultural Revolution pamphlet consisted of a lengthy extract from Marx's writings on *The Civil War in France* (Marx, 1871: 187–268). In public Marx welcomed the Paris Commune. For him the 'commune' embodied the idea of the masses taking the state into their own hands:

> The Commune – the reabsorption of the state power by society as its own living forces instead of as forces controlling and subduing it, by the popular masses themselves, forming their own force instead of the organized force for their suppression.
>
> (Marx, 1871: 250)

Marx warned repeatedly against premature risings of the proletariat before socio-economic conditions had matured. Writing in 1847 he said:

> If the proletariat brings down the domination of the bourgeoisie, its victory will be ephemeral, only a moment in the service of the bourgeoisie (just like *anno* 1794), so long as within the process of history, within its 'movement', those material conditions have not been created that make necessary the abolition of the bourgeois mode of production and therefore also the definitive fall of the political bourgeois domination.
>
> (Marx, article in *Deutsche Brusseler Zeitung*, November 1847, quoted in Avineri, 1968: 191)

Marx warned repeatedly that a communist revolution which attempted to realize itself by purely political means could never go beyond a formalistic egalitarianism, unaware of the creative possibilities offered by an unfolding civil society created by capitalism itself.

Although Marx offered enthusiastic public support for the revolutions of 1848 and 1871 he emphasized that the communist revolution was a long-term evolutionary process, quite different from a utopian socialist '*putsch*' in which there is a 'direct attempt of the proletariat to attain its own ends, made in times of universal excitement'(Marx and Engels, 1848: 89). Indeed, Marx was concerned that violent, premature and opportunistic seizures of power would have a 'necessarily reactionary character', which 'inculcated universal asceticism and social levelling in its crudest form' (Marx and Engels, 1848: 89). Privately, Marx discouraged the 1871 revolution. He regarded the Paris Commune as a mere political revolution, a '*putsch*', which could not possibly establish communism, because the conditions for this to take place were not yet mature in France: '[T]his was merely the rising of a city under exceptional conditions, the majority of the Commune was in no way socialist, nor could it be' (Marx, 1881a: 293). In 1893 Engels reflected on the defeat of the 1871 Paris Commune: '[N]either the economic progress nor the intellectual development of the mass of French workers had as yet reached the stage which would have made a social reconstruction possible' (Engels, 1893: 37). Marx was little known before his pamphlet *The Civil War in France* (1871). By the mid-1860s virtually nothing that Marx had written in the past was any longer in print. It was deeply ironical that Marx's name:

> ... became world-famous almost overnight not through his works and writings, but in connection with an insurrection which he opposed, whose downfall he foresaw and predicted, whose initiators were not his disciples, and which, according to him, was not and could not be socialist.
>
> (Avineri, 1968: 243)

Although Marx only discussed briefly rural communal forms of organization in the modern world, his observations were to be profoundly significant for the future of communism in developing countries.

In February 1881, Vera Zasulich, the Russian revolutionary and translator of the 1882 Russian edition of the *Manifesto,* wrote to Marx.[12] She asked him whether the Russian commune was destined to perish at the hands of rural capitalism and, if so, what this would mean for Russian socialists:

> If the commune is destined to perish, all that remains for the socialist is more or less ill-founded calculations as to how many decades it will take for the Russian peasant's land to pass into the hands of the bourgeoisie, and how many centuries it will take for capitalism in Russia to reach something like the level of development already attained in Western Europe. Their task will then be to conduct propaganda solely among the urban workers, while these workers will be continually drowned in the peasant mass which, following the dissolution of the commune, will be thrown on to the streets of the large towns in search of a wage.
>
> (Zasulich, 1881)

Marx agonized over his reply, composing and editing three successive lengthy drafts over several weeks (Marx, 1881b). His final reply to her was short and cautious, but he said that he believed that the commune might be the 'fulcrum for social regeneration in Russia' (Marx, 1881b). Marx's various drafts were lost, but rediscovered in 1911 and published in 1924. The timing of their publication was critically important, coming in the middle of the Soviet Union's 'Great Industrialization Debate' of the 1920s, in which the role of agricultural institutions was centrally important.[13] The different drafts were heavily worked upon, with substantial overlap. The intense re-working of the drafts, with arguments altered slightly from one draft to the next, betray the anxiety that the issue caused for Marx.

In the drafts of his letter to Vera Zasulich (Marx, 1881b), Marx considered two possible paths of Russian rural development. The first was the path of North American capitalist development under which communal property would be abolished and 'an intermediate class of a more or less prosperous minority of the peasants' would be created alongside a 'majority of proletarians'. However, a different path could be made possible due to the special features of the Russian peasantry:

> Alone in Europe, it has preserved itself not as scattered debris ... but as the more or less dominant form of popular life spread over a vast empire. While it has in common land ownership, the natural basis of collective appropriation, its historical context – the contemporaneity of capitalist production – provides it with ready-made material conditions for huge-scale common labour. It is therefore able to incorporate the positive achievement of the capitalist system, without having to pass under its harsh tribute. The commune may gradually replace fragmented agriculture with large-scale, machine-assisted agriculture particularly suited to the physical configuration of Russia. It may thus become the direct starting point of the economic system towards which modern society is tending.
>
> (Marx, 1881b)

Marx was concerned that a 'debilitating feature' of the Russian agricultural commune was its isolation and lack of connection between the lives of different communes. Although it was not a universal characteristic of the commune, Marx warned that 'wherever it does so appear, it leads to the formation of a more or less central despotism above the communes' (Marx, 1881b). He considered that this obstacle could be removed 'with the utmost ease'. All that was necessary was to 'replace the "*volost*", a government institution,[14] with a peasant assembly chosen by the communes themselves – an economic and political body serving their own interests' (Marx, 1881b).

In their preface to the Russian translation of the *Manifesto*, published in 1882, Marx and Engels returned to the issues raised in Marx's draft replies to Vera Zasulich. They identified two possible paths for Russian development. The first path would follow that of North America where European immigration:

> [fitted] North America for a gigantic agricultural production ... Step by step the small and middle landownership of the farmers, the basis of the whole political constitution, is succumbing to the competition of giant farms; simultaneously, a mass proletariat and fabulous concentration of capitals are developing for the first time in the industrial regions.
>
> (Marx and Engels, 1882)

However, Marx and Engels noted that in Russia, despite the development of capitalist farming, 'more than half the land is owned in common'. They asked the question:

> Can the Russian *obschina* (village community), though greatly undermined, yet a form of the primeval common ownership of land, pass directly to the higher form of communist common ownership? Or, on the contrary must it pass through the same process of dissolution as constitutes the historical evolution of the West?
>
> (Marx and Engels, 1882)

They gave the fateful, but carefully qualified, answer: 'If the Russian Revolution becomes the signal for a proletarian movement in the West, so that both complement each other, the present Russian common ownership of land may serve as the starting point for a communist development' (Marx and Engels, 1882).

Even in this qualified form, Marx and Engels' preface, reinforced by the publication in the 1920s of the drafts of his letter to Vera Zasulich, written at the very end of Marx's life, amidst intense physical and mental stress,[15] provided vital nourishment to twentieth century revolutionary movements led by 'vanguard' communist parties in developing countries and to the post-revolutionary collectivization of their rural populations (Nolan, 1988).

Communism and China

A profound adjustment is required in the West if there is to be a fruitful cooperation with the East in order successfully to build global institutions to meet the common interests of the whole of humanity ('all under heaven', *tian xia*). The West needs much better to appreciate the way in which it is viewed by the majority of the world's citizens. In recent years, in the West the level of hostility towards China has grown steadily. In part, this has ideological roots in anti-communism.[16] Mainstream Western thought, including the mass media, politicians and intellectuals, have a simplistic understanding of the term 'communism' that bears little relationship to Marx's own view. Their perspective is a relic of the Cold War. In fact, there are grounds for widely differing definitions of the word 'communism', most of which may differ radically from the type of political economy established in the former USSR.

In China itself at the time that the Chinese Communist Party (CCP) was founded in 1921 there was considerable debate about the way in which to translate the term 'communism'. The Chinese Communist Party decided to adopt the Chinese term *'gongchang zhuyi'* for 'communism', which literally means 'common property-ism', and *'gongchangdang'*, literally 'common property party', for the Chinese name of the communist party. However, there were other suggestions for the translation of the word 'communism', which is an English word that is itself derived from the French word 'commune' (*gongshe* in Chinese). These included *'gongtong zhuyi'* ('common-ism'), *'gongxiang zhuyi'* ('sharing together-ism'), and *'shetuan zhuyi'* ('mass-ism'). They also included the term *'datong zhuyi'*, which harks back to the ancient Chinese concept of *'datong'*, or 'great harmony' for 'all under heaven'. Using *'datong zhuyi'* as the translation of 'communism' indicates a society in which the pursuit of the 'common good' or the 'common interest' is the paramount goal, without specifying the particular means by which it might be achieved.[17] In the *Manifesto*, Marx and Engels stated: 'All previous historical movements were movements of minorities or in the interests of minorities. The proletarian movement is the self-conscious, independent movement of the immense majority, in the interests of the immense majority' (Marx and Engels, 1848: 58). A 'communism' which pursues the 'common interest' of 'all under heaven' (*tian xia*), both East and West, is a philosophical goal that all human beings might agree to.

Conclusion

Capitalist freedom to compete in the pursuit of profit has been at the heart of human progress since the dawn of human civilization. However, capitalist freedom is a 'two-edged sword' with great benefits and deep contradictions (Nolan, 2007). In the era of capitalist globalization since the 1970s, the pace of progress has reached a new highpoint, with unprecedented advances in technology stimulated by the invisible hand of competition, led by the competition between giant oligopolistic firms battling for leading positions on global markets. Better than anyone, Marx grasped the central contradictory character of capitalism. Throughout his life Marx was guided by the core concepts of *praxis* and *aufhebung*, with the mass of the human species taking control of the world they had created together. His understanding of communism was that it grows incrementally out of the contradictions of capitalist development. Far from being the logical path for establishing communism, a political *'putsch'* by a minority is an indication that the process of capitalist development has not yet fully developed communism within itself. Far from being an irrelevance today, both the West and China can together learn from Marx as each of them tries to get to grips with the challenges that global capitalism poses for them individually and collectively.

In the recent era of capitalist globalization the dynamic character that was fundamental to Marx's analysis of capitalism has reached new heights, bringing unprecedented benefits for the human species. However, the contradictions of capitalism have intensified. These include the threat to the natural environment, which was not foreseen by Marx, as well as the challenge of the global business revolution, the unequal global class structure, and the inherently unstable nature of the global financial system, all of which were foreseen by Marx. He was confident that the global spread of capitalism would erode national differences. Marx and Engels declared that 'the working men have no country' and their clarion call at the end of the *Manifesto* was: 'working men of all countries unite!' (Marx and Engels, 1848: 71 and 96). In fact, nationalism and capitalism have been mutually reinforcing. Among the central issues for the period ahead will be the relationship between the West and China. The outcome of this interaction will be critical in deciding whether the world can achieve a peaceful resolution of the deep contradictions of capitalist globalization that leads the human species haltingly towards communism rather than marching to a New Peloponnesian War, fought with cyber-and nuclear weapons[18] instead of swords and spears.

If human beings are to resolve the contradictions of capitalist globalization, it is necessary to establish global mechanisms to contain the Frankenstein monster of unconstrained global capitalism. However, to do so requires cooperation between nations, with national interests that often diverge. It also requires cooperation between groups of nations at different levels of economic development. The richer group of countries has many interests in common that often diverge from those of the developing countries. For most human beings, 'global' is not their framework of reference or source of identity. Apart from the family and religion, the 'nation' is the primary source of identity and the main forum within which they have a political voice. Although the forces of capitalist globalization are increasingly international, the national interest of citizens and national governments remains a potent force.

The challenges that are faced by human beings are the product of people's own purposive activities, expressed mainly through the economic system. It is within their collective power to resolve these contradictions. The very depth of the challenges they face may shock them into the action necessary to ensure the survival of the species. Alongside human beings' competitive and destructive instincts are their Darwinian instincts for species survival through cooperation. It may only be the approaching 'final hour' which finally forces human beings to grope their way towards the globally cooperative solutions that constitute the essence of communism in the twenty-first century. The falling of the 'dusk', as humanity looks into the abyss, may be the final impulse to produce the cooperative solution that is immanent within the unfolding of global capitalism: 'The owl of Minerva spreads its wings only with the falling of the dusk' (Hegel, 1820: 13). East-West cooperation to regulate global capitalism is the 'choice of no choice' (*mei you xuan ze de xuan ze*) for the survival of the human species. Instead of being the basis of ideological conflict Marx's insights into the evolution of communism within the pores of capitalism can be a source of enhanced mutual understanding. As the world gropes its way towards a 'great harmony' Marx's rich intellectual legacy can make a significant contribution to East and West establishing a common language and understanding of the task that they face together.

Notes

1. I am indebted to Dr Zhang Jin for suggesting that I write this chapter. I am grateful to Dr Zhang, Stephen Perry and Geoff Harcourt for their comments.
2. In *The Theory of Moral Sentiments* (Smith, 1761) and *The Wealth of Nations* (Smith, 1776).
3. The transformation of British capitalism between 1848 and the 1880s is summarized in Engels, 1892. Engels notes: 'The truth is this: during the period of England's industrial monopoly the English working class have, to a certain extent, shared in the benefits of the monopoly [of world trade]. These benefits were very unequally parcelled out amongst them; the privileged minority pocketed most, but even the great mass had, at least, a temporary share now and then. And that is the reason why, since the dying out of Owenism, there has been no Socialism in England' (Engels, 1892: 34).
4. This annual publication ceased in 2010.
5. During her term as US Secretary of State, Hillary Clinton appointed Alec Ross as 'Senior Advisor for Innovation'. He spearheaded the US government's '21st Century Statecraft' initiative: 'The Internet is a game-changer for statecraft ... Social media offers government a powerful tool to engage directly with people in a more local and organic fashion. Diplomacy is normally conducted in formal interactions between sovereign states ... In the twenty-first century the critical innovation in diplomacy is people to people. Using connection technologies and social media networks, the people of all nations can interact with one another on the pressing issues of our time ... The policy of the US government is to promote access and adoption of connection technologies as tools of human empowerment and progress' (Ross and Scott, 2011).
6. The development of cyber warfare has radically changed the shape of twenty-first century warfare.
7. See Chapter Four on the issue of how to translate the term 'class struggle' into Chinese.
8. They define middle class as a per capita income of between USD $4,000–7,000 (at year 2000 PPP dollars) and the rich as over $7,000. The global poor have an income of less than $4,000.
9. It is almost impossible to measure the impact of technical progress on mass welfare.
10. Foster (1974) provides one of the few detailed accounts of the richly textured and complex nature of class struggle during the British Industrial Revolution.
11. It is estimated that in the UK only 15 per cent of total financial flows go into investment (Turner, 2013) and that 40 per cent of the benefit from US quantitative easing has gone to the top 5 per cent of the population (Tett, 2013).
12. There is some confusion about whether Vera Zasulich was the translator of the 1882 Russian edition. G. V. Plekhanov later claimed that he was the translator.
13. The timing is so significant, and the apparent support they lent to the collectivization so obvious, that one might suspect that they were sophisticated forgeries. However, even the most severe critic of Soviet collectivization, Robert Conquest, does not doubt their authenticity (Conquest, 1986: 22).

14. Each *volost* incorporated a number of peasant communes. It was run by peasant elders and local magistrates controlled by the local officialdom (Shanin, 1983: 125).
15. Marx himself was gravely ill and his wife, Jenny, died in December 1881.
16. However, the growing hostility is related also to the West's fears at the prospect of a radical shift in the international balance of power in the twenty-first century, as developing countries in general, and China in particular, increase their economic, political and military strength. This process will bring to a close a relatively brief era in world history that began with the Industrial Revolution in late eighteenth century Britain, which heralded the West's global dominance for around 200 years.
17. Rousseau wrestled endlessly with this concept. In the *Social Contract and Discourses* he refers to the 'common interest', the 'common good', the 'general will', the 'will of all', the 'public will', the 'public interest', and the 'great society'. Ultimately, Rousseau regarded the supremacy of the great General Will as 'the first principle of public economy and the fundamental principle of government' (Cole, 1993: xliii). Rousseau's profound concern for the 'common interest', however that might be defined, is one reason for the popularity of his writings in China.
18. For a terrifying perspective on the threat of nuclear war that still looms over the human species, see Schlosser, 2013. Wang Lixiong (2008) has provided a highly realistic scenario under which such an apocalypse might occur.

Bibliography

Allen, G.C. and A. Donnithorne (1957) *Western Enterprise and Economic Development in Indonesia and Malaya*, London: Macmillan.

Avineri, S. (1968) *The Social and Political Thought of Karl Marx*, Cambridge: Cambridge University Press.

Avineri, S. (1969) *Karl Marx on Colonialism and Modernization*, New York: Anchor Books.

Bagchi, A.K. (1982) *The Political Economy of Development,* Cambridge: Cambridge University Press.

Baran, P. (1957) *The Political Economy of Growth*, New York: Monthly Review Press.

Berle, A. and G.C. Means (1991) *The Modern Corporation and Private Property*, New York: Harcourt, Brace and World, originally published 1932.

Birdsall, N. (2011) 'The (indispensable) middle class in developing countries Or, why it's the rich and the rest, not the poor and the rest', Washington, DC: Center for Global Governance.

Boston Consulting Group (BCG) (2009) *Wealth Markets in China: Delivering the Right Value Proposition for China's Wealthy*, Beijing: Boston Consulting Group.

Breman, J. (2009) 'Myth of the global safety net', *New Left Review,* no. 59.

Burke, E. (1968) *Reflections on the Revolution in France*, London: Pelican Books, originally published 1790.

Carson, R. (1962) *The Silent Spring*, New York: Houghton Mifflin.

Clark, L.G. (2000) *Pension Fund Capitalism*, Oxford: Oxford University Press.

Cole, G.D.H. (1993) Introduction, J.-J. Rousseau, *The Social Contract and Discourses*, London: Everyman.

Conquest, R. (1986) *Harvest of Sorrow,* London: Hutchison.

David, J.B., Sandstrom, S., Shorrocks, A. and E.N. Wolff (2008) 'The world distribution of household wealth', United Nations University – WIDER, Discussion Paper, no. 2008/3.

Department for Business Enterprise and Regulatory Reform (BERR) (2008) *The 2008 R&D Scoreboard*, London: BERR.

Department for Business Innovation and Skills (BIS) (2010) *The 2010 R&D Scoreboard,* London: BIS.

Drucker, P.F. (1976) *The Unseen Revolution: How Pension Fund Socialism Came to America,* New York: Harper and Row.

Engels, F. (1952) Preface to the English edition of *Manifesto of the Communist Party,* in Marx and Engels, *Manifesto of the Communist Party,* Moscow: Progress Publishers, originally published 1888.

Engels, F. (1952) Preface to the Italian edition of *Manifesto of the Communist Party,* in Marx and Engels, *Manifesto of the Communist Party,* Moscow: Progress Publishers, originally published 1893.

Engels, F. (1969a) 'French Rule in Algeria', *The Northern Star,* 22 January 1848, in Avineri, *Karl Marx on Colonialism and Modernization.*

Engels, F. (1969b) Preface to the first English edition of *The Condition of the Working Class in England,* Panther edition with Foreword by E. Hobsbawm, originally published in German 1845 and in English 1892.

Foster, J. (1974) *Class Struggle and the Industrial Revolution,* London: Methuen.

Frank. A.G. (1967) *Capitalism and Underdevelopment in Latin America,* New York: Monthly Review Press.

Friedman, T. (2006) *The World is Flat: The Globalized World in the Twenty-first Century,* London: Penguin Books.

Hegel, G.F. (1952) *The Philosophy of Right,* English edition, Oxford: Oxford University Press, originally published in German 1820.

Held, D. and A. Kaya, eds (2007) *Global Inequality,* Cambridge: Polity Press.

International Labour Organisation (ILO) (2002) *Decent Work and the Informal Economy,* Geneva: ILO.

Marshall, A. (1920) *Principles of Economics,* London: Macmillan, originally published 1890.

Marx, K. (1967) *Capital,* Vol. 1, New York: International Publishers, originally published 1867.

Marx, K. (1972) *Capital,* Vol. 3, London: Lawrence and Wishart, originally published 1894.

Marx, K. (1974) *The First International and After,* Political Writings, Vol. 3. London: Penguin Books, originally published 1871.

Marx, K. (1974) '*The Civil War in France*', in Marx, *The First International and After.*

Marx, K. (1971) Letter to F. Domela-Nieuwenhiuis in the Hague originally written in 1881a, reproduced in Marx and Engels, *On the Paris Commune,* originally published 1871.

Marx, K. (1975) *Early Writings,* London: Penguin Books, originally published 1843.

Marx, K. (1975) '*Critique of Hegel's Doctrine of the State*', in Marx, *Early Writings.*

Marx, K. (1983) Drafts and final version of a letter to Vera Zasulich, originally written in 1881b, reproduced in full in Shanin, *Late Marx and the Russian Road: Marx and the Peripheries of Capitalism.*

Marx, K. and F. Engels (1952) *Manifesto of the Communist Party,* Moscow: Progress Publishers, originally published in German 1848.

Marx, K. and F. Engels (1952) Preface to the Russian edition of *Manifesto of the Communist Party,* in Marx and Engels, *Manifesto of the Communist Party,* Moscow: Progress Publishers, originally published 1882.

Marx, K. and F. Engels (1961) *On the Paris Commune, (lun bali gongshe),* Beijing: Renmin chubanshe.

Marx, K. and F. Engels (1968) 'Revolution in China and Europe', in *Marx on China: Articles from the New York Daily Tribune, 1853–1860.* London: Laurence and Wishart, originally published 1853.

Marx, K. and F. Engels (1971) *On the Paris Commune,* Moscow: Progress Publishers, originally published 1871.

Means, G.C. (1930) 'The diffusion of stock ownership in the US', *Quarterly Journal of Economics*, no. 44: 561–600.

Milanovic, B. (2007) 'Globalisation and inequality', in D. Held and A. Kaya, eds, *Global Inequality,* Cambridge: Polity Press.

Minns, R. (1996) 'The social ownership of capital', *New Left Review*, Sept/Oct: 42–61.

Nolan, P. (1988) *The Political Economy of Collective Farms,* Cambridge: Polity Press.

Nolan. P. (2007) *Capitalism and Freedom: The Contradictory Character of Globalization,* London: Anthem Press.

Nolan, P. (2009) *Crossroads: The End of Wild Capitalism*, London: Marshall Cavendish.

Nolan, P. (2012) *Is China Buying the World?,* Cambridge: Polity Press.

Nolan, P., Jin Zhang and Chunhang Liu (2007) *The Global Business Revolution and the Cascade Effect,* Basingstoke: Palgrave.

Picketty, T. and E. Sasz (2012) 'Top Incomes and the Great Recession: Recent Evolutions and Policy Implications', *IMF Annual Research Conference*, 8–9 November.

Polanyi, K. (1957) *The Great Transformation,* Boston: Beacon Press.

Prahalad, C.K. (2004) *The Fortune at the Bottom of the Pyramid: Eradicating Poverty through Profits,* Upper Saddle River, NJ: Prentice-Hall.

Ross, A. and B. Scott. (2011) '21st Century statecraft', *NATO Review,* 17 November.

Rousseau, J-J. (1993) *The Social Contract and Discourses,* London: Everyman edition, originally published 1762.

Schlosser, E. (2013) *Command and Control*, London: Allen Lane.

Seabright, P. (2005) *The Company of Strangers,* Princeton: Princeton University Press.

Sessions, J. (2011) *By Plow and Sword: France and the Conquest of Algeria,* London: Cornell University Press.

Shanin, T., ed. (1983) *Late Marx and the Russian Road: Marx and the Peripheries of Capitalism,* New York: Monthly Review Press.

Smith, A. (1982) *The Theory of Moral Sentiments*, Indianapolis: Liberty Classics edition (revised edition), originally published 1761.

Smith, A. (1976) *The Wealth of Nations* (2 Vols.), Chicago: University of Chicago Press (Cannan edition), originally published 1776.

Tett, G. (2013) 'Insane financial system lives on post-Lehman', *Financial Times,* 13 September.

Towers Watson (2010) The *World's 500 Largest Asset Managers,* New York: Towers Watson.

Turner, A. (2013) 'Credit, money and leverage: What Wiksell, Hayek and Fisher knew, but modern macroeconomics Forgot', Stockholm: Stockholm School of Economics.

UNCTAD (2010) *World Investment Report*, Geneva: UNCTAD.

Wang, Lixiong (2008) *China Tidal Wave*, London: Oriental Global, originally published in Chinese in 1991 as *Yellow Peril* (*Huang Huo*).

Warren, B. (1980) *Imperialism: Pioneer of Capitalism*, London: Verso.

World Bank (2004) *World Development Indicators,* Washington DC: The World Bank.

World Bank (2007) *Global Economic Prospects,* Washington DC: The World Bank.

World Bank (2010) *World Development Indicators,* Washington DC: The World Bank.

World Bank (2012) *World Development Indicators,* Washington DC: The World Bank.

Zasulich, V. (1983) 'A letter to Marx' written in 1881, reproduced in Shanin *Late Marx and the Russian Road: Marx and the Peripheries of Capitalism.*

4 Translating the term 'class struggle' into Chinese[1]

The history of the proletariat in England begins with the second half of the last century, with the invention of the steam engine and of machinery for working cotton. These inventions gave rise as is well known to an industrial revolution, a revolution which altered the whole of civil society ... England is the classic soil of this transformation ... and England is, therefore, the classic land of its chief product also, the proletariat. Only in England can the proletariat be studied in all its relations and from all sides.

(Engels, 1845: 50)

Introduction

In the English language the term 'class struggle' is flexible and embraces a wide array of possible forms of 'struggle'. The German equivalent, '*Klassenkampf*', is equally ambiguous and can embrace a wide array of meanings.[2] The normal Chinese translation of 'class struggle' is *jieji douzheng*, which is much closer in meaning to 'class fighting' than the English term 'class struggle' or the German equivalent '*Klassenkampf*'. The term 'class struggle' was central to China's political campaigns between late 1957 and the death of Chairman Mao in 1976. The Cultural Revolution was imbued with the language of 'class struggle'. In fact, following the socialist transformation in the 1950s, class differentiation based on ownership of the means of production, or wide differences in income and wealth, no longer existed: 'exploiters were fundamentally eliminated as classes' (Eleventh CPC Central Committee, 1981: 163). However, the Cultural Revolution, which was 'initiated and led by Chairman Mao Zedong', was based on the proposition that it was necessary to have 'a great political revolution in which one class would overthrow another, a revolution that would have to be waged time and again' (Eleventh CPC Central Committee, 1981: 161).

In its reflection on the Cultural Revolution in June 1981, the Eleventh CPC Central Committee observed:

The history of the Cultural Revolution has proved that Comrade Mao Zedong's principal theses for initiating this revolution conformed neither to Marxism-Leninism nor to Chinese reality. They represent an entirely erroneous appraisal of the prevailing class relations and political situation in the

Party and the state ... The Cultural Revolution was defined as a struggle against the revisionist line or capitalist road. There were no grounds at all for this definition.

(Eleventh CPC Central Committee, 1981: 161)

It continued:

Under socialist conditions, there is no economic or political basis for carrying out a great political revolution in which 'one class overthrows another'. It decidedly could not come up with any constructive programme, but could only bring grave disorder, damage and retrogression in its train. History has shown that the Cultural Revolution, initiated by a leader labouring under misapprehension and capitalized on by counterrevolutionary cliques, led to domestic turmoil and brought catastrophe to the Party, the state and the whole people.

(Eleventh CPC Central Committee, 1981: 163–4)

The term 'class struggle' was central to Marx's understanding of the transformation of capitalism. The case of Britain was crucially important, not only because he lived most of his adult life in Britain, but also because it was the heart of global capitalism in the nineteenth century. In fact, the various ways in which class struggle can take place and evolve under capitalism constitute a continuum, ranging from inchoate protest to violent, revolutionary class warfare. The different parts of the spectrum can be observed in the case of the First Industrial Nation, Britain. The nature of 'class struggle' in Britain has evolved and changed character over the course of more than two hundred years, from the late eighteenth to the early twenty-first century. At least five phases can be distinguished, each of which represents a different aspect of the nature of class struggle. In the first phase (1750–1867) the British working class was deprived of the franchise. In the second phase (1867–1914) they gained the franchise but did not achieve political rule. The working class established their own political party, but it was far too small to govern the country. In the third phase (1914–1945) the workers' own political party was admitted as a partner in wartime coalition governments and governed for two brief spells as a minority government. In the fourth phase (1945–1979) , after World War II, the Labour Party finally achieved the position of a majority government and the legislative measures they passed formed the basis of the 'welfare state' that was the foundation of British political economy up until the 1970s. In the fifth phase (1979–2015) class relations in Britain have changed greatly in the face of the challenge of capitalist globalization since the 1970s, posing further complicated issues for class struggle.

1750–1867

During the whole of the first century of capitalist industrialization in Britain the working class was excluded from the electorate, denied a political 'voice' by the ruling class. In the long period of early capitalist industrialization Britain made the transition from a largely agricultural and commercial economy into the 'workshop of the world', by far the most urbanized, technologically advanced and industrially powerful country in the world. In the course of less than a century the balance of the world economy and military power was completely transformed. The decisive factor was the technological revolution that began in late-eighteenth-century Britain.

Even though Britain had only 2 per cent of the world population by the middle of the nineteenth century it held a dominant position in world industry that was 'much more pronounced than that of the United States in the mid-twentieth century' (Crouzet, 1982: 5). In the 1850s Britain accounted for 53 per cent of world iron production, 50 per cent of coal and lignite production, 49 per cent of raw cotton consumption, 34 per cent of merchant navy capacity, 27 per cent of energy consumption, and 25 per cent of exports. In 1850 Britain's stock of steam engines and locomotives totalled 1.29 million hp., compared with 700,000 for the five countries of Western Europe combined (Crouzet, 1982: 7), and it accounted for 40 per cent of the world's internationally traded manufactured goods (Crouzet, 1982: 343).

In 1813 Patrick Colquhoun published his famous study of the English class structure (reproduced in Hilton, 2006: 127). He estimated that in the years 1801 to 1803, the top 35 per cent of the British population had average family incomes of over £75, the top 11 per cent had family incomes of over £200, while the top 1 per cent had incomes of over £1,500. The top 1 per cent was composed mainly of large landlords, eminent merchants and bankers. At the other end of the income structure 64 per cent of the population had an annual household income of less than £55. Sir Frederick Eden's massive study of the English poor, which was published in 1797, estimated that a typical labourer's annual family budget was £39, of which no less than 64 per cent was spent simply on cereals and potatoes. In late eighteenth century and early nineteenth century Britain, the majority of the population fell into the category of the 'labouring poor'. Their life was 'extremely wretched':

> It was impossible for most of them to live a life of more than bare subsistence, and the natural disasters of their personal lives – unemployment, sickness, death of the breadwinner – left families in utter destitution … Poverty was regarded as an inexorable law of nature.
>
> (Plumb, 1963: 150–54)

In the late eighteenth century, alongside the emergence of a powerful merchant and manufacturing class, a large proportion of the urban population consisted of a property-less, unskilled and impoverished working class. They were unprotected by social welfare provision, without job security, and 'crowded into filthy courts, alleys and insalubrious garrets' (Rude, 1962: 6). In London, for the mass of citizens, 'life was hard, brutal and violent, a constant struggle against high disease, high mortality and wretched economic conditions' (Rude, 1962: 7). This 'very large and powerful body, which forms the fourth estate in the community … has been dignified by the name of the Mob' (Henry Fielding, quoted in Rude, 1962: 7).

For most of the time, the impoverished mass of the population endured their condition passively. Periodic bouts of violence were mostly disorganized. Their objective was not to achieve revolutionary change and mob riots were mostly contained with relative ease by the ruling class. In eighteenth century Britain 'popular rioting was endemic':

> In country districts and market towns, riots took place against rising food prices, against turnpikes, enclosures, work-houses, Smuggling and Militia Acts, and against Methodists' and Dissenters' chapels; above all they broke out in years of shortage, when the prices of wheat and flour and bread were appreciably above the average.
>
> (Rude, 1962: 13)

By far the most severe of these were the Gordon Riots in London, which were initiated by mass protest against the Papists Act (1778) that removed many of the anti-Catholic discriminations. The petition delivered to the House of Commons on 29 May 1780 erupted into a huge riot, which lasted for several days and involved an enormous crowd of people ransacking central London. Although the riot had its origins in anti-Catholic sentiment, it had a distinct class character. The targets of the mob's wrath were 'generally among the more substantial citizens and very rarely among the poor' (Rude, 1952: 329). Homes of prominent Catholics were attacked and destroyed. The Bank of England was attacked. Newgate, The Fleet and other prisons were badly damaged and large numbers of prisoners allowed to escape. The Lord Mayor of London, Brackley Kennett, was afterwards examined by the Privy Council. They found him guilty of acting with 'great timidity' and he was fined £1,000. By 6 June the civil authority had completely lost control of London. So widespread was the violence, rioting and destruction on 7 June that it became known as 'Black Wednesday'. The army acted with extreme force to quell the disorder. Almost three hundred rioters were shot dead and many hundreds more were wounded. Over four hundred rioters were arrested, and sixty-two were sentenced to death, though some of these were subsequently reprieved. Twenty-five of the rioters were hanged publicly, not only at Tyburn, but also at specific buildings linked to the actions of the individual convicted felons.

The French Revolution erupted only a few years later. The Revolution began as an aristocratic rebellion against royal taxation in 1789 and transformed into a middle class rebellion from 1789–91. The Declaration of the Rights of Man was promulgated by the Constituent Assembly on 26 August 1789. It declared that 'all men are born equal and free in respect to their rights'. However, the Assembly had 'no intention of sharing its political authority with the lower social strata' (Cobban, 1963: 167). It decided that voting rights for the new Legislative Assembly should be limited to 'active citizens' who paid taxes equivalent to more than three days' labour, and that a much higher property qualification was required in order to stand for election to the Assembly: 'In this way it was hoped that the principle of democratic sovereignty would have the sting taken out of it and effective power remain in the hands of the propertied classes' (Cobban, 1963: 167). The Assembly also passed the Le Chapelier Law, which drastically restricted workers' rights to take industrial action against their employers.[3]

Between 1792 and 1794 the Revolution entered a chaotic and violent phase. In August 1792 the revolutionary Paris Commune, with forty-eight local 'sections', was established. These formed the basis for mobilizing a mass insurrection in Paris. Throughout the final two convulsive years of the French Revolution, the Commune 'so effectively controlled France that it was frequently referred to as the "Parisian Dictatorship"' (Horne, 1990: 293). In the 'Revolution of 10 August' in 1792 over 1,000 people died during a mass attack on the Tuileries. The Legislative Assembly was replaced by a new Convention, which was elected on the basis of 'universal suffrage'. However, the election took place under such chaotic conditions that only a tiny fraction of the population voted. The two wings of the Convention were the Jacobins, who included Robespierre, Marat and Danton, and the Girondists. They engaged in a bitter ideological and factional struggle. Although they both theoretically respected the 'sovereignty of the people', they also believed in the 'sacred rights of private property and a free market economy', and neither of them regarded the 'people' as including the property-less proletariat (Cobban, 1963: 223). During the 'September Days' of 1792 mobs broke open several of the prisons in Paris and massacred over 1,000 prisoners who were alleged to be 'royalist plotters', supposedly supporting the invasion of France by anti-revolutionary forces. The Convention abolished the monarchy and Louis XVI was executed on 21 January 1793. The political and economic situation deteriorated. France faced the possibility of foreign invasion, rebellion in the Vendée in Western France, price inflation and food riots. The survival of the fledgling revolutionary state appeared in danger. In this turbulent atmosphere in the Spring of 1793, the Convention established a Revolutionary Tribunal to judge traitors with the right to order summary execution of those found guilty, as well as establishing the Committee of Public Safety. These two bodies became the instruments of the Great Terror. France was turned into a police state with a vast machinery of spies and informers who defended the Revolution against its alleged enemies: 'the whole country including the small ruling faction and its adherents [were] stifled in a miasma of suspicion and fear' (Cobban, 1963: 238). As many as 300,000 people were arrested for alleged political crimes. Between June 1793 and July 1794 almost 3,000 people were executed. The Revolution ended in August 1794 with the arrest and execution of Robespierre and ninety-two of his supporters.

Prior to the French Revolution there was a group of English radical thinkers, mainly 'Dissenters', who were excluded from the universities and from government office and included people such as Joseph Priestly (1723–1804), John Wilkes (1725–1797) and Richard Price (1723–1791). They argued for radical political reform, including universal male suffrage, annual parliaments, and secret ballots. However, the Gordon Riots and the vastly more dramatic events of the French Revolution profoundly affected the British ruling class, reinforcing their deep-seated fear of the 'mob'. Indeed, during the Gordon Riots, John Wilkes shouldered a musket in defence of the Bank of England and shot down rioters. A few years later he greeted with horror the outbreak of the French Revolution

(Rude, 1962: 192). The Treason and Sedition Acts of 1795 and 1799 increased greatly the government's powers to quell radical activities. Groups such as the Corresponding Societies were suppressed. The fears of political upheaval were reflected in Edmund Burke's *Reflections on the Revolution in France* (1790), which had a long-lasting impact on British political thought, as well as Thomas Carlyle's *The French Revolution* (1837), and Charles Dickens' *Barnaby Rudge* (1841) and *A Tale of Two Cities* (1859).

Throughout the first century of capitalist industrialization in Britain, the mass of the population was excluded from the electorate. Membership of the House of Lords was based mainly on inherited landed property. Up until the 1830s the electoral system for the House of Commons was based on a very narrow franchise, with corrupt elections: 'Narrow electorates were the basis on which the eighteenth century system of Parliamentary corruption was reared. The monied men stepped in to control this system, made safe against democracy' (Hill, 1969: 142). In the rural areas 'the country gentlemen decided county elections among themselves', and in the urban boroughs, the local government was 'dominated by families of self-perpetuating oligarchies, who also in effect, chose MPs' (Hill, 1969: 218). So tightly knit was the eighteenth-century ruling class that it was commonplace for an MP to have fifty relatives who were also members of Parliament: 'It is doubtful if any member of the ruling class, no matter how odd or eccentric his political views, was ever kept out of Parliament, if he really wanted to get in' (Plumb, 1963: 41).

The 1832 Reform Act eliminated many of the corrupt features of Parliamentary elections. However, it introduced stringent property qualifications for voting, which formalized political control for the propertied middle class. The size of the electorate increased only marginally, from 473,000 to 670,000, out of a total population of over sixteen million people. It was not until 1867 that a second Reform Act was introduced. Thus, throughout the whole of the first century of capitalist industrialization in Britain, the electorate excluded the mass of the working population. As seen in Chapter Three, Polanyi observed:

> In England it became the unwritten law of the constitution that the working class must be denied the vote ... The Chartists [in 1848] fought for the right to stop the mill of the market which ground the lives of the people. But the people were only granted rights when the awful adjustment had been made.
>
> (Polanyi, 1957: 266)

The economic condition of the working class was 'so bad as to render impossible their steady cooperation with other classes in a purely political programme' (Trevelyan, 1965: 251).

Private property was protected far more securely during the Enlightenment than in earlier periods. The laws protecting property became increasingly savage. Between 1688 and 1780 the number of offences which carried the death penalty rose from about fifty to nearly five times that number (Hill, 1969: 223). The vast majority of these were offences against property. A total of nearly 7,000 people were hanged in Britain between 1735 and 1799. The majority of offenders, in London at least, were under twenty-one years of age. The law 'was both dispassionate in its adjudication of substantial property rights and passionately vengeful against those who transgressed against them' (E.P. Thompson, quoted in Hill, 1969: 223). During the Enlightenment a man was hanged for stealing one shilling, a boy for stealing three shillings, six pence and a penknife, a girl for stealing a handkerchief. A boy of eleven was hanged for setting fire to his master's house (Hill, 1969: 223). Numerous people were sentenced to transportation to the colonies for offences against property.

In the seventeenth and eighteenth centuries the old relationships between master and workers, which were based on guilds and apprenticeships, broke down, to be replaced by an increased separation of the interests of owners and workers. As early as the seventeenth century workers had 'combined' for the purpose of mutual insurance against sickness, old age or death. The early forms of worker combinations were mainly confined to skilled artisans, rather than labourers. Workers' combinations expanded in the eighteenth century in order to bargain over wages and conditions of work with the capitalist employers who occupied a growing space in the British economic system. However, employers put pressure on Parliament to pass laws that protected them against combinations. Numerous acts were put into place during the Enlightenment which prohibited workers' 'combinations' against employers. In 1719 when keelmen went on strike in Newcastle, a regiment of soldiers and a man-of-war were sent to break the strike. In 1720 after a strike by around 7,000 journeymen tailors in London, combination was forbidden in that industry by Act of Parliament. In 1726, following riots and loom-breaking in the West country in the weaving and wool-combing industry, workers' combination was forbidden in that industry, in 1749 in the silk, linen, cotton, fustian, iron, leather and other industries and in 1777 among hatters (Hill, 1969: 267).

The Combination Acts of 1799 and 1800 provided for summary trials of workers who were deemed to have broken the 'combination acts' passed in the preceding decades.

The Acts made the combinations of workmen in clubs and societies for the purposes of improving working conditions and wages, a conspiracy: 'Time and again the Acts were invoked to suppress savagely and indiscriminately the movement towards trade unionism' (Plumb, 1963: 158). The Combination Acts caused no comment in political circles: 'It was a general conviction that the working man was a savage, unprincipled brute who naturally thirsted to overturn a society so obviously not to his advantage' (Plumb, 1963: 158). In the eighteenth century workers could be sentenced to fourteen years transportation for use of violence in labour disputes, and sentenced to death for machine-breaking (Hill, 1969: 266). While there were severe laws against workers' 'combinations', there were none against employers, as Adam Smith noted:

> The masters, being fewer in number ... can combine much more easily; and the law besides, authorizes or at least does not prohibit, their combinations, whilst it prohibits those of the workmen. We have had no acts of parliament against combining to lower the price of labour; but many against combining to raise it. In all such disputes, masters can hold out much longer ... Many

workmen could not subsist a week, few could subsist a month, and scarce
any a year without employment.

(Smith, 1776, 74–5)

Despite the existence of the Combination Acts, there were widespread efforts by
workers to combine against their employers. Already, by the end of the eighteenth
century, worker combinations extending across substantial geographical areas
had emerged. This was the case, for example, with the Association of Weavers
in Lancashire. By 1799 the Association included several cities in Lancashire. In
1804 the Attorney-General, Spencer Percival, observed that 'combinations exist
in almost every trade in the kingdom' (quoted in Pelling, 1963: 27). In 1816 the
Home Secretary, Lord Sidmouth, noted the 'alarming extent to which the combinations of workmen in the different branches of trade and manufactures have been
carried' (quoted in Pelling, 1963: 28). The fact that peaceful combination was
impossible meant that it was 'not unnatural for desperate men to resort to violence'
(Pelling, 1963: 29). During and immediately after the Napoleonic Wars there was
widespread machine-breaking by workers in handicraft trades, especially in the
lace and woolen industries, by skilled workers displaced by machines. In 1811–12
a wave of worker unrest across much of the Midlands and northern England tied
down 12,000 regular troops for the best part of a year (Foster, 1974: 40).

In the social and economic dislocation after the Napoleonic Wars there was a
wave of strikes, minor riots and mass meetings. These often ended in confrontation with the local authorities, who made use of the local 'yeomanry', a body of
armed and mounted volunteers from the local ruling class, and could even include
an appeal to the military to intervene. The most violent outcome was the mass
demonstration in support of political reform in Manchester in 1819 ('Peterloo').
The armed yeomanry charged the crowd. Around fifteen people were killed and
a much larger number wounded. In the wake of these disturbances, a Select
Committee of the House of Commons was set up in 1824. It concluded: '[The
Combination Laws] had a tendency to produce mutual irritation and distrust, and
to give a violent character to the Combinations, and to render them highly dangerous to the peace of the community' (quoted in Pelling, 1963: 30). As a result a new
Combination Law was passed which declared the act of combination should no
longer be illegal. However, it also authorized summary jurisdiction for 'persons
using 'violence to the person or property' or 'threats of intimidation' in pursuit of
the interests of the combination.

The passage of the Bill coincided with an upsurge in workplace struggle. The
sudden crop of strikes was accompanied by 'far-reaching demands for the regulation of conditions of work, exclusion of non-society men' as well as 'a certain
amount of violence' (Pelling, 1963: 31). The most intense struggle took place in
the shipbuilding and shipping industries. In the face of this upsurge in workers'
actions, Parliament made provisions against violence and intimidation: 'Molesting'
or 'obstructing' persons at work was forbidden and the definition of a legal combination was narrowed to questions of wages and hours of labour. However, the
principle of legal combination was reaffirmed. The Home Secretary, Robert Peel,

said: 'Men who ... have no property except their manual skill and strength, ought to be allowed to confer together, if they think it fit, for the purpose of determining at what rate they will sell their property' (quoted in Pelling, 1963: 32).

By the 1820s the term 'combination' had begun to be replaced by the term 'union'. Some of the 'unions', such as the West Riding Fancy Union, had several thousand members. Attempts to establish larger 'general unions' typically ended in failure. This was the case with the 'Grand General Union of the Operative Spinners of Great Britain and Ireland', established in 1829. It quickly spread to include spinning workers across a number of towns. Their strike in 1831 against reductions in wages failed and the union broke up. In 1834 the 'Grand National Union' was established with the hope of coordinating the demands across many industries and districts for increased wages and assistance for strikes to resist wages reductions. It attempted also to put into practice Robert Owen's ideas for cooperative production. However, the efforts were unsuccessful and the union broke up in 1837. Most union organization were local and small scale. The most long-lasting unions were composed of skilled workers.

By 1841, 54 per cent of Britain's population lived in cities. In 1861 less than one-fifth of the working population was employed in agriculture. The ready availability of the rural 'reserve army of labour' meant that there was little improvement in real wages in Britain until the 1840s.[4] As rural migrants flooded in to rapidly expanding urban areas the conditions for the early generations of urban residents were shocking. Friedrich Engels' account of the conditions of the English working class was published in 1845. It remains by far the most important account of the condition of English workers at this point in the evolution of capitalism. His meticulous account laid bare in graphic fashion the conditions of life and work for the large majority of the English population. Engels was the son of a wealthy German businessman. He came to Britain in the early 1840s as a young man in his early twenties and spent almost two years collecting material for his study. In the Foreword to the first edition he records the warmth of his reception during his fieldwork:

> I wanted more than a mere abstract knowledge of my subject. I wanted to see you in your own homes, to observe you in your everyday life, to chat with you on your condition and grievances, to witness your struggles against the social and political power of your oppressor.
>
> (Engels, 1845: 32)

Engels wrote in a clear and accessible fashion, in 'plain English'. However, the book was originally published only in German and not widely available to an English audience until 1892.[5]

He put himself in the position of the mass of poor people thronging the streets of the 'Great Towns' of Britain:

> The very turmoil of the streets had something repulsive, something against which human nature rebels. The hundreds of thousands of all classes and ranks crowding past each other, are they not all human beings with the

> same qualities and powers, and with the same interest in being happy? ...
> The dissolution of mankind into monads, of which each one has a separate
> essence, and a separate purpose is here carried to its utmost extreme.
>
> (Engels, 1845: 68–9)

However, the position of different social strata in this turbulent world was radically
different:

> [T]he social war, the war of all against all, is here openly declared ... Every
> where barbarous indifference, hard egotism on one hand, and nameless mis-
> ery on the other, everywhere social warfare, every man's house under siege,
> everywhere reciprocal plundering under the protection of the law, and all so
> shameless, so openly avowed that one shrinks before the consequences of
> our social state as they manifest themselves here undisguised, and can only
> wonder that the whole crazy edifice still hangs together.
>
> (Engels, 1845: 69)

Already in the 1840s there was a 'labour aristocracy', for whom there was a 'temporarily endurable existence for hard work and good wages' (Engels, 1845: 108).
However, the majority of the urban working class had negligible property, and
'live wholly upon wages, which usually go from hand to mouth' (Engels, 1845:
108). Combinations and friendly societies that might support workers in times of
illness, unemployment or old age had limited funds and were not available for
most of the working class. Most of the working class was 'constantly exposed to
loss of work and food'. The main part of Engels' study (Engels, 1845: 68–158)
provides a raw and brutally realistic examination of the living conditions of daily
life for the mass of the population in the Great Towns:

> The dwellings of the workers are everywhere badly planned, badly built,
> and kept in the worst condition, badly ventilated, damp, and unwholesome.
> The inhabitants are confined to the smallest possible space, and at least
> one family usually sleeps in each room. The interior arrangements of the
> dwellings are poverty-stricken in varying degrees, down to the utter absence
> of even the most necessary furniture. The clothing of the workers is gener-
> ally scanty, and that of the great multitude is in rags. The food is, in general,
> bad; often unfit for use, and in many cases, at least at times, insufficient in
> quantity, so that in extreme cases, death by starvation results.
>
> (Engels, 1845: 108)

He devoted special attention to Manchester, 'the first manufacturing city of the
world'. Ducie Bridge looks down upon the River Irk, which runs through Manchester's Old Town:

> The view from this bridge ... is characteristic for the whole district. At the
> bottom flows, or rather, stagnates, the Irk, a narrow, coal-black, foul-smelling

stream, full of debris and refuse, which it deposits on the lower right bank. In dry weather, a long string of the most disgusting blackish-green slime pools are left standing on this bank, from the depths of which bubbles of miasmatic gas constantly arise and give forth a stench unendurable even on the bridge forty or fifty feet above the surface of the stream ... Above the bridge are tanneries, bone mills, and gasworks, from which all drains and refuse find their way into the Irk, which receive further the contents of all the neighbouring sewers and privies ... Below the bridge you may look upon the piles of debris, the refuse, filth, and offal from the courts on the steep left bank; here each house is packed close behind its neighbour and a bit of each is visible, all black, smoky, crumbling, ancient, with broke panes and window frames.

(Engels, 1845: 89)

On re-reading his account of the Old Town of Manchester he writes:

[I]nstead of being exaggerated, it is far from black enough to convey a true impression of the filth, ruin, and uninhabitableness, the defiance of all considerations of cleanliness, ventilation, and health which character-ize the construction of this single district, containing at least twenty to thirty thousand inhabitants ... The industrial epoch alone has built up every spot between these old houses to make a covering for the masses whom it has conjured hither from the agricultural districts and from Ireland; the industrial epoch alone enables the owners of these cattle-sheds to rent them for high prices to human beings, to plunder the poverty of the workers, to undermine the health of thousands, in order that they only, the owners, may grow rich.

(Engels, 1845: 92)

Engels provides detailed consideration of the death rates of different segments of the population. Official government statistics for 1839 through 1840 recorded the average national death rate as one per forty-five people. In Manchester, the overall figure was one per thirty-three people. However, in Class I streets the figure was one death per fifty-one to fifty-five people, in Class II streets, one per thirty-eight to forty-five people, and in Class III streets the figure was one per twenty-five to thirty-six people (Engels, 1845: 136). In Liverpool in 1840, the average life expectancy of the upper classes, gentry, professional men, and so on, was thirty-five years, compared with twenty-two years for business men and better-placed craftsmen, and fifteen years for the 'operatives, day labourers and the service-able class' (Engels, 1845: 136). Among working class children in Manchester, the death rate of children below the age of five was 57 per cent, compared with 20 per cent for children of the upper classes (Engels, 1845: 137). Working class chil-dren were susceptible to a wide range of illnesses, with negligible medical care, poor diet and frequent parental neglect due to both parents working long hours in factories (Engels, 1845: 137).

Engels devotes meticulous attention to the nature of the labour process. He considers in detail the 'demoralizing' consequences of the factory system: 'As voluntary, productive activity is the highest enjoyment known to us, so is compulsory toil the most cruel' (Engels, 1845: 145). The division of labour has 'multiplied the brutalizing influences of forced work': 'In most branches the worker's activity is reduced to some paltry, purely mechanical manipulation, repeated minute after minute, unchanged year after year' (Engels, 1845: 146). The introduction of the steam engine reduced the sheer physical demands in many occupations, but 'the work itself becomes unmeaning and monotonous to the last degree' (Engels, 1845: 146).

Engels analyses closely the physical details of a wide variety of different types of industrial work and their consequences for the workers. For example:

> [I]n many rooms of the cotton and flax-spinning mills, the air is filled with fibrous dust, which produces chest affections [*sic*] especially among work-
> ers in the carding and combing rooms ... The most common effects of this breathing of dust are blood-spitting, hard noisy breathing, pains in the chest, coughs, sleeplessness – in short all the symptoms of asthma, ending in the worst cases of consumption.
>
> (Engels, 1845: 181)

In the knife grinding industry in Sheffield, 'by far the most unwholesome work is the grinding of knife-blades and forks, which, especially when done with dry stone, entails certain early death': 'The unwholesomeness of this work lies in part in the bent posture, in which the chest and stomach are cramped; but especially in the quantity of sharp-edged metal dust particles freed in the cutting, which fill the atmosphere, and are necessarily inhaled' (Engels, 1845: 214). Engels subjects the separate branches of the mining industry to close examination, including the tin, lead, iron and coal mines. In each branch of the industry the same physical deformities appear, including 'distortions of the legs, knees bent inwards and feet bent outwards, deformities of the spinal column and other malformations' as well as 'almost universal rupture' and 'numerous painful and dangerous affections of the lungs' (Engels, 1845: 252–3). Among all the industries, 'there is no occupation in which a man may meet his end in so many diverse ways' as in the coal mining industry, which is 'the scene of a multitude of the most terrifying calamities ... Explosions take place, in one mine or another almost every day' (Engels, 1845: 253). In the 1840s around 1,400 workers were killed annually as a result of coal mining accidents (Engels, 1845: 254).

Engels gives a detailed account of the struggles of the working class against their employers. Innumerable strikes took place in the 1830s and 1840s. However, the history of the unions in this period was a 'long series of defeats of the working class interrupted by a few isolated victories' (Engels, 1845: 226). Most strikes were small scale. They were typically of short duration and ended in victory for the employers. Union strike funds were quickly exhausted. Employers often called in non-union labour ('knobsticks' or 'black sheep' labour) and if any unlawful act was committed by the strikers prosecution quickly followed. A small number of strikes were more widespread and longer-lasting. Among the most remarkable was the coal miners' strike over pay and conditions of work. The main centre of the strike was Northumberland and Durham. Around 40,000 mine workers came out on strike in March 1844. In July the employers turned the families of most of the striking miners out of their homes. The miners' strike funds eventually were exhausted. Moreover, the mine owners brought in 'black-sheep' workers from Ireland and 'remote parts of Wales'. By the end of September the strike collapsed. The growth of machine-based agriculture in the countryside also stimulated discontent. In the 1830s there was extensive rick-burning and machine-breaking.

In his account of the numerous strikes in the 1830s and 1840s Engels observes:

> The incredible frequency of these strikes proves best of all to what extent the social war has broken out all over England. No week passes, scarcely a day, indeed, in which there is not a strike in some direction, now against reduction, then against a refusal to raise the rate of wages, again by reason of the employment of knobsticks or the continuance of abuses, sometimes against new machinery, or for a hundred other reasons.
>
> (Engels, 1845: 232)

Engels believed that the 'decisive battle between bourgeoisie and proletariat is approaching':

> It is too late for a peaceful solution. The classes are divided more and more sharply, the spirit of resistance penetrates the workers, the bitterness intensifies, and soon a slight impulse will suffice to set the avalanche in motion ... Before too long goes by, a time almost within the power of man to predict, the deep wrath of the whole working class ... against the rich must break out into a revolution in comparison with which the French Revolution, and the year 1794, will prove to have been child's play.
>
> (Engels, 1845: 64 and 233)

Prior to the 1860s there were some radical British writers and trade union leaders who, like Engels, believed that it was possible and desirable to wage violent 'class warfare' against the ruling class, and that such a political revolution was imminent. However, they were a small minority within the British radical tradition. The much more influential radical mainstream included such figures as William Cobbett (1763–1835), Robert Owen (1771–1858), Henry Hunt (1773–1834), William Lovett (1800–1877), Francis Place (1771–1854), Feargus O'Connor (1794–1855) and Francis Burdett (1770–1844). They were in broad agreement that workers should be free to bargain with employers for improved pay and conditions of work and that the reform of the unjust system of Parliamentary elections should be altered radically in order that power be passed into the hands of the people. They also agreed that Parliamentary legislation was a key channel for the amelioration of the conditions for the mass of working people. Following the passage of the 1832 Reform Act, great efforts were put into extending the franchise. The People's Charter of 1838 called for manhood suffrage, secret ballots, equal electoral districts, payment of members of Parliament, abolition of the property qualification to stand for election, and annual Parliaments. A series of huge meetings were held in support of the Charter and the petition, signed by more than one million people, was presented to the House of Commons. MPs voted by a large majority not to hear the petitioners. Angry demonstrations took place. The demonstration in South Wales, which has been called the 'last armed uprising against the state in Britain', ended in a violent confrontation with armed soldiers, and it was reported that more than twenty people were killed. A second petition, which reportedly had more than three million signatures, was presented in 1842. It was again rejected by Parliament. A third petition was presented to Parliament in 1848 following a mass meeting at Kensington Common in London.

Whereas the year 1848 in Britain was relatively peaceful, in France it was incredibly violent. Revolutionary forces seized control of large parts of Paris. They were crushed by the army. Around 1,500 people were killed in the fighting and a further 3,000 were slaughtered in the aftermath of the defeat (Hobsbawm, 1977: 30). Around 12,000 people were imprisoned or deported. The French Revolution of 1848 left a deep imprint on European politics in the mid-decades of the nineteenth century. In Britain the Chartist movement faded into near-oblivion.

Although the mass of the population were excluded from the franchise right up until 1867, a wide array of pressures was exerted on Parliament to address the appalling conditions of life and work for a large majority of the working class. Pressures for social reform came from the trade unions themselves, which exerted continuous pressure for social reform. Pressure came also from a wide range of radical political figures, including a small number who had been elected MPs, from literary figures such as Charles Dickens, whose vivid accounts of the lives of ordinary people inspired sympathy among segments of the ruling class, and from penetrating social commentary such as that of Henry Mayhew (1861). There was also a growing acceptance within the capitalist class that if the conditions of the working population were not ameliorated, there was a possibility of violent 'social warfare'.

Between the 1830s and the 1860s a succession of Acts of Parliament contributed to a slow amelioration of the conditions of life and work for the working class. The 1835 Municipal Corporations Act established a new structure under which local governments elected by ratepayers were empowered to levy local rates, which could be used to fund municipal lighting, drainage, paving, water and police (Trevelyan, 1965: 244). The 1833 Factory Act fixed legal limits for working hours for children and young persons and prohibited the employment of children, except in silk mills. It also instituted a system of factory inspectors to enforce the law. The legislation was passed by Parliament in the face of opposition from the majority of factory owners, politicians from all sides, as well as from 'doctrinaire political economists' (Trevelyan, 1965: 247). The Mines Act of 1842 came about as a result of a Royal Commission of Enquiry into conditions in coal mines. The details contained in the report shocked the British public. The Act prohibited women and boys from working underground in coalmines. The second set of Factory Acts was passed between 1844 and 1847. The 'Ten Hours Bill' limited the daily work of women and youths in factories, which effectively limited the working day to ten hours, as it was impossible for males to carry on by themselves, given the integrated nature of factory work. This had been a key objective of the working class for many years. The industrial towns of the nineteenth century were constructed without sanitary codes: 'The jerry-builder and the thrifty manufacturer in a hurry had covered England with slums; trout streams had become sewers; rubbish-heaps festered unregarded till cholera or some milder epidemic threatened the well-to-do' (Trevelyan, 1965: 275). In 1848 Parliament passed the Public Health Act under which a General Board of Health was set up for the whole country, and it imposed upon local authorities compulsory requirements for provision of public health facilities: 'A system of constant and delicate interaction between central and local authorities grew up after the middle years of the nineteenth century', which became 'one of the most important elements of [Britain's] State machinery' (Trevelyan, 1965: 276). Despite their limited nature, these measures to advance social welfare constituted a considerable degree of regulation of the free market economy. In the early 1870s J. S. Mill observed:

> The present system is not, as many Socialists believe, hurrying into a state of general indigence and slavery from which only socialism can save us. The evils and injustices of the present system are great, but they are not increasing; on the contrary, the general tendency is towards their slow diminution.
>
> (Mill, 1879: 112)

In 1832 an Act of Parliament reduced by two-thirds the number of crimes punishable by death. A succession of Acts of Parliament in 1861 reduced to five the number of crimes punishable by capital punishment, namely murder, treason, espionage, arson in royal dockyards and piracy with violence. The era in which crimes against private property could be punished by the death sentence was over. In 1866 an Act of Parliament ruled that executions should only take place in prisons.[6]

Prior to the 1867 Reform Act, as well as social progress (albeit painfully slow, achieved through Parliamentary legislation), there was also an appreciable advance in real incomes of British workers. This took place before the advance of mass trade unionism in the final decades of the nineteenth century. In his posthumously published study *On Socialism* (Mill, 1879) J. S. Mill recognized the deplorable conditions of the working class across Europe: '[I]t is unhappily true that the wages of ordinary labour, in all the countries of Europe, are wretchedly insufficient to supply the physical and moral necessities of the population in any tolerable measure' (Mill, 1879: 98). However, he argued that '[t]here is much evidence of improvement, and none, that is at all trustworthy, of deterioration, in the mode of living of the countries of Europe' (Mill, 1879: 99). Despite the large increase in European population Mill considered that '[s]ociety as at present constituted is not descending into that abyss [of poverty and over-population], but gradually, though slowly, rising out of it, and this improvement is likely to be progressive if bad laws do not interfere with it' (Mill, 1879).

Modern research in British economic history supports Mill's view. The main forces driving up average real earnings were exhaustion of the rural labour surplus, the growing skill level of the workforce, and advances in capital accumulation, technical progress and labour productivity. Between 1801 and 1851 the size of the labour force in Britain increased from 4.8 million to 9.7 million (Tranter, 1981: 206). In the same years, the share of agriculture in total employment fell from 36 per cent to 22 per cent, while the share of manufacturing, mining and industry rose from 30 per cent to 43 per cent. The structure of the workforce grew increasingly complex, with greatly increased demands for skilled labour. This was reflected in the fact that between 1755 and 1851 there was a substantial widening of earnings differentials between different categories of workers (Lindert and Williamson, 1981: Table 9.2). During the first century of the Industrial Revolution in Britain capital accumulation occurred at a historically unprecedented rate. Investment as a proportion of GNP rose from 8 per cent in the 1750s to 13 per cent in the 1850s, and fixed capital formation increased from £6.5 million per annum (at 1851–60 prices) to £58.0 million (Feinstein, 1981: 131). Technical progress permitted output per worker to more than double from £26 (at 1851–60 prices) in 1760 to £60 in 1860 (Feinstein, 1981: 139). Between 1790 and 1850 real wages increased by 74 per cent (O'Brien and Engerman, 1981: 169). Real consumption per person is estimated to have more than doubled between the 1760s and the 1850s, rising from £9.6 (at 1851–60 prices) to £22.9 (Feinstein, 1981: 137).

1867–1914

Between the 1860s and the First World War the British working class was permitted to expand its political 'voice' through gradual extension of the electoral franchise. By the early twentieth century it had established its own political party, but the party still was far too small to form the government.

Although only a minority of workers were members of trade unions, in the mid-nineteenth century the unions played a crucial role in pressuring Parliament for reform of the franchise. In 1865 the Reform League was founded, with the objective of winning the franchise for the working class, and most of the union leaders played a full part in its activities. The middle-class National Reform Union also supported extension of the franchise. Following the rejection of the Reform Bill in 1866 there were massive popular demonstrations in major cities, including a mass rally in Hyde Park in May 1867. In 1867 after fierce debate both inside and outside Parliament, the Second Reform Act was passed. Pressure from trade unionists, both at the 1865 general election, and in the subsequent popular demonstrations, played a vital role in the passage of the Act. Almost the whole of the middle class was enfranchised, as were the better-off artisans. The property qualification was reduced to include all urban ratepayers. The electorate was extended from 1.3 million to 2.5 million, out of around seven million adult males in the total population. The Third Reform Act of 1884 further extended the franchise, increasing the electorate to 5.5 million people, which constituted over three-fifths of the adult male population, but still excluded all women from the franchise.

J.S. Mill (1806–1873) was arguably the most influential British political thinker in the nineteenth century. He was one the strongest supporters of electoral reform. Even though the 1867 Reform Act did not enfranchise all members of the working class, he considered it to be of great long-term significance for the evolution of Britain's economic and political system:

> The great increase of electoral power which the act places within the reach of the working classes is permanent ... It is known even to the most inobservant, that the working classes have, and are likely to have, political objects which concern them as working classes, and on which they believe, rightly or wrongly, that the interests and opinions of other powerful classes are opposed to theirs ... [I]t is as certain as anything in politics can be, that they will before long find the means of making their collective electoral power effectively instrumental to the promotion of their collective objects.
>
> (Mill, 1879: 58)

It was at Mill's instigation that the Labour Representation League was established in 1869 with the objective of carrying out a national campaign to secure the return of working people to Parliament. In the 1874 Parliament the League put forward twelve working men as candidates, of whom two (Thomas Burt and Alexander MacDonald) were elected as MPs.

Mill was severely critical of the greed and injustice of the raw capitalist system in mid-nineteenth century Britain. He believed that socialists such as himself were right to hold out the possibility of achieving a radically egalitarian society:

> [O]ur ideal[7] of ultimate improvement went far beyond democracy, and *would class us decidedly under the general designation of socialists* ... [W]e looked forward to a time when society would no longer be divided into the idle and the industrious; when the rule that they who do not work shall not eat, will be applied not to paupers only, but impartially to all; when the division of the produce of labour, instead of depending, in so great a degree as it now does, on the accident of birth, will be made in concert, on an acknowledged principle of justice; and when it will no longer either be, or be thought to be, impossible for human beings to exert themselves strenuously in procuring benefits which are not exclusively their own, but to be shared with the society they belong to. The social problem of the future we considered to be, how to unite the greatest individual liberty of action, with a common ownership in the raw materials of the globe and an equal participation of all in the benefits of labour.
>
> (Mill, quoted in Riley, 1993: xvi-xvii) (emphasis added)

However, Mill considered that achievement of such a socialist future would require an 'immense change of character ... in both the uncultivated herd who now compose the labouring masses and in the immense majority of employers':

> [B]oth these classes must learn by practice to labour and combine for generous, or at any event for public and social purposes, and, not as hitherto,

for narrowly interested ones ... [the] capacity to do this has always existed in mankind, and is not, nor is likely ever to be, extinguished ... The deep-rooted selfishness which forms the general character of the existing state of society, is *so* deeply rooted only because the whole course of existing institutions tends to foster it.

(Mill, quoted in Riley, 1993: xvii)

Although Mill was deeply critical of the 'existing state of society', he believed that the transition to a superior organization of the economy and society should be 'brought into operation progressively', and that it should 'prove its capabilities by trial' (Mill, 1879: 116). He argued against attempting to leap into a system with 'the management of the whole resources of the country by a single central authority. ... [T]he very idea of conducting the whole industry of a country by direction from a single centre is so obviously chimerical, that nobody ventures to propose any mode in which it should be done' (Mill, 1879: 116 and 134). He argued strongly against rash attempts to:

... substitute the new rule for the old at a single stroke, and to exchange the amount of good realized under the present system, and its large possibilities for improvement, for a plunge without any preparation into the most extreme form of the problem of carrying on the whole round of the operations of social life without the motive power which has always hitherto worked the social machinery.

(Mill, 1879: 116)

He warned that such a transformation of the economy and society was deeply irresponsible, based on the 'hope that it holds out to the enthusiasts of seeing the whole of their aspirations realized in their own time and at a blow' (Mill, 1879: 117).

However, Mill considered that the leaders of the English working classes were 'unlikely to rush into the reckless extremities of some of the foreign Socialists' (Mill, 1879: 61). Rather, he considered that they were 'better aware than their Continental brethren that great and permanent changes in the fundamental ideas of mankind are not to be accomplished by a *coup de main*', but, instead, they 'direct their practical efforts towards ends which seem within easier reach, and are content to hold back all extreme theories until there has been experience of the operation of the same principles on a partial scale' (Mill, 1879: 61). Indeed, at the International Working Men's Association meetings in 1866 and 1869, the English trade union representatives 'refused to be drawn into the destructivism of the European revolutionary socialists' (Feuer, 1976: 38). When the Second International was established in 1889, it was 'so obviously a political rather than an industrial organization, that most of the leaders of the Trades Union Congress (TUC) would have nothing to do with it' (Pelling, 1963: 119). Most British trade union leaders of this period 'prided themselves that their approach to industrial problems was of a practical rather than a theoretical character': '[O]ut and out dogmatic Marxism ... was very much a minority creed in Britain ... and the moderate socialism of a rather larger proportion of unionists did not prevent their unions from adopting highly conservative policies on many issues' (Pelling, 1963: 119–21). The lack of receptiveness of the mainstream of the British working class to violent revolution is reflected in the fact that the key works of Marx and Engels were not published in English until long after they were published in German.[8]

The Paris Commune of 1871 played a significant role in shaping the attitudes of the British working class towards class struggle in their own country. The Commune was established following France's humiliating defeat by Prussia in 1870 and the siege of Paris by Prussian troops. Its leaders included Blanquists, who 'based their creed on Proudhonist theories of a decentralized society composed of small property-owners'; Jacobins, who 'were wedded to abstract ideas of political liberty … but constantly looked back to their namesakes of '93 for guidance'; 'diverse members of the International' and a 'nebula of assorted anarchists, intellectuals, Bohemians, Gambettists, disgruntled petty bourgeois, general layabouts, *déclassés*, and unclassifiables' (Horne, 1990: 298). The Commune lasted only two months until it was crushed by the army of the French government that had retreated to Versailles following its defeat by Prussia. In its brief life the Commune passed a wide array of 'revolutionary' legislation, including selection of Commune officials by universal suffrage, subject to the right of recall at any time by the electors. The public officials included the police and the bureaucracy. The standing army was dissolved and replaced by the 'armed people'. The Commune imposed strict limits on the officials' salaries. They were to be paid only workmen's wages and all financial privileges for bureaucrats were abolished. The Commune also drew up plans for the operation of factories by the workers, their organization into cooperative societies joined together in 'one great union' (Engels, 1871: 27).

The French Government forces suppressed the Commune with fantastic ferocity. The government itself reported that 17,000 people were killed but the real figures were far in excess of this, probably around 25,000, but may even have been as high as 40,000 (Horne, 1990: 418). The *London Times* reported:

> Human nature shrinks in horror … The French are filling up the darkest page in the book of their own or the world's history. The charge of ruthless cruelty is no longer confined to one party or class of persons. The Versailles troops seem inclined to outdo the Communists in their sheer lavishness of human blood.
>
> (quoted in Horne, 1990: 417)

Although the decision to establish the Commune was not supported by Karl Marx, it was widely regarded as a 'Red Revolution' with Marx as its architect. In 1881 Marx reflected that 'this was merely the rising of a city under exceptional conditions … and the majority of the Commune was in no wise socialist, nor could it be' (Marx, 1881: 293). The fact that such staggering violence could take place across the channel from Britain helped to reinforce the apprehensions of British socialists about pursuing political revolution to overthrow the ruling class.

The Paris Commune was to assume a key role in Lenin's political outlook:

> The Commune taught the European proletariat to pose concretely the tasks of the socialist revolution ... The thunder of the cannon of Paris awakened the most backward sections of the proletariat from their deep slumber, and everywhere gave the impetus to the growth of revolutionary socialist propaganda.
>
> (Lenin, quoted in Marx and Engels, 1971: 9)

After the February Revolution Lenin closely studied Marx's writings on the Paris Commune. The Commune was centrally important for his *State and Revolution*, published in August 1917. He wrote: 'We cannot imagine democracy, even proletarian democracy, without representative institutions, but we can and must imagine democracy without parliamentarianism if our criticisms of bourgeois society are not mere empty words for us' (Lenin, 1917: 43). He concluded that the central task of the proletarian revolution was to:

> ... smash the old bureaucratic machine at once and to begin immediately to construct a new one that facilitates the gradual eradication of all bureaucracy: this is not utopia, this is the experience of the Commune, this is the direct, immediate task of the revolutionary proletariat ... We ourselves, the workers, will organize large-scale production on the basis of what has already been created by capitalism, relying on our own experience as workers, establishing strict, iron discipline supported by state power of the armed workers.
>
> (Lenin, 1917: 44)

After the Bolshevik's seizure of power in the October Revolution, Lenin is said to have counted each day that it outlived the Paris Commune.

The Paris Commune occupied an important place during the Chinese Cultural Revolution. An article by Zheng Zhisi on 'The Great Lessons of the Paris Commune', published in *Hong Qi* ('Red Flag') in April 1966, helped to launch the widespread attack on government officials. Zheng argued:

> [The violent destruction of the Paris Commune] was a bitter lesson written in blood ... It teaches us that the proletariat must carry the revolution through to the end; that fleeing bandits must be pursued and destroyed, that drowning rats must be beaten to death; that the enemy must not be given the chance to regain his breath.
>
> (Zheng Zhisi, 1966: 99)

Under the name of class struggle (*jieji douzheng*) the Cultural Revolution descended into chaotic and violent factional struggle. By January 1967:

> [R]epeated factional clashes and battles [brought] China precariously close to the brink of civil war ... [It became] difficult to disentangle the myriad

threads of factional alliances spun out by mass organizations and cliques at every level throughout the land ... Everybody seemed to call themselves 'rebels' and fought under the same political slogans ... [Uprisings across the country] were sometimes accompanied by destruction of state property and valuable cultural treasures, bloodletting, even loss of life, and humiliation of party and state officials.

(Nee, 1973: 355)

The extension of the franchise in 1867 had opened up for the British working class the prospect of using Parliament to achieve further social reforms, which planted the seeds for the Labour Party to follow the path of a peaceful 'Parliamentary Party' rather than a violently revolutionary one. Under the 1870 Education Reform Act a school was 'placed within the reach of every child, at a very low charge' and in 1880 primary education was made compulsory for all and in 1891 it was offered free of all expense (Trevelyan, 1965: 344). Between 1870 and 1890 average school attendance rose from one and a quarter million to four and a half million. In 1868 the first annual meeting of the TUC took place. In 1871 the TUC set up the Parliamentary Committee and in the 1874 election, a milestone was passed with the election to Parliament of two trade union candidates, standing as Liberal Party candidates. In 1874 an Act of Parliament reduced the legal maximum working week from sixty to fifty-six and a half hours. In 1872 the Mines Regulation Act made progress in the development of safety precautions and mines inspection. In 1875 the Conspiracy and Protection of Property Act and the Employers and Workmen Acts were passed. The former ruled that the law of conspiracy could not be applied to trade disputes unless the actions concerned were criminal in themselves, and peaceful picketing was made legal. Under the latter act the penalty for breach of contract was limited to civil damages (Pelling, 1963: 75–6).

In the last two decades of the nineteenth century, tremendous progress took place in 'municipal socialism': 'The self-governing towns of England became employers of labour on a large scale' (Trevelyan, 1963: 388). Municipal governments across the length and breadth of the country built baths and washing-houses, public libraries, parks, gardens, open spaces, allotments and lodging houses for the working classes, maintained out of local rates. Tramways, gas, electricity and water, were in many places provided by the municipal government. In 1887 Sir William Harcourt shocked the House of Commons by saying: 'We're all socialists now'.

Bitter workplace struggles continued alongside slow but steady progress to ameliorate conditions for the English working class. The late 1880s saw the emergence of 'new unionism', which catered mainly to the unskilled and poorly paid workers, and used aggressive strike tactics. The new unionism was strongly influenced by the rise of a more aggressive Socialist movement, influenced by their interpretations of the ideas of Marx and Engels. In 1889 the London dockworkers undertook a five-week strike, at the end of which the employers conceded that the dockers would be paid sixpence an hour – 'the full round orb of the dockers' tanner'. In the gas industry in many towns there were bitter strikes to try to achieve the eight-hour day.

One of the main aims of the new unionists was to influence local politics. In 1898 West Ham in East London became the first local authority to be controlled by organized labour, through local trades councils. In the 1890s there was growing interest among trade unionists in establishing an independent political party at the national level. One of the results of the new unionism was the foundation in 1893 of the Independent Labour Party (ILP), led by Kier Hardie. In the general election of 1892 the number of workers' candidates increased to thirteen. Of these ten stood as Liberal party candidates and three as independents. In that year the TUC raised the issue of using the Parliamentary Committee as the instrument to obtain labour representation in Parliament through a political party. However the TUC hesitated to form a new political party for the working class. To a considerable degree this was due to the fact that at the 1893 TUC Conference, through vigorous argument the Socialists had persuaded the congress to pass a resolution urging the unions to support only those candidates who pledge to 'the collective ownership of the means of production, distribution and exchange' (Pelling, 1963: 107). The resolution was carried again in 1894. Up until this point voting had been by show of hands. At the 1895 Congress it was decided that in future voting would be in proportion to the number of members that were in each delegate's union. In 1900 a meeting of the Parliamentary Committee decided to establish the Labour Representative Committee.

Bitter struggle over the legal position of trade unions continued into the twentieth century. In 1903 in the Taff Vale case the House of Lords ruled that trade unions were liable for damages inflicted by their officials, which had the potential to curtail strike action drastically. The decision spurred the trade unions' determination to establish an independent political party to represent in Parliament the interests of the working class. In the general election of 1906 fifty-four representatives of the working class were elected, of whom twenty-nine were members of the Labour Representative Committee and the rest were workers standing as Liberal candidates ('Lib-Labs'). Following the election they changed their name to the 'Labour Party' with the formal apparatus of officers and whips. The new Parliament passed an Act that reversed the Taff Vale Judgment. It gave trade unions recognition as legal entities, together with provision for separation of strike funds from benefit funds, so that benefit funds would be immune from damages. The Act also restored unions' right to conduct peaceful picketing. Thus 'the unions had secured from the ballot box the respect for their privileged position which had been denied them in the courts' (Pelling, 1963: 127).

Further Parliamentary Acts to the advantage of the working class were passed in the following years. In 1909 an Act of Parliament established labour exchanges, with trade unions officials included in the supervisory mechanism. Measures were introduced to improve health and unemployment insurance. Friendly societies and unions were designated as agents or 'approved societies' for the operation of the state-run system. As a result of these measures union membership, especially among unions that catered for lower-skilled workers, rose rapidly, increasing from 2.6 million in 1910 to 4.1 million in 1914 (Pelling, 1963: 262). In 1909 an Act of Parliament established trade boards to fix wages in the 'sweated trades', which were notorious for the employment of cheap female labour.

Conflict over the political role of trade unions was exacerbated by the House of Lords' 'Osborne Judgment' of 1909. It ruled that it was illegal for unions to contribute funds to the Labour Party. In 1913 the judgment was reversed substantially by an Act of Parliament, which ruled that trade unions could support the Labour Party through ring-fenced 'political funds', though members had the right to opt out of the political levy and a majority of the members needed to be secured before the union was allowed to contribute to Labour Party funds.

In the years immediately before the First World War there was a marked increase in the incidence of strikes. In part this was due to the growing influence of Marxist ideas. After the turn of the century the 'syndicalist' and 'workers' control' movement gained influence among the working class. The high water mark of the influence of the movement was the pamphlet *The Miners' Next Step,* produced in 1912 by the South Wales Miners' Federation. The pamphlet urged 'political action, both local and national, on the basis of complete independence of, and hostility to, all capitalist parties, with an avowed policy of wresting whatever advantage it can for the working class'. It called for all workers to:

> ... amalgamate into one National and International Union, to work for the taking over of all industries, by the workmen themselves ... The suggested organization is constructed to fight rather than to negotiate ... Our objective begins to take shape before your eyes. Every industry thoroughly organized, in the first place, to fight, to gain control and then to administer that industry. The coordination of all industries in a Central Production Board, who, with a statistical department to ascertain the needs of the people, will issue its demands on the different departments of industry, leaving it to the men themselves to determine under what conditions and how, the work should be done. This would mean real democracy in real life, making for real manhood and womanhood. Any other form of democracy is a delusion and a snare.
>
> (Unofficial Reform Committee, 1912)

In the 1890s a number of industries established boards of conciliation to enable employers and employees to reach agreement on wages and conditions of work. The Conciliation Act of 1896 conferred powers on the Board of Trade to appoint conciliators at the request of the parties concerned in labour disputes. The number of conciliation and arbitration boards increased from 64 in 1894 to 325 in 1913. In 1911 there were prolonged strikes among dockers and seamen, and the first national rail strike took place. In response, the government appointed a Royal Commission to examine the conciliation boards and revised the boards' mode of operation to increase trade union representation.

The English edition of the *Condition of the English Working Class* was not published until 1892. Engels' Preface to the English edition recognized the enormous changes that had taken place in Britain since 1845. The 'social warfare' that he had predicted in 1845 had not come about. However, Engels explained that he would not 'strike out of the text the many prophecies, among others that of an imminent social revolution in England, which my youthful ardour induced me to venture upon' (Engels, 1892: 41). The 'People's Charter' had actually become 'the political programme of the very manufacturers who opposed it to the last': 'The "Abolition of the Property Qualification" and "Vote by Ballot" are now the law of the land. The Reform Acts of 1867 and 1884 make a near approach to universal suffrage' (Engels, 1892: 44).

The British economy had not experienced the catastrophic economic and political crisis that Engels predicted in 1845. The revolution in the means of transport had opened up vast tracks of the world:

> No wonder England's industrial progress was colossal and unparalleled, and that the status of 1844 now appears to us as comparatively primitive and insignificant ... The previous astounding creations of steam and machinery dwindled into nothing compared with the immense mass of productions of the twenty years from 1850 to 1870, with the overwhelming figures of exports and imports, of wealth accumulated in the hands of capitalists and of human working power concentrated in the large towns.
>
> (Engels, 1892: 38 and 44)

Engels acknowledged that the move towards large-scale firms had 'moralized' the manufacturing industry:

> [T]he larger the concern, and with it the number of hands, the greater the loss and inconvenience caused by every conflict between master and men; and thus a new spirit came over the masters, especially the larger ones, which taught them to avoid unnecessary squabbles, to acquiesce in the existence and power of trade unions, and finally even to discover in strikes – at opportune times – means to serve their own ends. The largest manufacturers, formerly the leaders of the war against the working class, were now the foremost to preach peace and harmony.
>
> (Engels, 1892: 38–9)

The Factory Acts, 'once the bugbear of all manufacturers, were not only willingly submitted to, but their expansion into acts regulating almost all trades tolerated' (Engels, 1892: 43). Trade unions, 'hitherto considered the invention of the devil himself, were now petted and patronized as perfectly legitimate institutions, and as a useful medium of spreading sound economical doctrines among the workers' (Engels, 1892: 43). The worst urban slum conditions, which he described in detail in the original 1845 edition, had been removed: 'Drainage has been introduced or improved, wide avenues have been opened out athwart many of the worst "slums"' (Engels, 1892: 39). The condition of the English working class had improved significantly since the 1840s:

> The truth is this: during the period of England's industrial monopoly the English working class have, to a certain extent, shared in the benefits of the monopoly. These benefits were very unevenly parcelled out among them;

the privileged minority pocketed most, but even the mass had, at least a temporary share now and then. And that is the reason why, since the dying out of Owenism, there has been no socialism in England.

(Engels, 1892: 47)

From the 1860s up until 1914 the British economy experienced a succession of crises, and its global dominance was challenged by the industrialization of Continental Europe and the United States. However, over the long term the country experienced increases in capital accumulation and technical progress that permitted increased output per worker. The revolution in transport technologies and the opening up of large parts of the world to foreign investment permitted greatly increased British imports of food and raw materials with falling long-term real prices. These developments allowed for long-term progress in living standards for the British working class. Despite the widespread progress a large section of the unskilled working class remained in deep absolute poverty. However, the structure of the 'working class' altered greatly. By the beginning of the twentieth century class identities had become much more complex than they had been in the middle of the nineteenth century. Over the long term the proportion of white-collar occupations expanded. The share of the workforce employed in trade and transport increased from 15.5 per cent in 1851 to 21.5 per cent in 1911, while the proportion employed in public services and professional occupations increased from 5.2 per cent to 8.1 per cent (Baines, 1994: 54). Although they were not manual workers, in terms of their income and wealth, the mass of lower level clerical and service sector workers were much closer to the 'labour aristocracy' among blue collar workers than to the professional stratum of doctors, lawyers, senior bankers, officers in the armed forces and business leaders. The proportion of domestic and personal service sector workers rose from 5.2 per cent in 1851 to 14.0 per cent in 1911 (Baines, 1994: 54). Most of the workers in these occupations had incomes that were on a par with or even lower than those of ordinary manual workers.

Although the British economy grew less rapidly than the 'latecomer countries' such as Germany, France or the United States, it still experienced considerable growth in the late nineteenth and early twentieth century. Real GDP grew at 1.2 per cent per annum in 1873–99 and at 0.5 per cent per annum in 1899–1913 (Floud and McCloskey, 1981: 16). Between 1870 and 1914 real per capita income in Britain increased by 44 per cent (Mackinnon, 1994: 271). Although a large fraction of the working class still lived in absolute poverty, the 'average' British working class family on the eve of the First World War 'consumed many more goods and services than their hypothetical grandparents in the 1870s' (MacKinnon, 1994: 290). Infant death rates fell from 154 per 1,000 live births in 1870–1874 to 109 per 1,000 in 1910–1914 (Mackinnon, 1994: 281), while life expectancy rose from forty years in the 1850s to fifty years in 1901 (Floud and McCloskey, 1981: 7).

The growth of mass education had produced a largely literate population with a much stronger sense of national identity than before the Industrial Revolution. The great expansion of the newspaper industry strongly reinforced the sense of a shared national culture. The era of extension of the suffrage to the majority of the

British working class coincided with a massive extension of the British Empire, including the 'Scramble for Africa' and consolidation of British rule in India. Across the developed countries the era of industrialization was accompanied by intensification of national identity, reinforced symbiotically by military rivalry. The growth of nationalism was closely associated with the rise of giant, modern industrialized military machines by land and sea. The construction of huge instruments of mass destruction, such as Britain's 'Dreadnought' battleship, was a source of national pride. There was negligible working class opposition to the wild expansion of British colonial rule. British workers were major beneficiaries of the expansion of the country's military machine, including the army, navy, dockyards and arms factories. Schools, newspapers and politicians took pride in the British Empire, and the pride was widely shared among the working class. The British working class almost universally supported the declaration of war with Germany in August 1914. The only sustained opposition came from the Independent Labour Party and Ramsay MacDonald, chairman of the Labour Party. The extent of working class enthusiasm to volunteer and serve 'king and country' exceeded even the expectations of the government. In the first month of the war, 500,000 men, mainly working class, volunteered to fight, and altogether there were more than three million volunteers to fight in the British army.

1914–1945

During the First World War the Labour Party was drawn deeply into the apparatus of government as a partner in the wartime coalition. In the general election of 1918 Ramsay MacDonald was defeated and all the Independent Labour Party socialists were defeated, 'owing to voters' hostility to pacifists' (Pelling, 1963: 159). In 1924 the Labour Party formed the Government for the first time, albeit briefly, as a minority government. It did so again in 1929–31, during which time the Great Depression erupted. In the Second World War the Labour Party and trade unions were drawn even more deeply into the Government apparatus as coalition partners.

During the First World War class struggle continued during the hostilities. A powerful factory-level shop stewards' movement emerged for the first time, and there were major strikes in both the mining and engineering industries. However, during the war the working class became closely involved in the process of governing the country. This took place through the trade unions as well as through the Labour Party, which joined the wartime coalition government. The overall level of strikes was much below the pre-war years. Labour MPs were invited to join the coalition government. Throughout the war the Government exercised enormous powers over the munitions industry and its workers. It authorized the compulsory arbitration of disputes and the suspension of trade practices, and strictly controlled the profits of armaments firms. In Lloyd George's government, formed in 1916, Arthur Henderson, who was chairman of the Parliamentary Labour Party, joined the War Cabinet, and two other Labour MPs, John Hodge and George Barnes, became respectively, Minister of Labour and Minister of Pensions. Several other Labour MPs were appointed as junior ministers. The Labour MPs in the wartime coalition government had all been trade union officials. Under Lloyd George's coalition government state control was established over mines and shipping. There was strict control of food supplies and the Ministry of Labour was established.

In February 1918 Parliament passed by a large majority the Representation of the People Act, which widened the franchise to include almost the whole of the adult male population and women over the age of thirty. This increased the size of the electorate from 7.7 million in 1912 to 21.4 million. The final step of extending the franchise to all adult women took place in 1928.

In 1918 the Labour Party revised its constitution to include 'Clause IV'. It read:

> To secure for the workers by hand or by brain the full fruits of their industry and the most equitable distribution thereof that may be possible upon the basis of the common ownership of the means of production, distribution and exchange, and the best obtainable system of popular administration and control of each industry or service.

The phrase 'common ownership' was ambiguous. The way in which to interpret it was the subject of fierce controversy right through to its removal from the Constitution in 1995. In the 'khaki election' of 1918 the Labour Party election manifesto included a demand for 'the immediate nationalization and democratic control of vital public services, such as mines, railways, shipping, armaments and electric power; the fullest recognition and utmost extension of trade unionism, both in private employment and in the public services'. The Labour Party won only fifty-seven seats in Parliament, representing only a small advance on the 1910 election.

After the brief post-war boom the economy encountered serious difficulties in 1920 and by mid-1921 unemployment reached 17.8 per cent of the insured workforce. Trade union membership grew from 5.4 million in 1917 to 8.3 million in 1920, and there was a sharp rise in industrial militancy. The number of days lost through strikes rose from 2.5 million in 1916 to 85.9 million in 1921 (Pelling, 1963: 262). The Railwaymen and Transport Workers agreed to join the Mineworkers in a 'Triple Alliance' to resist the coal owners' attempt to cut miners' wages and maintain profits. However, on 15 April 1921 ('Black Friday'), before the planned strike had begun, the Railwaymen and the Transport Workers cancelled their plan to support the Mineworkers. The Miners decide to go ahead with their strike but by the end of June they were forced to give way and accept wage cuts. The level of industrial militancy fell sharply and the unofficial shop stewards' movement was 'finally broken by the heavy unemployment of the 1920s' (Pelling, 1963: 166).

In the general election of 1922 the Labour Party increased the number of seats in Parliament to 142. Following internal disputes within the Conservative government, a further election was held in December 1923, in which the Labour Party won 191 seats, compared with 158 for the Liberals and 258 for the Conservatives. With the support of the Liberal Party, the Labour Party formed the Government. For the first time in British history the party that represented the interests of the British working class, especially through its deep connections with the trade unions, became the governing party. However, the Labour Party lacked government experience and had to face the reality that it was a minority government that could be overturned at any point if the Liberals disagreed with their policies. The Prime Minister, Ramsay MacDonald, turned to the experienced Philip Snowden to be Chancellor of the Exchequer. However, he included several ministers from outside the Labour Party, and the Cabinet contained only seven trade unionists out of a total of twenty members. In spite of the organic link of the unions with the Labour Party, the minority government had little choice other than to 'behave singularly like other governments': 'The Government felt that it ought to take an independent view of industrial problems ... [and] place the national interest before sectional loyalties' (Pelling, 1963: 169). In the face of two major strikes the Labour Government prepared to use 'Emergency Powers' involving employment of troops to ensure maintenance of essential services. In fact, neither strike took place, but the fact that a Labour Government had signalled its preparedness to use troops in the 'national interest' caused great disquiet in the Labour Party and among the rank and file of the trade unions. The Labour Government did not attempt to pass any significant legislation and it fell in October 1924 after less than a year in office. In his reply to left-wing criticism of the Labour Party, Philip Snowden replied that it was not possible to pursue more radical legislation due to the Government's reliance on Liberal Party support. In the ensuing General Election the number of Labour MPs fell to 151, compared with 412 for the Conservatives.

In 1925, faced with deteriorating conditions in export markets the coal owners attempted to enforce a reduction in miners' wages and the restoration of the eight-hour working day. The Conservative Government set up a Royal Commission to investigate wages and working hours in the mines. Its report, published early in 1926, supported the mine owners, arguing that the reduction of wages was necessary in order for the mining industry to make a profit in the face of difficult market conditions. The General Council of the TUC supported a call for a 'General Strike', involving coal miners, transport workers, print workers, workers in the iron and steel, heavy chemical and power industries. The General Strike began on 4 May, and within a week engineering and shipbuilding workers were called out on strike. In all the major urban centres 'the strike was a strange and even eerie experience' (Pelling, 1963: 174). The government used troops, police and special constables to ensure the maintenance of essential supplies. Large numbers of students volunteered to attempt to drive trains and load and unload ship cargoes, as well as performing other jobs. The period of the General Strike was mainly peaceful, with only occasional conflicts between strikers and the police. On 12 May, just nine days after the strike began, the General Council of the TUC decided to accept the terms of the Royal Commission. It represented a 'complete surrender' to the Government. The strikers' 'nine days' solidarity had ended in humiliating defeat with the strikers having 'failed to secure the slightest concession from the Government' (Pelling, 1963: 177). The extent of support for the General Strike demonstrated how deeply rooted trade unionism had become in the fabric of British society. The 'abject surrender' of its leaders showed how 'fundamentally devoid of political purpose it was'. In her diary entry just after the strike ended, Beatrice Webb wrote: 'The failure of the General Strike shows what a *sane* people the British are' (quoted in Pelling, 1963: 180).

In 1927 following the General Strike the Government passed the Trade Disputes and Trade Union Act, which declared illegal any strike action other than 'within the trade or industry or industry in which the strikers are engaged' or 'attempts to coerce the government either directly or by inflicting hardships on the community'. The Act also declared various forms of industrial action to constitute 'intimidation' and, therefore, to be illegal. It introduced a system under which trade unionists needed to 'contract in' to pay the political levy to the Labour Party. The Act was widely resented across the trade union movement.

In the second half of the 1920s the British economy grew slowly and unemployment remained at almost 10 per cent of the insured workforce. In the general election of 1929 the Labour Party for the first time became the largest single party, with 287 seats compared with 260 for the Conservatives and fifty-nine for the Liberals. The Labour Party formed the Government, but was still reliant on the Liberals for support, which constrained their independence. The Government was composed almost entirely of people from within the labour movement. Philip Snowden was once again appointed as Chancellor of the Exchequer.

Within months of taking office the economy began its steep decline into the Great Depression. The Labour Party's advisors in the Treasury argued strongly to cut government spending, especially in order to reassure foreign investors. Despite fierce opposition from the trade union movement the Labour Government followed the Treasury's advice. The General Council of the TUC argued vigorously against this response to the crisis. In this they were influenced by J.M. Keynes, who advised the Economic Committee of the General Council. In March 1931 the General Council published a comprehensive statement on economic policy arguing for measures that would sustain consumer spending.

Between 1929 and 1931 national output fell by 3 per cent per year and by 1931 the national unemployment rate had risen to 17 per cent of the insured population. In his budget speech of February 1931 Philip Snowden created a sensation. He proposed that the Government should balance the budget in part through cuts in social services and unemployment benefit. The Liberal Party, on whom the Labour Party depended for its survival, insisted on the appointment of a Committee on National Expenditure. When it reported in May 1931 it recommended further heavy cuts in Government expenditure. Almost immediately a foreign exchange crisis developed. Foreign investors began to withdraw their gold deposits from the London money market. The Cabinet responded by announcing even further cuts in Government spending. The TUC General Council declared their hostility to the cuts and to the whole course of economic policy followed by the Labour Government in response to the crisis. The Cabinet was split and the Prime Minister, Ramsay McDonald, resigned. He was invited by the King to form a National Government with Conservative and Liberal support. McDonald accepted the offer and Snowden stayed on as Chancellor of the Exchequer, along with two other Labour Cabinet members (J. H. Thomas and Lord Sankey). However, there was deep opposition within the trade union movement and the

Labour Party to McDonald and Snowden's decision. In September 1931 the Labour Party voted to expel McDonald and the other Labour Party Ministers from the Party. In the face of this dramatic development, McDonald was forced to concede to the Conservative Party's demand for a general election. The election was a disaster for the Labour Party. It won only forty-six seats, compared with 470 seats for the Conservative Party.

In 1933 the Labour Party's National Executive Council presented plans for the next occasion when it might be in office. It envisaged the formation of public corporations managed by people selected for their ability as administrators or technicians. It proposed that there should be trade union representation on the boards of nationalized industries. In response to pressure for a commitment to 'workers' control' on the shop floor the plan stated bluntly that the day-to-day administration of industrial concerns 'is quickly becoming a profession, and the persons undertaking this work will have to be trained business administrators' (quoted in Pelling, 1963: 202).

In the general election of November 1935 the Labour Party recovered its position somewhat and won 154 seats in Parliament, still far behind the Conservatives, who won 429 seats.

During the 1930s trade union membership expanded, reaching 6.3 million in 1939. There were still many industries that were largely non-unionized, including domestic servants, clerks and typists, agricultural workers, the distributive trades and the unskilled and general labour. However, among the main body of the manual workforce a large fraction of workers were members of a trade union. Overall, around one-third of the total workforce was a member of a trade union (Brown, 2003: 2). The TUC, to which most trade unions were affiliated, 'advanced its status both with the Government and with the public' (Pelling, 1963: 208). Both employers and trade unions adopted cautious policies that prevented large scale conflicts taking place, during the depths of the Depression and later in the 1930s as economic conditions improved. In the years 1934 through 1939 the number of days lost due to strikes only once exceeded two million, far below the levels between 1919 and 1926. Trade union leaders displayed a 'steady constitutionalism'. They were 'quite undoctrinaire about the possibilities for cooperation with the Government even when Labour was out of office' (Pelling, 1963: 208). The closeness of the relationship between union leaders and the Government is reflected in the fact that two of the trade union leaders, Arthur Pugh and Walter Citrine, accepted knighthoods. Trade union leaders were gradually drawn into the machinery of government which accompanied state intervention in industry, including the Government's efforts to restructure the cotton and fishing industries. The Labour Party Conference of 1936, with the strong support of the TUC, committed the party to support for national rearmament and in 1938–9 the TUC General Council worked closely with the Government in preparing plans for war mobilization and air-raid precautions.

International developments had a major impact upon the outlook of the British labour movement in this era. Russia's 1917 February Revolution was widely supported. However, the October Bolshevik Revolution produced a more complicated response. There was a wide opposition among the British working class to Western intervention to support the White Russian forces. Following the mutiny of British troops at Murmansk in 1918–19 British troops were withdrawn from Russia. However, the ferocity of the Civil War (1917–1921) reinforced deep-seated fears about the violence associated with a revolutionary overthrow of the bourgeois ruling class. During the period of New Economic Policy in the 1920s it appeared that the Soviet Union was going down the path of a mixed economy, with a wide diversity of political opinion albeit under Communist Party rule. The defeat of Trotsky and the emergence of Stalin as the undisputed leader of the Soviet Union sharply changed British opinion. During 'collectivization', which involved 'liquidation of the *kulaks* as a class' large numbers of people were killed and many more starved to death. During the 'Great Purge' Stalin directed extreme violence against his opponents, including the execution of ninety-eight out of 139 members of the 1934 Central Committee of the Communist Party of the Soviet Union (CPSU). Although rapid Soviet industrialization in the 1930s won admiration in the midst of the Great Depression and the slow economic recovery, to most British socialists the political price paid for this achievement appeared far too high.

The Communist Party of Great Britain (CPGB) was founded in 1920–1921 following the Bolshevik Revolution. It joined the 'Third Communist International' (Comintern), which was established in 1919 at the initiative of the Soviet Union and was widely viewed as being an instrument of Soviet foreign policy. Membership of the CPGB expanded from 12,000 in 1927 to 16,000 in 1939, still a tiny fraction of the politically active British population. Membership of the Labour Party rose from 215,000 in 1927 to 447,000 in 1939. Although the CPGB was committed to a Leninist revolutionary seizure of power and state ownership of the means of production, distribution and exchange, it also fielded candidates for election to Parliament. In general elections between the two world wars the CPGB never had more than one MP. In the election that took place in the depth of the Great Depression in 1931 the CPGB fielded twenty-six candidates, but none was elected. Following the electoral debacle of 1931, the CPGB proposed a united front with the Labour Party. The National Joint Council of the TUC and Labour Party responded with the publication in 1933 of the document *Democracy and Dictatorship*, which reaffirmed its belief in constitutional principles and its opposition to both communism and fascism. It was followed in 1934 by the so-called 'Black Circular' from the General Council, which advised unions to exclude communists from posts of responsibility and made exclusion of communists mandatory upon trades councils that wished to retain formal recognition by the TUC. Repeated requests in the 1930s by the CPGB to become affiliated with the Labour Party were rejected.

The rise of fascism in Spain, Italy, Germany and Japan was at least as important as Soviet communism in its impact on the political outlook of the British labour movement. In the inter-war period the scale of industrial enterprises in developed countries greatly increased alongside the spread of mass production. Progress in information technologies, including radio, cinema, newsreels, mass distribution newspapers, news photography, mass advertising and microphones and loudspeakers for mass meetings, opened up new avenues for the manipulation of public opinion through propaganda (Bernays, 1928). The rise of Stalin, Mussolini, Franco and, above all, Hitler, greatly reinforced fears within the British labour movement of the dangers of 'totalitarianism' crushing individualism in a society with a single mass political party that exercised a monopoly over the means of communication, organized the economy through central planning, and used terror and the secret police as instruments of social control. This nightmare vision infused a wide range of literature between the two world wars, such as Yevgeny Zamyatin's *We* (1920), Olaf Stapledon's *Last and First Men* (1930), Aldous Huxley's *Brave New World* (1932), and H.G. Wells' *The Shape of Things to Come* (1933), as well as films, such as Fritz Lang's *Metropolis* (1927) and Charlie Chaplin's *Modern Times* (1936). Olaf Stapledon, for example, foresaw a point in history 380 terrestrial years in the future, with a 'unified Americanized planet':

> The new order consisted of a vast system akin to guild socialism, yet at bottom individualistic. Each industry was in theory democratically governed by all its members, but in practice was controlled by its dominant individuals. Coordination of all industries was effected by the World Industrial Council, whereon the leaders of each industry discussed the affairs of the planet as a whole ... But the real seat of power was not the Council, not even an inner ring of the Council, but the Financial Directorate. This consisted of a dozen millionaires, with the American President and the Chinese Vice-President at their head.
>
> (Stapledon, 1930: 70–71)

Apprehension about the development of 'totalitarianism' under both fascism and Soviet communism had a profound impact on the British labour movement in the inter-war period. The idea that fascism and Soviet communism were both 'totalitarian' was first advanced by Trotsky in *Revolution Betrayed* (1937). He described the Soviet Union as a totalitarian regime that shared common features with fascism: 'Stalinism and fascism, in spite of deep differences of social foundations, are symmetrical phenomena. In many of their features they show a deadly similarity' (Trotsky, 1937: 278). This idea was developed in Franz Borknau's *The Totalitarian Enemy* (1940), James Burnham's *Managerial Revolution* (1941) and Hannah Arendt's *The Origins of Totalitarianism* (1951). Most British workers found it hard to distinguish between the 'totalitarian' violence unleashed on the one hand by Stalin against the *kulaks* and his opponents with the CPSU, and on the other hand, that unleashed by Hitler against Jews and communists in Germany. Their apprehensions about totalitarianism reinforced the views of the main body of British workers about the virtues of parliamentary democracy compared with the Leninist revolutionary path of social and economic change.

In the inter-war period George Orwell was, arguably, the most influential writer who addressed the issue of class struggle in Britain. His impact on British political thought resonated through into the post-1945 era of the Cold War and beyond. Orwell's sympathy with the British working class is reflected in the fact that he undertook two long journeys of 'fieldwork'. One was among the poor and destitute in Paris and London (*Down and Out in Paris and London*) (1933). The other was among the British industrial working class in northern England (*The Road to Wigan Pier*) (1937). Orwell was passionately committed to the belief that the injustice and inequality of a capitalist society would be replaced by socialism:

> There is no chance of righting the conditions [of the English working class] unless we can bring an effective Socialist party into existence. It will have to be a party with genuinely revolutionary intentions, and will have to be numerically strong enough to act.
>
> (Orwell, 1937: 202)

Despite measurable advances in average levels of real consumption and improvements in aspects of mass welfare, the conditions of work and living for the majority of working people in the 1920s and 1930s were far behind those that were reached in the 1960s and 1970s. Orwell's account of England's northern industrial towns emphasizes the arduous nature of manual occupations and the poor conditions of housing for the majority of the population. A programme of slum clearance and council house building had begun in cities like Manchester and Sheffield, but in the 1930s most workers in northern industrial towns still lived in 'labyrinths of little brick houses blackened by smoke, festering in planless chaos round miry alleys and little cindered yards where there are stinking dust-bins and lines of grimy washing and half-ruinous WCs (Orwell, 1937: 44). The majority of houses in Britain's northern industrial towns were 'fifty or sixty years old at least', and 'great numbers of them are not by any ordinary standards fit for human habitation': '[T]he houses are poky and ugly, and insanitary and comfortless ... distributed in incredibly filthy slums round belching foundries and stinking canals and slag-heaps that deluge them with sulphurous smoke' (Orwell, 1937: 45).

Orwell considered that the only way to engage with the mass of the working population, not only manual workers, but also with the large and growing number of clerical and service sector workers, was to use clear and simple language, devoid of Marxist jargon, with less about 'class consciousness', 'expropriation of the expropriators', 'bourgeois ideology', and 'proletarian solidarity' and 'more about justice, liberty and the plight of the unemployed' (Orwell, 1937: 202). Orwell opposed the idea of a 'vanguard party':

> The truth is that, to many people calling themselves Socialists, revolution does not mean a movement of the masses with which they hope to associate themselves; it means a set of reforms which 'we', the clever ones, are going to impose upon 'them', the Lower Orders.
>
> (Orwell, 1937: 157)

Orwell was implacably hostile to the centralist, authoritarian nature of Soviet communism. Nor did he believe that this kind of society held much attraction for the mass of the British working class. For Orwell, the communist movement in

Western Europe began as 'a movement for the violent overthrow of capitalism, and degenerated within a few years into an instrument of Russian foreign policy' (Orwell, 1940: 141). This could not have happened if 'any real revolutionary feeling had existed in the industrialized countries':

> In England, for instance, it is obvious that no such feeling has existed for years past. The pathetic membership of all extremist parties show this clearly ... [I]n any Western country a Party is always unstable and usually very small. Its long-term membership really consists of an inner ring of intellectuals who have identified with the Russian bureaucracy, and a slightly larger body of working-class people who feel loyalty towards Soviet Russia without necessarily understanding its policies.
>
> (Orwell, 1940: 142)

Orwell's hostility to fascism was reflected in the fact that he volunteered to fight in Spain against the fascist forces and was wounded in doing so (Orwell, 1938). He was influenced profoundly by the socialist ideals he encountered among segments of the anti-fascist forces. At the Aragon front Orwell fought with the workers' militias, based on the trade unions and each composed of people with approximately the same opinions, which had the effect of 'canalizing into one place all the most revolutionary sentiment in the country':

> Up here in Aragon one was among tens of thousands of people, mainly, though not entirely, of working class origin, all living and mingling on terms of equality. In theory it was perfect equality, and even in practice it was not far from it. There is a sense in which it would be true to say that one was experiencing a foretaste of Socialism, by which I mean that the prevailing mental atmosphere was that of Socialism. Many of the normal motives of civilized life – snobbishness, money-grubbing, fear of the boss etc. – had simply ceased to exist ... The thing that attracts ordinary men to Socialism and makes them willing to risk their skins for it, the 'mystique' of Socialism, is the idea of equality; to the vast majority of people Socialism means a classless society or it means nothing at all.
>
> (Orwell, 1938: 102)

Orwell was afraid that totalitarianism might become global. In the 1930s he thought that this was more likely to emerge from fascism than from Soviet communism: 'Fascism is now an international movement, which [is] groping ... towards a world system. For the vision of the totalitarian state is being substituted for the vision of a totalitarian world' (Orwell, 1937: 189). As the threat from fascism receded in 1945, Orwell focused on the degenerate nature of Soviet communism. *Animal Farm* (1945) is unquestionably directed against Stalinism. However, *1984* (1949) can best be interpreted as a critique of totalitarian tendencies within capitalism as much as a critique of the Soviet Union. In 1945 Orwell wrote: 'Capitalism leads to dole queues, the scramble for markets and war. Collectivism leads to concentration camps, leader worship, and war. There is no way out of this unless a planned economy can be combined with the freedom of the intellect' (Orwell, 1944: 144).

Despite his hostility to Soviet communism, Orwell never wavered in his hopes for socialism, even though he admitted that it would be a hard battle to achieve this. The pursuit of socialism was central to Orwell's philosophy throughout his life:

> Everyone who uses his brain knows that Socialism, as a world system and wholeheartedly applied, is a way out ... of a world in which nobody is free, in which hardly anybody is secure, in which it is almost impossible to be honest and remain alive ... Socialism is such elementary common sense that I am sometimes amazed that it has not established itself already. The world is a raft sailing through space, with, potentially, plenty of provisions for everybody; the idea that we must all cooperate and see to it that everybody does his fair share of the work and gets a fair share of the provisions, seems so blatantly obvious that one would say that no-one could possibly fail to accept it unless he had some corrupt motive for clinging to the present system.
>
> (Orwell, 1937: 149–150)

In his view the only places where democratic socialism as an idea existed on a large scale was Western Europe:

> Only in these countries are there still large numbers of people to whom the word 'Socialism' has some appeal and for whom it is bound up with liberty, equality and internationalism ... [A] Socialist United States of Europe seems to me the only worthwhile political objective today. Such a federation would contain about 250 million people, including perhaps half the skilled industrial workers of the world.
>
> (Orwell, 1947: 425)

Immediately after the outbreak of World War II the Labour Party joined Neville Chamberlain's wartime coalition Government. When Winston Churchill replaced Chamberlain as Prime Minister and leader of the Conservative Party, the Labour Party was offered a larger role in the Government than was warranted by the number of Labour MPs. This reflected the importance of securing the support of the labour movement for the war effort. Clem Attlee and Arthur Henderson, respectively Leader and Deputy Leader of the Opposition, were invited to join the War Cabinet, which initially consisted of only five members. In addition there were several other Labour ministers, including Ernest Bevin as Minister of Labour and National Service. Bevin formed a Joint Consultation Committee, which consisted of seven employers and seven trade union leaders. He also held a mass meeting of 2,300 trade union officials asking them for their support for the war effort. The Emergency Powers (Defence) Act gave the Government 'complete control over persons and property', and the Defence Regulations Act 58A gave it 'enormous powers of control of labour' (Pelling, 1963: 213). Order 1305 declared strikes and lock-outs to be illegal. A 'new spirit of cooperation in industry' was developed and in 1940 the number of strikes was the lowest on record. By 1941 'the trade union leadership was heavily committed to the Government's policy and involved in its administration at every level' (Pelling, 1963: 215). Union officials 'served on innumerable committees for the encouragement of production, for the operation of rationing schemes, and for a wide range of other purposes' (Pelling, 1963: 215). In 1942 the Ministry of Production was established and new national and regional production boards were set up. The boards involved representatives of employers and trade unions working closely with government officials. The following two years saw 'a remarkable development of consultative machinery at the factory level in order to increase output' (Pelling, 1963: 214). From May 1940 onwards trade union officials 'worked unceasingly to improve industrial relations and to increase output' (Pelling, 1963: 218). The Government did not attempt to control wages directly. Instead it appealed for unions to be restrained in their wage demands and during the whole period of war there was only a small increase in real wage rates.

Trade union membership rose from 6.1 million in 1938 to 7.8 million in 1945. By the end of the war the 'big six' unions contained over half of the total membership of the TUC. In 1945 at the end of the war trade union leaders felt that they had 'earned a right to have a say in the reconstruction of British society and industry' (Pelling, 1963: 221).

High levels of unemployment during the Great Depression caused great hardship for a substantial part of the British population. However, over the whole inter-war period the economy continued to grow. A wide array of new industries emerged, including electrical consumer goods, mass-produced automobiles, consumer goods made from petrochemicals, and commercial aircraft. Between 1911 and 1937 output per worker grew at 0.9 per cent per annum (Crafts, 2014: 28). Between 1913 and 1951 average real earnings grew at 1.5 per annum (Gazeley, 2014: 153).

A rudimentary system of health provision was put in place by the establishment of National Health Insurance in 1911 and the patchwork system was expanded and modified in the inter-war period. The system offered benefits to contributors below a certain level of income and excluded the contributor's dependents. Contributions were paid for on a fifty-fifty basis by employees and employers. Contributors were entitled to free but limited care from a doctor on a local list or 'panel', but were only entitled to hospital treatment for severe illnesses, such as tuberculosis. Local governments gradually expanded hospital provision for local ratepayers and alongside these were voluntary hospitals supported by charitable donations. Many workers had no health insurance and had no choice but to resort to self-medication and over-the-counter medicines. Overall, the 'threat of being asked to pay was a significant barrier to receiving treatment' (Harris, 2014: 143).

Although the rate of progress was slow and levels of provision were far below those of later years, there was significant progress in social welfare provision before 1945 (Harris, 2014: 142–43). The Liberal Government of 1906–1914 introduced the provision of free school meals by local authorities (1906), old age pensions (1908) and the creation of national schemes for unemployment and health insurance (1911). At the end of World War I the Government introduced a national network of municipal maternity and child welfare services (1918) and of subsidized public housing (1919). Unemployment insurance was expanded rapidly (1920–21). Expenditure on social services rose from 1.9 per cent of GDP in 1890 to 10.7 per cent in 1938, and the share of economic and environmental services increased from 1.3 per cent to 3.6 per cent (Harris, 2014: 142).

In the mid-1930s a typical unemployed family with children received around thirty shillings per week on the 'dole', with a strictly enforced Means Test. On this level of income a family were 'not far from the starvation line', but they could 'make a home of sorts' (Orwell, 1937: 71). Families living on the dole 'lived a reduced version of their former lives' and 'instead of raging against their destiny they ... made things tolerable by lowering their standards' (Orwell, 1937: 78). Life for the unemployed was rendered more palatable by the arrival of mass cinema (four pence for a double bill), the radio and cheap mass-produced 'luxuries', including cheap, fashionable clothing:

> You may have three halfpence in your pocket and not a prospect in the world, and only the corner of a leaky bedroom to go home to; but in your new clothes you can stand on the street corner, indulging in a private daydream of yourself as Clark Gable or Greta Garbo, which compensates you for a great deal.
>
> (Orwell, 1937: 79)

The rise of organized mass gambling in the form of the Football Pools, with the participants drawn mainly from the working class, provided the 'cheapest of all luxuries': 'Even people on the verge of starvation can buy a few days' hope ... by having a penny on the sweepstake' (Orwell, 1937: 79).

By the late 1930s 'literally everyone in England had access to a radio', which presented the 'queer spectacle of modern electrical science showering miracles upon people with empty bellies': 'Whole sections of the working class who have been plundered by all they really need are being compensated, in part, by cheap luxuries which mitigate the surface of life' (Orwell, 1937: 80). These developments meant that the poor and unemployed 'neither turned revolutionary nor lost their self-respect': 'The alternative would be God knows what continued agonies of despair; or it might be attempted insurrections, which, in a country strongly ruled like England could only lead to futile massacres and a regime of savage repression' (Orwell, 1937: 80). The development of cheap mass-produced luxuries served a vital function for British social and political stability in the face of the economic crisis of the 1930s: 'It is likely that fish-and-chips, art silk stockings, tinned salmon, cut-price chocolates, the movies, the radio, strong tea, and the Football Pools have averted revolution' (Orwell, 1937: 80). The supply of 'cheap palliatives' did not take place as an 'astute manoeuvre' by the governing classes to 'put the unemployed down'. Rather, it took place as an 'unconscious process', the 'quite natural interaction between the manufacturer's need for a market and the need for half-starved people for cheap palliatives' (Orwell, 1937: 80).

1945–1951

The Labour Party won a landslide victory in the election of 1945, winning 393 seats, with 48 per cent of the total votes, compared with 197 for the Conservatives, with 36 per cent of the total votes. With over three-fifths of the seats in the House of Commons, for the first time in history the party of the British working class had a clear majority of seats. The Communist Party fielded twenty-one candidates, but won only two seats. The Labour Party's campaign was closely coordinated with the trade unions. One hundred twenty-four of the Labour MPs were union-sponsored. The Labour Party also won a large number of seats in mainly middle class constituencies. Six of the twenty cabinet members were union-sponsored MPs. One of the first measures of the new Government was the repeal of the 1927 Trade Disputes Act. The most important consequence of this was that the trade unions were now required to 'contract out' rather than 'contract in' to the political levy to the Labour Party. This measure increased the membership of the Labour Party by over one-half and provided a considerable increment to Labour Party funds.

Since the introduction of Clause IV into its constitution, the Labour Party had been committed to 'common ownership of the means of production, distribution and exchange'. The Labour Government entered upon a programme of extensive nationalization of assets. Its aim was 'public control of industry rather than workers' control as such'. The boards of the nationalized industries were to contain people of 'wide experience and knowledge of workpeople's interests', at the same time 'care should be taken to avoid the creation of dual responsibility'. In other words, union representatives on the boards of nationalized industries should be freed from all their union duties (Pelling, 1963: 223).

In 1946 the Labour Party nationalized the Bank of England. In 1947 it nationalized the coal industry, bringing the entire mining industry under the National Coal Board. In 1947 it established the British Transport Commission, which took control of the railways, canals and road haulage. In 1948 it established the British Electricity Authority to run the electricity industry and in 1949 it set up the British Gas Council to run the gas industry. In 1951 it took over the firms in the iron and steel industry and placed them under a public authority. By 1951 about one-fifth of the British economy had been taken into public ownership.

During the years of Labour Government the trade unions 'passed from the era of propaganda to one of responsibility'. The union leadership became 'closely integrated with the Government at every level': 'In return for the privilege of being consulted and of taking part in innumerable administrative decisions, it gave up, albeit temporarily the right to strike' (Pelling, 1963: 231). The union leaders became 'deeply committed to many of the processes of management' including cooperation in the introduction of 'scientific management' (Pelling, 1963: 231). The period 1946–51 saw a low level of strike activity, with a maximum of 2.5 million working days lost through strikes. Trade union membership grew to 9.5 million by 1951.

During this period there was also a power struggle within the union movement. Although the CPGB was extremely weak politically, winning just two seats in the 1945 general election, it expanded its influence in the trade union movement, gaining complete control of some unions, including the Electrical Trades Union, and with significant influence in others, including the Mineworkers and the Amalgamated Engineering Union (AEU). In 1948 the General Council of the TUC issued the document *Defend Democracy*. It urged all trade unions to act in order to prevent communists from holding key posts, arguing that communist penetration of the British trade union movement was directed by the international communist movement, which was heavily influenced by the Soviet Union. In 1949 a 'decisive battle' took place in the Transport and General Workers Union (TGWU), which had an enormous membership. The union's conference carried a resolution to prevent communists from holding office in the union.

The Labour Government of 1945–51 put into place a wide array of social welfare measures that came to be collectively thought of as the 'Welfare State'. However, these measures did not originate with the Labour Government. The central ideas emerged from the Beveridge Report of 1942 (Abel-Smith, 1992). The Report was commissioned by the wartime coalition government, in which the Conservative Government was by far the dominant partner, with much the largest number of seats in Parliament. Beveridge was the son of a judge and educated at Oxford University. Before entering the wartime administration he had been Director of the London School of Economics. Although he was attracted by social-ist ideas, he never joined the Labour Party. In 1945 he was elected as a Liberal MP. The initial impetus for the Report came from the trade unions' dissatisfaction with the bewildering variety of different provisions for social welfare benefits. In the middle of the war the Government felt that it was necessary to listen to the trade unions' views and established a committee under Beveridge's chairmanship. The war reinforced the sense of a single national community in which rights and duties extended across all members of society. In 1940 the *Times* wrote:

> If we speak of democracy, we do not mean a democracy which maintains the right to vote, but forgets the right to live and work. If we speak of freedom, we do not mean a rugged individualism which excludes social organization and economic planning. If we speak of equality, we do not mean a political equality nullified by social and economic privilege. If we speak of economic reconstruction, we think less of maximum production (though that too will be required) than of equitable distribution.
>
> (quoted in Tawney, 1951: 26)

Beveridge pushed the scope of the committee's investigations far beyond the Government's original intention. The Beveridge Report recommended a sweep-ing plan to comprehensively transform the welfare system:

> The plan for social security is put forward as part of a general programme of social policy. It is one part only of an attack upon five giant evils: upon the physical Want with which it is directly concerned, upon Disease which often causes Want and brings many other troubles in its train, upon Ignorance which no democracy can afford among its citizens, upon Squalor which

arises mainly through the haphazard distribution of industry and population, and upon Idleness which destroys wealth and corrupts men ... The
proposals in the report are concerned not with increasing the wealth of the
British people, but with so distributing whatever wealth is available to them
in total, as to deal first with first things, with essential physical needs ... The
object of government in peace and in war is not the glory of rulers or races,
but the happiness of the common man ... The purpose of victory is to live in
a better world than the old world.

(quoted in Abel-Smith, 1992: 5–6)

The very title of the Report – 'Full Employment in a Free Society' – was arresting.
The Report argued: 'Now, when the war is abolishing landmarks of every kind,
is the opportunity for using experience in a clear field. A revolutionary moment
in the world's history is a time for revolutions, not for patching' (quoted in Abel-
Smith, 1992: 7). The Report shocked many people with its statement concerning
liberty and private property:

The list of essential liberties ... does not include liberty of a private citizen
to own means of production and to employ other citizens in operating at a
wage. Whether private ownership of means of production to be operated by
others is a good economic device or not, it is to be judged as a device.

(quoted in Tawney, 1951: 245)

The Report recommended unification of the sickness and unemployment benefit
system. Both contributions and benefits were to be flat rate. The whole system
was to be administered centrally, rather than by local authorities: 'no longer would
any part of the task of providing income to the poor be left to local authorities'
(Abel-Smith, 1992: 10). The central goal of the social security system was to
be the elimination of poverty. The Report also recommended the introduction of
family allowances and a free health service, with full employment enshrined as a
central policy goal.

The reception by the general public when the Report was published in
December 1942 was euphoric, tapping a wellspring of popular sentiment. The
Times said that it was 'a momentous document which should and must exercise
a profound and immediate influence on the direction of social change in Britain'.
The *Daily Telegraph* said that it was 'a consummation of the revolution begun by
David Lloyd George in 1911'. The Archbishop of Canterbury said that it was 'the
first time anyone had set out to embody the whole spirit of the Christian ethic in
an Act of Parliament' (quoted in Barnett, 2001: 30). A number of reasons explain
the enthusiasm with which the general public responded to the Report. The high
taxation necessary to pay for the war, along with full employment and rationing
had brought a much greater degree of equality of income and welfare. One and a
half million mothers and children had been evacuated during the war. They had
been billeted without regard to social class. In the cities all social classes had
had to share the same air raid shelter. Around eight million people were in the

armed forces, the Home Guard or the Civil Defence, and the patriotic fervour of the war all contributed to a new sense of 'equality of sacrifice' and 'fair shares' for all citizens (Abel-Smith, 1992: 12). Detailed plans based on the Report were not produced until 1944. Although there was considerable debate in Parliament about the financial implications of putting into place the whole package of recommendations, there was broad cross-party agreement about the basic philosophy of the Report. In his broadcast of March 1943 the prime minister, Winston Churchill, spoke of the need for a 'national compulsory insurance for all classes, for all purposes, from the cradle to the grave'. He spoke also of the need to establish 'a national health service on broad and solid foundations'. In fact, it fell to the Labour Party to implement many of the key ideas in the Report.

Although progress was made before 1939 in expanding access to health services, the system remained 'a patchwork of institutions which were not accessible according to need'. Under the National Health Service Act (1946) the Labour Government established the 'National Health Service', which provided a service that was 'comprehensive and universal, and free at the point of use' (Harris, 2014: 143). The preceding complicated structure of insurance schemes was abolished and all members of the population were given the opportunity to register with a general practitioner. General practitioners, dentists, opticians and pharmacists were registered as independent contractors providing services to the NHS. The voluntary hospitals were nationalized and the whole hospital system was placed under central control. Community services (maternity and child care, health visitors, midwives, vaccination, immunization and ambulance services) were placed under local authorities. The entire range of health care services was provided free at the point of use. The whole system was funded out of taxation rather than insurance. The share of social service expenditure in GDP rose from 10.7 per cent in 1938 to 14.1 per cent in 1950 (Harris, 2014: 142).

Large advances in popular welfare took place between 1945 and 1951. In 1895–1900 the infant mortality rate stood at 156 per thousand live births, and more than one hundred per 1,000 live births between 1900 and 1920. By 1946–48 it had fallen to thirty-nine per 1,000 (Tawney, 1951: 129 and 232). The height and weight of schoolchildren increased and many ailments that formerly afflicted them disappeared. The expectation of life at birth rose from about forty-three years in the 1870s to sixty-five years in the late 1940s. Unemployment averaged over 14 per cent of the insured population between 1921 and 1938. In the later 1940s the unemployment rate was 'reduced to a negligible level'. There was 'substantial improvement in the provision for victims of unemployment as well as for those affected by sickness, accidents and old age (Tawney, 1951: 233).

The Labour Government implemented important new programmes in housing and education. Between 1945 and 1950 over one million new homes were built, 80 per cent of which were council houses with subsidized rents. In 1944 the wartime government passed the Butler Education Act, the provisions of which were put into place by the Labour Government. Free secondary education became a right for the first time and the school leaving age was raised from fourteen to fifteen. A system of secondary modern schools was established alongside grammar schools. A selection exam at age eleven (the eleven-plus) determined which of the two systems pupils went to for their secondary education. Expenditure per person on social services more than doubled, increasing from £7.4 in 1936 to £15.5 in 1949–50 (at 1936 prices) (Tawney, 1951: 217).

In 1951 Britain was still a highly unequal country. However, compared with the 1930s there had been a large reduction in income inequality. Inequality in the distribution of pre-tax income had fallen, due to such factors as changes in the occupational distribution of the workforce and the impact of full employment on the bargaining power of organized labour. The Gini coefficient of inequality in original incomes, without tax or benefits, declined from 0.37 in 1937 to 0.26 in 1949 (Gazeley, 2014: 174). Compared with the 1930s a wide range of cash benefits were now distributed, broadly speaking, in relation to need. The Gini coefficient of income including cash benefits fell from 0.33 in 1937 to 0.21 in 1949. In part also the reduction in income inequality was due to the effect of progressive income tax. In 1948 the share of pre-tax income taken in income tax was 5.6 per cent for those with an annual income of £250-£499 (74 per cent of total income earners), 14.6 per cent for those with incomes of £500-£999 (20 per cent of income earners), 25.6 per cent for those with £1,000-£1,999 (4.7 per cent of income earners), 42.6 per cent for those with £2,000-£9,999 (1.8 per cent of income earners), and 75.9 per cent for those with over £10,000 (0.09 per cent of income earners) (Tawney, 1951: 214). The Gini coefficient of income distribution after direct taxes fell from 0.29 in 1937 to 0.16 in 1949, and the Gini coefficient of income inequality after taking account of taxes and benefits in kind fell from 0.28 in 1937 to 0.14 in 1949 (Gazeley, 2014: 174). In other words, the combined impact of increased progressive taxation and benefits in kind reduced income inequality in Britain to around one-half of its pre-war level.

Few scholars addressed so directly and forcefully the nature of British class struggle in mid-twentieth century as did R.H. Tawney. Few did so with comparable passion or in such an informed and balanced fashion.[9]

The foundation of Tawney's approach was the idea that freedom and equality are intimately connected. He considered that '[f]reedom for the strong is oppression for the weak … and oppression is not less oppressive when its strength is derived from superior wealth, than when it relies on a preponderance of physical force' (Tawney, 1951: 228). He believed that 'there is no such thing as freedom in the abstract, divorced from a particular time and place … [F]reedom means the ability to do, or to refrain from doing, definite things, at a definite moment, in definite circumstances or it means nothing at all'(Tawney, 1951: 228). He cautioned that 'when steps to diminish inequality are denounced as infringements of freedom, the first question to be answered is one not normally asked. It is: freedom for whom?' (Tawney, 1951: 228). He argued that a society is free:

> … only insofar as within the limits set by nature, knowledge and resources, its institutions and policies are such as to enable all its members to grow to their full stature, to do their duty as they see fit, and – since liberty should not be too austere – to have their fling when they feel like it … Insofar as the

opportunity to lead a life worthy of human beings is needlessly confined to a minority, not a few of the conditions applauded as freedom would be more properly denounced as privilege. Action which causes such opportunities to be more widely shared is, therefore, twice blessed. It not only subtracts from inequality, but adds to freedom.

(Tawney, 1951: 235)

Despite enormous social progress the British class structure still remained highly unequal. The twin pillars of the class structure were the distribution of wealth and the educational system.

Despite the equalizing impact of death duties the distribution of wealth was still highly unequal. In 1911–13 the top 1 per cent of the British population had held 65 per cent of wealth. By 1946–47 their share had fallen to 50 per cent (Tawney, 1951: 243). By 1951–56 this had fallen further, but the top 1 per cent of the population still owned 42 per cent of personal net capital, and the top 5 per cent owned 67.5 per cent (Titmuss, 1964:16): 'The fact remains that the transmission of more than a minimum of wealth from generation to generation has … little more to commend it than would have the right to travel in perpetuity in first class coaches' (Tawney, 1951: 223).

Tawney fiercely attacked inequality in the distribution of educational opportunity. He argued that the 'realities of child-life' should be 'the criterion by which all educational arrangements should be tested' and that the government's educational policy should be 'merciless to the pretensions of different classes' (Tawney, 1951: 142). The focus of his attack was the private fee-paying school ('public school') system: 'The hereditary curse upon English education is its organization upon lines of social class'. He deplored the 'barbarous association of differences of educational opportunity with distinctions of wealth and social position':

The public school boy is encouraged to regard himself as one of the ruling class, which, in politics, administration and business will govern and direct – to acquire in short the aristocratic virtues of initiative and self-reliance, as well as frequently the aristocratic vices of arrogance, intellectual laziness and self-satisfaction.

(Tawney, 1951: 142)

Tawney drew attention to the remarkable class dominance of people whose parents had paid for them to attend a small number of elite public schools. In pre-war Britain almost all the bishops, three-quarters of the highest positions in the legal profession, the civil service, and the banks, were occupied by people who had attended public schools (Tawney, 1951: 247) and this had changed little by the 1950s (Tawney, 1951: 224). The British system of private schools accessible mainly through the wealth of a child's parents is 'socially disastrous' and 'does more than any other single cause, except capitalism itself, to perpetuate the division of the nation into classes of which one is almost unintelligible to the other' (Tawney, 1951: 145). The educational reforms of the 1940s did nothing to change the class-based distinctions in the British educational system. In Tawney's view 'the 'English educational system will never be one worthy of a civilized society until the children of all classes in the nation attend the same schools' (Tawney, 1951: 144). In Tawney's view the goal of educational policy should be to make 'the common school of the whole population so excellent and so generally esteemed that all parents will desire their children to attend it' (Tawney, 1951: 224).

Up until the 1940s progress in state provision of social welfare had been slow. Moreover, it was often undertaken for short-term political gain rather than ethical conviction. Nevertheless, even by the late 1930s Tawney could perceive the 'rise of this rudimentary communism' which had 'taken place without design and almost unconsciously' (Tawney, 1951: 133). Prior to 1938 through 'a long series of cautious and limited reforms ... politicians unseduced by the equalitarian mirage were led by the invisible hands of humanity, common sense and electoral expediency to promote ends which were no part of their design' (Tawney, 1951: 219). The reforms of the post-war Labour Government built upon and enlarged the scope and extent of 'communal provision'. Tawney applauded the 'increased money and services at the disposal of the lower income groups' (Tawney, 1951: 220). He drew attention to the fact that their children now had 'access to a schooling improved in quality and longer in duration'. The reforms meant that people with lower incomes would be 'less exposed in manhood to loss of livelihood and status through involuntary unemployment'; not be 'deprived by a lack of means of treatment in illness required by themselves or their dependents'; 'would, if injured at work, receive benefit as a matter of course'; and 'be assured in unemployment, incapacity and old age a less inadequate pension than in the past on terms compatible with his self-respect' (Tawney, 1951: 221).

Tawney noted that these 'advances towards the conversion of a class-ridden society into a community in fact, as well as in name, have taken place ... with almost melodramatic sedateness'. However, 'they have been effected without excursions and alarms, after prolonged debate in Parliament and the press, by the pedestrian and unspectacular process of democratic Government' (Tawney, 1951: 223). He observed that if a 'majority of the nation' wished the government to enact measures to 'turn one-class private "public" schools into institutions serving the public, to tax capital gains as well as incomes', to establish 'more stringent controls of monopolies' or to 'extend the area of public ownership', then Parliament and the Civil Service 'will do the job for it' (Tawney, 1951: 224). It need not fear that the 'political machine will break in its hand'. However, 'if these laudable improvements leave the British public cold, an enlightened minority has neither the right nor the power to force them down reluctant throats' (Tawney, 1951: 224).

Tawney was emphatic about the necessity of state intervention to regulate the market, but he was pragmatic and flexible in the methods necessary to achieve this. In his view the post-war British economic system was a 'power system', with 'a hierarchy of authority' in which 'those who hold its levers of power exercise, consciously or unconsciously, a decisive influence on human lives' (Tawney, 1951: 230). He considered that such a power was 'too great to be entrusted to private persons actuated primarily ... by considerations of their own and their shareholders' pecuniary gain or loss'. However, although this system 'cannot, for technical reasons be abolished or broken up' ... 'it can cease to be arbitrary and autocratic': 'It can, in short, be converted into a responsible public or semi-public function in the traditional English manner, by its submission to public control, whether in the form of regulation or ownership'. He observes that the idea of 'regulation', which was 'stubbornly contested in the recent past, appears today to meet, in principle, with general acquiescence'. However the idea of 'public ownership' retains its 'pleasing power to provoke hysterics'. Tawney notes that in reality there are a 'dozen different forms' of regulation and public ownership, that they are 'different forms of one genus' and at the edges they 'melt into one another' (Tawney, 1951: 230).

1951–1979

Between 1945 and 1951 the Labour Party introduced wide-ranging legislation to advance social welfare, reduce inequality and nationalize large segments of the economy. By any measure this was an enormous political achievement. It resonated deeply with the wishes of a large section of the British population and to a considerable degree it was a response to widely held beliefs, which had been reinforced by the experience of World War II. Instead of a renewal of the popular mandate in the General Election of 1950, the Labour Party's Parliamentary majority over the Conservatives was reduced from 196 seats to just seventeen. Within eighteen months the Labour Party was forced to call another election in which the number of seats shrank further and it was ejected from office. The Conservative Party won three successive general elections, ruling from 1951 until 1964. However, the orderly transfer of power through general elections resulted in the return of the Labour Party to government in 1964. Between 1964 and 1979 it governed for all but four years.

Throughout the period from the early 1950s until the late 1970s (and afterwards) the left-wing of the Labour Party continued to argue that the reason for the Party's failure after 1950 to cement its position as the natural party of government supported by the majority of the labour movement, was its decision not to advance a more radical Socialist agenda of 'class struggle'. In this view, the government of 1945 to 1950 should have been used as the springboard for more radical polices to extend nationalization in order to attack the class structure at its root, redistribute income and wealth more seriously, undertake more radical measures to advance social welfare and implement root and branch reform of the educational system. Throughout the period between 1918 and 1995 the Labour Party maintained 'Clause IV' in its constitution. For those on the left-wing of the Party, nationalization of the means of production, distribution and exchange was the centrepiece of class struggle and essential to the achievement of socialism. Leading left-wing intellectuals such as Ralph Miliband were fiercely critical of Soviet communism, but at the same time they deplored the timidity of the Labour Party leadership in failing to put nationalization at the centre of their political programme.

The vision of a state-owned economy based on expropriation of the capitalist class, with the economy run in a planned and rational fashion continued to be centrally important for the left wing of the Labour Party and for left-wing groups outside the Party. Ralph Miliband was one of the most articulate exponents of this view. His study *Parliamentary Socialism* (Miliband, 1961) is a sustained critique of 'revisionism' in the Labour Party, which he blamed for the Labour Party's failure to become the natural party of government with the support of the mass of the working population. Miliband was a left wing scholar with a deep knowledge of the British political system. He joined the Labour Party in 1951. In 1955 he spoke at the Labour Party Conference and argued:

> We are a socialist party engaged on a great adventure ... [W]e have a vision which the Tories have never had and never will have ... [W]e are concerned with building that kind of socialist commonwealth which our forebears wanted and which millions of people in our movement have tried to build ... We want this party to state that it stands unequivocally behind the social ownership and control of the means of production, distribution and exchange.
>
> (quoted in Simkin, 2014: 7)

He criticized the Labour Party for its timidity in the pursuit of 'real' socialist goals. He believed that the core reason for this was the Party's 'devotion' to the parliamentary system:

> [T]he leaders of the Labour Party have always rejected any kind of political action (such as industrial action for political purposes) which fell, or which appeared to them to fall, outside the framework and conventions of the parliamentary system. The Labour Party has not only been a parliamentary party; it has been a party deeply imbued by parliamentarianism.
>
> (Miliband, 1961: 13)

International developments affected the British labour movement's view of the domestic class struggle, helping to reduce their sympathy for 'revolutionary' political ideas. In the late 1940s the emergence of communist rule in Eastern and Central Europe under strong influence from the Soviet Union strengthened popular fears about communist 'totalitarianism'. Under the Labour Government Britain waged a ferocious guerrilla war against 'Communist Terrorists' in Malaya and in 1950 the Labour Government took Britain into the Korean War, fighting alongside American troops against both Korean and Chinese forces. The Chinese revolution, China's involvement in the Korean War and a perception that China was supporting communist-led independence struggles in Southeast Asia, helped to reinforce popular fears about communist revolution. The Sino-Soviet split bewildered most ordinary British workers. The Cultural Revolution bewildered them further. Throughout the period from 1945 until the late 1970s in the minds of the mainstream of the British labour movement 'communism' was equated with the regimes in the Soviet bloc and in China. A small and dwindling minority of the labour movement sympathized with either Soviet or Chinese communism. The net effect of international developments in the communist world was to reinforce support among British workers for the British 'Parliamentary Road to Socialism'.

There were serious and growing doubts also in the main body of the Labour Party about the desirability of a centrally controlled economic system based on state ownership as a long-term goal for the Labour Party. There was mounting evidence against the argument that 'central planning' and comprehensive state ownership of the means of production were useful mechanisms for the achievement of socialist ends. The Soviet economy achieved high speed growth in the 1930s and it achieved tremendous long-term advances in the provision of education, healthcare and housing for the mass of the population. By the late 1950s life expectancy in the Soviet Union had caught up with that in the industrialized West (World Bank, 1979: 166–7). However, it became increasingly clear from the 1950s onwards that a system which attempted to eliminate the profit motive and the price mechanism resulted in large problems in achieving innovation and efficiency in resource use.

The core of the 'planned economy' was the idea of the 'whole economy as a single enterprise'. This fundamentalist view of the nature of a 'communist' economy was expressed as follows by Bukharin and Preobrazhensky:

> The basis of communist society must be the social ownership of the means of production and exchange. All these means of production must be under the control of society as a whole, and not, as at present, under the control of individual capitalists or combines ... In these circumstances society will be transformed into one huge organization for cooperative production. There will be neither disintegration of production nor anarchy of production. In such a social order, production will be organized. No longer will one enterprise compete with another; the factories, mines and other productive institutions will be subdivisions, as it were, of one vast people's workshop, which will embrace the entire national economy.
>
> (Bukharin and Preobrazhensky, 1922: 114)

A great paradox of the 'planned' economy in the USSR and in other 'communist' countries is that the system of commands issued to enterprises failed to establish an economy which was any less anarchic and therefore any less alienating than the capitalist system (Nolan, 1995: Chapter 3). At least as much as under capitalist competition the system that people themselves had created exercised control over them. It remained, in a fundamental sense, anarchic. The adjective 'planned' is inappropriate to describe the Stalinist system of state ownership and commands deriving from the construction of material balances. The central elements of 'planning' are 'looking ahead', 'co-ordination', and 'the attainment of deliberate aims'. The Stalinist system was an 'administered', an 'instruction' or a 'command' rather than a 'planned' economy.

Instead of working as a 'team' pulling towards common goals, agents at different levels of the 'planning' system struggled to maximize individual self-interest and failed to provide truthful information to higher levels of the 'planning' system. In the absence of market information the task of checking the information provided by agents at each level became impossibly complex. Moreover, even if all agents had provided planners with truthful information, the iterations and feedback effects involved in constructing a material balance plan were impossibly complex. Consequently, as is well known, the administratively 'planned' economy had built into it a permanent imbalance of supply and demand.

A high degree of self-sufficiency was produced at every level of the system. The system resulted in a pervasive tendency towards hoarding, with a vicious circle of 'suction' and hoarding feeding off each other in an atmosphere of uncertainty about supplies of intermediate inputs. The advanced capitalist economies were reducing inventories per unit of final product, culminating in 'just-in-time' supplies of needed inputs. The Soviet economy experienced rising stocks of inventories per unit of final product. The system produced little interest among producers in the usefulness of their output. Pervasive shortage meant that there existed a seller's market for a large proportion of output. Specification of output targets in simple physical terms led to a tendency towards the narrowing of product range towards those products which were easiest to produce. Thus, the mix of consumer goods notoriously failed to respond to consumer signals and there was a high rate of breakdowns of consumer durables. The real welfare provided by a given bundle of consumer goods was much less than might have been the case under competitive conditions. Moreover, throughout the system, capital goods were unsuitable to the task for which they were supplied and/or broke down frequently.

Far from overcoming the key shortcomings of the capitalist system, the communist 'planned' economy produced many of these shortcomings in an even more acute form. Far from abolishing waste it produced waste on a grand scale. It abolished production for profit but was unable to replace it with production for use. It abolished the short-termism produced by competitive capitalism but substituted for this an even more profound short-termism of current plan fulfillment. It steered economic activity in directions that were widely acknowledged as being socially undesirable, but was unable to shift away from this pattern of economic behaviour. In sum, it was a system that was more 'anarchic' than competitive capitalism.

Moreover, there was wide apprehension about the relationship between a highly centralized system of economic control under state ownership and concentration of political power. The identification of public control of the means of production, distribution and exchange as a necessary aspect of socialism was increasingly called into question. The mainstream of the labour movement came increasingly to regard regulation of a market economy as the most effective way to combine equity with economic efficiency.

The mass of the British population demonstrated little appetite for Leninist 'revolutionary' organizations. During the 1950s the parties to the left of the Labour Party disappeared from Parliament. In the general election of 1950 the Communist Party of Great Britain (CPGB) fielded a hundred candidates, but they attracted only 92,000 votes and failed to win a single seat. The CPGB failed to win a single seat in any of the general elections from the 1950s to the late 1970s. In the 1979 election the CPGB fielded thirty-eight candidates and attracted just 17,000 votes across the whole country. At its peak during World War II the CPGB had over 60,000 members. The membership declined after the war. The party's weakness was reflected in their decision to formally renounce a Leninist 'revolutionary' path and follow a 'reformist' path, which accepted that in Britain the transition to socialism would take place through parliamentary methods. This was formalized in the document *The British Road to Socialism*, published in 1952. Around 7,000 CPGB members resigned over the Soviet crushing of the Hungarian uprising in 1956 and a further 6,000 resigned over the Soviet crushing of the Prague Spring in 1968 in Czechoslovakia. The images of Soviet tanks repressing the popular uprisings in Hungary and Czechoslovakia were lodged indelibly in the popular imagination in Britain. The Sino-Soviet split led to a further decline in membership. The 'first past the post' system of British elections disadvantaged small parties. The CPGB's electoral performance was far worse than that of the Liberal Party, which won between six and fourteen seats in Parliament in the elections between the 1940s and the late 1970s.

Membership of the other left-wing groups, such as the International Socialists (later the Socialist Workers' Party, SWP) and the International Marxist Group (IMG), was even smaller than that of the CPGB. The 'revolutionary' organizations were mainly 'Trotskyist', who considered that the USSR was a 'state capitalist' country. They were heavily critical of the CPGB, which had a close relationship with the Soviet Union. At their respective peaks the International Socialists may have had over 3,000 members, while the IMG had around 1,000 members at its peak. There was a proliferation of smaller 'revolutionary' groups, each with only a handful of members, including tiny groups such as the British and Irish Communist Organisation (B&ICO) and the Revolutionary Communist Group (RCG). They typically were formed due to ideological differences that led to their expulsion from or their decision to 'split' from the main 'revolutionary' organization. Indeed, splits over ideological differences absorbed a great deal of energy of the ultra-left groups. Universities were their main source of recruitment and an important location for their activity, including distribution of their journals and magazines. The ultra-left organizations constituted a sort of club, mainly for young intellectuals from relatively privileged backgrounds. Their leaders were typically much older, often with charismatic personalities. Their members frequently gravitated out of the ultra-left groups into mainstream, non-revolutionary occupations, often involving a dramatic change of political outlook. Some of Britain's leading journalists and politicians were once members of the SWP or IMG. The 'ultra-left' groups posed no threat to British political stability. Their membership was tiny. A large part of their energy was devoted to doctrinal disputes about the interpretation of the legacy of Marx, Engels and Lenin, and how to classify the USSR and China in terms of 'Marxist' theory. Their language was typically obscure and unconnected with the realities of daily life for the main body of the working population. Their political influence was small. The British government treated them tolerantly despite their allegedly 'revolutionary' purpose. There was no British equivalent of America's McCarthyism or the West German *'Berufsverbot'* law (1972), which banned members of ultra-left organizations from positions in public employment, including universities.

As early as 1950 a group of Labour Party MPs produced a pamphlet (*Keeping Left*) which argued that the Labour Party should move away from its preoccupation with changing the ownership structure:

> Most early socialists thought that the job of changing the nature of society was exclusively a matter of changing the proprietors of industry. For them the ownership of the means of production, distribution and exchange was the sole criterion of whether the community was a capitalist or a socialist one. They therefore identified socialism with public ownership and believed that all the world's ills could be dispersed through the formula of nationalization. In the last few years we have learned to distinguish the means of socialism from the ends, and the tools of social revolution from their uses.
>
> (quoted in Crosland, 1956: 366)

Increasingly during the 1950s the leadership of the Labour Party pursued a 'new revisionism', which argued that 'in a "post-capitalist society" nationalization had become largely irrelevant' (Miliband, 1961: 332). The 'essential difference between Right and Left' in the Labour Party was the fact that 'the former envisaged an economic system in which the "private sector" was to retain by far the dominant share of economic power, while the latter wanted precisely the opposite' (Miliband, 1961: 333). In 1957 the Labour Party conference adopted the document *Industry and Society*. It stated:

> The Labour Party recognizes that, under increasingly professional managements, large firms are as a whole serving the nation well ... and no organization, public or private, can operate effectively if it is subjected to persistent and detailed interventions from above. We have, therefore, no intention of interfering in any firm which is doing a good job.
>
> (quoted in Miliband, 1961: 338)

Anthony Crosland was the most powerful exponent of revisionism in the Labour Party. He argued:

> A higher working-class standard of living, more effective joint consultation, better labour relations, a proper use of economic resources, a wider diffusion of power, a greater degree of cooperation, or more social and economic equality – none of these now primarily requires a large-scale change in ownership for their fulfilment; still less is such a change a sufficient condition of their fulfilment.
>
> (Crosland, 1956: 365)

The Conservative Party realized that there was deep-rooted public support for the welfare state. It made no attempt to dismantle it during its long years in government. The welfare state ensured socio-economic stability. It allowed the elite to continue to occupy its privileged position safely, without the threat of radical measures to overthrow them, such as through a root-and-branch attack on private education. This constituted an implicit contract between the British elite and the mass of the working population.

As the Labour Party moved away from a dogmatic interpretation of Clause IV towards a more pragmatic approach, the ideological differences between the Labour and Conservative Parties narrowed. Under the Labour Government nationalization was extended to the steel industry (1967), British Leyland (automobiles), British Shipbuilding and British Aerospace (all in 1977). However, these decisions were guided less by an ideological belief in nationalization than in the weak condition of these industries. The main criterion distinguishing the two main political parties in the eyes of the electorate became their perceived competence to manage the mixed economy effectively rather than fundamental ideological difference. Indeed, it was Edward Heath's Conservative Government (1970–74) that implemented the main advance towards a more egalitarian state education system. Under the Labour Government of 1964 to 1970 the process was begun to transform the two track system of grammar schools and secondary modern schools into a unified 'comprehensive school' system, which abolished the eleven-plus. All pupils in state secondary schools would now attend the same type of school. However, it was Mrs. Thatcher, Minister of Education in Edward Heath's Government, who implemented the transformation of the state secondary school system into one based on comprehensive schools. Although large inequalities remained within the state educational sector, the measure had a significant impact on the British class structure.

Between 1939 and 1979 membership of trade unions climbed to new heights, increasing from 6.2 million to 12.6 million. By 1980 trade union density in Britain was 54 per cent of the employed workforce, compared with 41 per cent in Germany, 22 per cent in the United States, and 17 per cent in France (Brown, 2003: 400). In the 1950s labour relations were remarkably stable, with a high degree of industrial peace. Throughout the 1950s and 1960s less than four million working days were lost annually through industrial action (Brown, 2003: 400). An important part of the stability of the industrial relations system was the centralized system of central bargaining over wages and conditions of work that had evolved over decades. The structure of worker-employer negotiation was heavily influenced by the wartime experience. During the war no less than forty-six national bargaining bodies – the 'joint industrial councils'– had been established. In the 1950s and 1960s over three-quarters of pay-fixing arrangements were carried out either by industry level multi-employer agreements or by wages councils (Brown, 2003: 402). It was a 'remarkably centralized national bargaining system' (Brown, 2003: 406). It was also a 'voluntary' one, in which the courts were 'effectively excluded from collective bargaining and industrial disputes' (Brown, 2003: 405). The spread of collective bargaining contributed to a narrowing of pay distribution, and the spread of trade union membership to less-skilled workers helped to narrow skill differentials (Brown, 2003: 408).

In this period the trade union movement, both official and unofficial, steadily gained strength. A number of factors contributed to the growing self-confidence of ordinary workers. Independently of which party was in power, government spending on social services rose steadily from the early 1950s to the late 1970s. The share of social services spending as a share of GDP increased from 14.1 per cent in 1950, to 16.9 per cent in 1960, 20.0 per cent in 1970 and reached 25.4 per cent in 1980 (Harris, 2014: 142). Despite serious deficiencies in the state sector and the continued existence of a significant private sector, the era witnessed great overall progress in educational provision for the mass of the population. The school-leaving age was raised to sixteen in 1972, and the number of pupils in state secondary schools rose from two million in 1951 to 4.1million in 1970 (Millward, 2014: 401). Despite serious issues surrounding the nature of public sector housing, including the construction of huge 'council estates' remote from city centres and the move towards high-rise blocks, there was large progress in working-class housing. The share of public sector employment rose throughout the era. Employment in the government sector increased from 8 per cent of the total workforce in 1937, to 14 per cent in 1951 and reached 21 per cent in 1979 (Millward, 2014: 391 and 411). If employment in the nationalized industries is included, the share of the public sector in total employment in 1981 was 27.4 per cent (Glynn, 2006: 44). The public sector provided an unprecedented degree of security of employment for a large fraction of the British working population. Low levels of unemployment reinforced workers' sense of security. The standard of living of the British working population continued to rise throughout this period. Underpinning the rise in the standard of living was accelerated growth of GDP. The average annual growth rate rose from 1.3 per cent in 1911 to 1950 to 2.3 per cent in 1950 to 1990 (Broadberry, 2014: 325). The rate of growth of average real earnings accelerated, rising from an annual average of 1.47 per cent between 1913 and 1951 to 2.72 per cent between 1951 and 1973 (Gazeley, 2014: 153). These factors helped to increase the self-confidence of the British working population.

The international context also played a central role in facilitating the increased bargaining power of trade unions. Throughout the period from 1945 to 1979 British firms and their employees were relatively insulated from international competition within their home market. The giant economy of the Soviet bloc was inward-looking, with its own internal division of labour, specialization and exchange within COMECON (The Council for Mutual Economic Assistance). The countries of the Soviet bloc had little interest in, or capability of, competing in any Western market. China, with hundreds of millions of workers, was even more isolated from the global economy. By the time Chairman Mao died in 1976 it was a minnow in terms of global economic power. India was locked into an inward-looking pattern of development, heavily influenced by the Soviet Union, which supplied the core of its state-owned, heavy-industrial plants. Its large state-owned sector and powerful, but heavily protected, private-sector industrial groups were incapable of competing in Western markets. Large parts of the rest of the developing world, including potential giants such as Brazil, pursued import-substitution behind protectionist barriers. Their indigenous firms were almost invisible in Western markets.

A large segment of the British economy, including both manufacturing and services, was owned by the state. Competition with foreign firms was almost absent from these sectors. The world's largest private sector manufacturing firms, including British ones, had their main markets within their own national boundaries, as did the service sector firms for whom they were their main customers. Cross-border mergers and acquisitions were only a small part of international business practice, constrained by large cultural differences, capital controls and government protectionism. Consequently, production by foreign subsidiaries formed only a small share of the total output of the world's largest firms in the developed countries. In the case of the UK, in 1980 the stock of inward Foreign Direct Investment (FDI) amounted to 12 per cent of GDP and the stock of outward Foreign Direct Investment amounted to 15 per cent (UNCTAD, 1996: 262). With the notable exception of the auto industry, where Ford and GM subsidiaries were important parts of the UK economy, there were few sectors in which foreign firms held a large market share. Equally, with the notable exception of the oil industry, there were few British firms that had a large market share in other developed economies.

In the 1960s there developed a tendency for bargaining over pay and conditions of work to take place increasingly at the enterprise level, with a greater role for grass-roots unofficial trade union leaders, the so-called 'shop stewards'. The trend towards plant-level bargaining was accompanied by increasing industrial militancy. The process was widely perceived to contribute to wage inflation. In order to address the issue, a succession of governments, both Labour and Conservative, attempted to establish national-level bodies that contained representatives of trade unions, employers and government. These included the Conservative Government's National Economic Development Council (established in 1962), as well as the Labour Party's National Board for Prices and Incomes (established in 1964) and the Commission on Industrial Relations (established in 1968). However, the level of strike intensity reached new heights in the early 1970s, culminating in the national miners' strikes of 1972 and 1973. The 1972 strike caused immense disruption due to the impact on electricity supply. The 1973 strike was accompanied by 'flying pickets', which were mobile groups that organized blockades of coal storage depots. Faced with the threat of another national miners' strike in 1974, Edward Heath's Conservative government called a general election, which it lost.

Heath's 'defeat at the hands of the miners' stimulated wide public debate about the relationship of trade unions to society and politics. The Labour Government (1974–1979) attempted to solve the 'problem of industrial relations' through the so-called 'Social Contract', which proposed a statutory ceiling on pay rises in return for a package of rights, including the Employment Protection Act (1974), the Sex Discrimination Act (1975) and the Race Relations Act (1976). A core part of the Contract was the establishment of the Advisory, Conciliation and Arbitration Service (ACAS). Its objective was to 'ensure that industrial relations disputes remained in the hands of the industrial relations specialists and out of the normal courts' (Brown, 2003: 411). However, when the Labour Government proposed in 1978 an 'ambitiously low target for pay increases' there followed the 'Winter of Discontent' with massive nationwide strikes in the country's public services, including essential services such as refuse collection. The defeat of the Labour Government in the 1979 General Election, which resulted in a large majority for the Conservative Government, ushered in a fundamentally new era of class struggle in Britain.

1979–2015

The 1970s marked a watershed for class struggle in Britain, as indeed, across all of the high-income countries. The era of 'capitalist globalization' witnessed bewildering changes that transformed class relations and the nature of class struggle in Britain. The competitive environment in which British business operated changed dramatically after 1979, which had profound consequences for class relations. Class struggle in Britain became more deeply inter-connected than ever with global class struggle. The emerging shape of this struggle is still only dimly visible and weakly understood by politicians and the mass of the working population alike.

Developments within the 'communist' countries strongly influenced the outlook of the British labour movement during this period. A wide array of publications and media discussions helped shape perceptions of 'communism' not only among the general public in the UK, but also within the left-wing of British politics. A large body of Western scholarly literature identified the period of War Communism (1917–1921) as the critical era in which the system of inter-twined, centralized economic and political power was established in the Soviet Union (e.g., Carr, 1950, 1952; Shapiro, 1970; and Liebman, 1975). The same system formed the institutional foundations of other countries ruled by communist parties. They were almost all heavily influenced by the Soviet Union in constructing their 'Marxist-Leninist' ideologies and constitutions, as well as their political and government structures. Publications such as Robert Conquest's *The Great Terror* (1968) and *Kolyma: The Arctic Death Camps* (1978), and, especially, Alexander Solzhenitsyn's *Gulag Archipelago* (English edition, 1974), reinforced apprehensions within the left-wing of British politics about one-party communist rule. In the early 1980s it became increasingly clear from China's own national census data that the country had experienced a demographic disaster after the 'Great Leap Forward'. Western scholars used the data to estimate that as many as 25–30 million people had died during the famine. At the same time information emerged about the horrors committed by the Communist Party of Kampuchea (Khmer Rouge) during their rule over Cambodia between 1975 and 1979. By the mid-1980s little sympathy remained even among the left-wing of British politics for a 'Leninist revolution' led by a communist 'vanguard' party. Ultra-left, non-parliamentary organizations shrank into insignificance.

The problems of 'centrally planned' economies became increasingly clear from the 1960s onwards. Hungary attempted to move towards a form of 'market socialism' in 1968, with the introduction of the New Economic Mechanism. The

USSR implemented a succession of partial reforms in an unsuccessful effort to reverse the trend of decline in the rate of economic growth and stagnation of living standards after the 1960s. From the late 1950s through to the mid-1970s a succession of Chinese policy makers expressed their disagreement with the effort to suppress market forces and run the economy through administrative planning. They mostly suffered politically and personally for their views. Reform began as soon as Chairman Mao died in 1976. The intention to 'reform and open up' was formalized at the Third Plenum of the Eleventh Central Committee of the Chinese Communist Party in December 1978. The Chinese Communist Party set out on a 'New Long March' to reform fundamentally the economic system following the experimental approach of 'groping for stones to cross the river'. In 1986 the new Soviet leader Mikhail Gorbachev set in motion the policies of *'glasnost'* and *'perestroika'* that led quickly to the destruction of the CPSU and the disintegration of the Soviet Union as a political entity. This laid the foundation for the comprehensive dismantling of the centrally planned economy and facilitated comprehensive political and economic reform throughout Eastern Europe. The cataclysmic changes in the communist world dealt the final death blow within the mainstream of the Labour Party to the idea that a necessary condition of socialism was state ownership and central planning to replace the power of market forces and the profit motive. In 1995 the Labour Party finally removed the original Clause IV from the Party's Constitution. The move was regarded by the dwindling left wing both inside and outside the Labour Party as a 'setback for the general struggle for' and an indication that the Labour Party had 'abandoned the great historical aim of socialism' (Taffe, 1995).

Britain's role in the global economy shrank dramatically in this era. From being the 'workshop of the world' in the mid-nineteenth century, the UK was reduced to a relatively small part of the global economy. In 1988 the UK's GDP was 89 per cent greater than China's, its manufacturing value-added was 26 per cent greater and its exports were almost four times as great (World Bank, 1990). By 2010 the UK's gross national income (in PPP dollars) was 22 per cent of China's, its manufacturing value-added was 13 per cent of China's and its exports were 26 per cent of China's (World Bank, 2012). By 2010 the UK accounted for just 2.9 per cent of global gross national income (in PPP dollars), 2.7 per cent of world exports and 2.3 per cent of global manufacturing value-added (World Bank, 2012).

Beginning with Mrs. Thatcher's Conservative Government (1979–1990) Britain took the lead globally in the privatization of state-owned assets. The mainly institutional shareholders, who now dominated ownership of the former state-owned enterprises, placed strict performance requirements on the privatized companies, which radically altered their method of operation. Privatization in the state-owned manufacturing sector included British Steel, British Leyland (automobiles and trucks), British Shipbuilders, British Aerospace, British Coal, Rolls Royce and BP. The privatization process included also the public utilities in gas, electricity, water, telecommunications, railways, ports, airports, bus transport, airlines and mail service. The implications for competition were enormous. Profit-seeking private utilities were interested in procuring the best value equipment and services irrespective of the nationality of the supplier. Across large swathes of government services, including hospitals, police, army, prisons and local government, provision of services such as garbage collection and municipal swimming pools was contracted out to private sector firms. These changes revolutionized the nature and intensity of competition in the British economy, with profound implications for the workforce.

The impact of widespread privatization and outsourcing upon the nature of employment was combined with a drastic change in Britain's relationship with the international economy. Liberalization of international trade was spearheaded by the General Agreement on Tariffs and Trades (GATT) and its successor body the World Trade Organization (WTO). In the case of the UK the impact of trade liberalization was relatively muted, as it was already a relatively open economy in terms of the conduct of trade relations. However, the share of exports in GDP increased from 24 per cent in 1990 to 30 per cent in 2010, and over the same period the share of imports increased from 27 per cent to 33 per cent (World Bank, 2004 and 2012). The share of manufactured imports in total domestic demand rose from 25 per cent in 1980 to 62 per cent in 2006 (Brown, 2011), which greatly intensified international competition for the British manufacturing sector.

The transformation of international capital flows was of even greater importance for the UK's class structure and the nature of class struggle. The privatization of large swathes of the economy across much of the world together with liberalization of constraints on international capital flows facilitated a revolutionary transformation in the nature of the large firm. The ownership of large British firms changed drastically during the era of globalization. Between 1975 and 2010 the share of individual shareholders in the ownership of UK quoted firms declined from 38 per cent to 12 per cent. Institutional shareholders of one kind or another now account for 82 per cent of the ownership of UK companies. Between 1975 and 2010 the share of foreign (mainly institutional) shareholders rose from 6 per cent to 41 per cent (Chambers, 2014: 263). Shareholder pressure upon 'British' firms is now global in nature and highly concentrated. For example, in 2013 the top fifty asset management firms accounted for 63 per cent of the $76.4 trillion of funds managed by the five hundred largest global asset managers (Towers Watson, 2013). The top fifteen asset management firms each have over one trillion dollars of assets under management. The top asset manager, Blackrock, has $4.3 trillion of assets under management, compared with the UK's 2012 stock market capitalization of $3.0 trillion.

In 1980 the UK's stock of inward FDI amounted to $63 billion, which was equivalent to 11.7 per cent of the UK's GDP. By 2013 the stock of inward FDI had increased to $1,605 billion (i.e., investment $1.6 trillion), which was equivalent to 63.3 per cent of the UK's GDP (UNCTAD, 1996 and 2014). Multinational firms built their UK businesses both through organic growth and Merger and Acquisition (M&A). In this period a succession of major UK companies was acquired by international firms including Abbey National (Santander), Allied Domeq (Pernod Ricard), Autonomy (HP), BAA (Ferrovial), Barings (ING), Bentley Automobile (VW), BOC (Linde), British Paper Board (St Gobain), British Energy (EDF),

British Steel (Tata), Cadbury (Kraft), Foden Trucks (Paccar), Hanson (Lafarge), ICI (Akzo Nobel), Invensys (Schneider/Siemens), International Power (GDF-Suez), Jaguar-Land Rover (Tata), Jewson (St Gobain), Leyland Trucks (Paccar), Marconi (Ericsson), Midland Bank (HSBC), O2 (Telefónica), Perkins Diesel (Caterpillar), Pilkington Glass (NSG), Rolls Royce Automobile (BMW), Scottish and Newcastle Breweries (Carlsberg/Heineken), Scottish Power (Iberdrola), Smith's Aerospace (GE) and Wellstream (GE). In 2013 there were 45,000 UK subsidiaries of overseas-headquartered companies. They employed more than three million people and they accounted for at least 36 per cent of total UK value-added (Fast Track, 2014). The top fifty subsidiaries of foreign companies employed 785,000 people in the UK.

At the same time that major international firms built their business systems in the UK, firms with their headquarters in the UK expanded their international operations through both organic growth and M&A. In 1980 the UK's stock of outward FDI amounted to $80 billion, equivalent to 14.9 per cent of the UK's GDP. By 2013 the stock had risen to $1,885 billion (i.e., $ 1.9 trillion), equivalent to 74.3 per cent of the UK's GDP (UNCTAD, 1996 and 2014). For most of the UK's leading firms their 'domestic' operations in the UK today constitute a small share of their global operations. Leading 'British' firms such as Anglo-American, Astra Zeneca, BAE Systems, BAT, BP, GKN, GSK, HSBC, Rexam, Rio Tinto, SABMiller, Shell, Standard Chartered, Unilever, Vodafone, and WPP, have at least three-fifths of their assets, employment and sales outside the UK. In addition, a number of leading international companies moved their headquarters and their primary stock market listing to the UK. These included HSBC (from Hong Kong), Anglo-American, SABMiller and Old Mutual (all from South Africa).

These changes in the nature of large firms raise difficult questions about the relevance of traditional approaches to the national identity of firms and about national industrial policy.

The nature of class struggle in the UK is especially complicated due to the role of the financial sector. In 1986 the Conservative Government took the decision to remove the web of protection that had surrounded the City of London's financial institutions. In the early 1980s the leading stockbrokers and merchant banks were all British. The 'Big Bang' opened the City of London to global financial firms and new methods of conducting business, including electronic, screen-based trading. Within a few years almost all the major names of British investment banking had been acquired by global banks, including Morgan Grenfell (Deutsche Bank), Warburg's (UBS), Kleinwort (Dresdner), Smith New Court (Merrill Lynch), Barings (ING), Schroders (Citigroup), Flemings (Chase Manhattan) and Cazenove (JPMorgan). The Midland Bank was acquired by HSBC, which moved its global headquarters to London. The City of London was regulated with a 'light touch' by the UK government with the intention of making the City of London as attractive as possible for global banks. The City of London was already powerful prior to the Big Bang. With hindsight, the Conservative Government correctly understood the potential for the City of London to play a central role in the process of globalization, which had finance at its core. In the process the UK economy has become more 'financialized' than any other major economy. In 1975 the total assets of UK banks, both domestic and foreign, were around the same size as the UK's GDP. By 2013 total bank assets had grown to 4.5 times the size of the UK's GDP. If present trends were to continue, by 2050 total banks assets would be 9.5 times the size of UK GDP (Mark Carney, Governor of the Bank of England, quoted in *Wall Street Journal*, 6 December 2014). The financial services sector accounts for around one-tenth of UK GDP and employs a total of around one million people. If the firms that supply goods and services to the financial services industry and its employees were included, then the share of total UK output and employment dependent on the financial services industry would be far larger.

It is hard to imagine how the financialization of the UK economy could be reversed through 'industrial policy' and the UK returned to an economy such as Japan or Germany in which the share of manufacturing in GDP is 18 per cent and 22 per cent respectively, compared with 10 per cent in the UK (World Bank, 2014). In the 1980s the UK chose to follow a path that built it into arguably the world's leading financial centre. The UK sits at the financial heart of the global-ized economy, intimately connected with the other two great financial centres, New York and Hong Kong. The connection takes place through global, mainly American, financial firms. The connection is not only human and financial but also physical, in the shape of the information technologies supplied mainly by American IT companies. Given the impossibility of going 'back to the future' and re-creating a manufacturing-based economy in the UK, the UK needs to ensure that the price of serving as a core of the world financial system is the education of its population to enable its citizens to obtain high-quality occupations within the long value chain of global financial services. At the same time, the UK has more interest than almost any economy in ensuring not only that the financial system in the UK is well regulated, but also that of the whole global financial system, since the UK is tied to this system irrevocably. A global financial disaster would have especially serious consequences for the UK; however, there is a danger that the short-term interests of highly organized global financial firms, with the American firms at their core, hinder the effective regulation of both the UK's and the global financial systems. This is 'class struggle' indeed!

During the era of globalization the City of London has grown into arguably the world's leading financial centre, with major operations for global banks. In many sectors London is more important than any other financial centre, including even Wall Street. For example, in foreign exchange trading, London accounts for 37 per cent of total foreign exchange transactions, compared with 18 per cent for New York (*Financial Times*, 1 September 2010). The banking sector employs around 100,000 people in central London, mainly in the old City of London and Canary Wharf. Banks with headquarters in other countries employ a large number of people in their London offices. These include 10,000 employees at JPMorgan, 8,000 at Bank of America, 7,000 each at Deutsche Bank and Citigroup, 6,000 each at Goldman Sachs, Morgan Stanley, Crédit Suisse and UBS. International bank employees account for three-quarters of the total banking sector employment in the City of London (*Financial Times*, 14 May 2012). In 2013 in the UK's financial services sector as a whole overseas firms accounted for 47 per cent of all firms with an annual revenue of over £100 million (UKTI, 2014). Close to one-half of the foreign firms in the financial services industry are US-headquartered. The remuneration of the top employees of global banks in London is stratospheric. In 2014, 738 senior staff at five top banks earned a total of £1.3 billion, amounting to £1.8 million per person (*Financial Times*, 2 January 2015). The banks all had their headquarters in the USA: Goldman Sachs, Morgan Stanley, JPMorgan Chase, Bank of America Merrill Lynch, and Citigroup. The highest remuneration was at Goldman Sachs, which paid its 121 leading UK-based staff an average of £3 million each in 2014, of which 85 per cent came from bonuses. In 2011–12 only 2 per cent of UK taxpayers earned a pre-tax income above £100,000 and the top 1 per cent had an average of £147,000 (HM Revenue, 2013).

Many global companies in the non-financial sector also chose to locate core financial operations in London. In addition, there are large operations in London for global firms that service the financial sector. These include global audit companies, such as EY, DeLoitte, KPMG and PWC; global financial information companies, such as Reuters and Bloomberg; global consultancy companies, such as McKinsey, Accenture, Cap Gemini and Boston Consulting Group; global business software companies, such as Oracle and SAP; global telecoms firms, such as BT, Vodafone, Telefónica (O2) and France Télécom (Orange); global media and marketing firms, such as WPP, Omnicom, Interpublic and Publicis; and global law firms, such as Linklaters, Freshfields, Baker McKenzie and DLA Piper. Greater London has around 360,000 people working in the broadly defined financial services sector.

Numerous firms, both indigenous and foreign, provide a wide array of other services for the financial services sector and its employees in London. These include entertainment such as high-end restaurants, concert halls, opera houses, art galleries, auction houses and corporate sports entertainment (e.g., Wimbledon, Lords, Twickenham, Arsenal and Chelsea). In London during globalization there have developed 'external economies of entertainment', which interact symbiotically with the development of global financial sector occupations, to make the city increasingly one of the most desirable locations for the global elite. The services for the global elite include also prosaic daily needs, such as five-star hotels, fast-food outlets, coffee shops, clothes shops, luxury goods shops, gyms, contract cleaners, home helps, nannies, taxis and estate agents. A large fraction of the service workers who work for firms that supply the financial sector and its employees are without fixed contracts, do not belong to a trade union and work for the minimum wage. For every one of the global financial elite in London there may be at least twenty people employed on £10–15,000 per annum, who provide them with services.[10] The high property prices in central London mean that ordinary, low-paid service workers must travel from further and further away in order to meet the needs of the elite who work in and around the financial industry.

The City of London has long been centrally important within the British class structure. Traditionally, the vast bulk of employees were British. At the highest levels of the banking industry, which formerly gravitated around Lombard Street, there was a form of 'gentlemanly capitalism' (Augur, 2000). Leading bankers were drawn from a narrow range of English public schools and mainly were Oxbridge graduates. Since the 1970s the financial elite in London has radically changed in character, with its members drawn from a much wider circle of the global financial elite. Large parts of central London have changed character radically under the influence of the global financial elite residing in London. Their relationship with the rest of British society has become progressively more distant. London does not need to 'declare independence' and control 'immigration' to the city. Inflation of Central London property prices far ahead of the rest of the UK has accentuated the sense of colonization by a global elite, with financial services at the core. The 'voice' of the City of London in British politics was always important. However, the 'voice' is decreasingly a 'British' voice and increasingly the 'voice' of the global financial elite with only the shallowest of roots in British society and politics.

British universities perform a vital function within the global class structure. Thirty years ago non-UK students formed a small share of the UK's post-graduate population. In the UK in 2013 there were 179,000 students studying for full-time higher taught degrees, of whom only 29 per cent were domiciled in the UK and 71 per cent were foreign-domiciled students. Twelve per cent of the total were from Europe and 40 per cent from Asia. Over 60 per cent of the graduate students in Oxford and Cambridge are foreign. A large fraction of the international graduate students studying at UK universities are from high-income and wealth groups within their own country. Graduate study at a leading UK university, especially at Oxford or Cambridge, provides a pathway to employment within the global elite. It provides advanced skills gained through the medium of English, which is the language of the global elite. It also provides a platform of networks that nurtures and sustains a career within the global elite.

During the era of globalization dramatic changes have taken place in the relationship between workers and employers in Britain.

Mrs. Thatcher's Conservative government (1979–90) came to power following the 'winter of discontent'. The new government made clear its intention to contain trade union power. Over the course of the 1980s there were 'many highly publicized and bitter trade union defeats' (Brown, 2003: 415). Increasingly confident employers were backed by the government in their confrontation with the trade unions. The most important defeats for trade union strike action were in the state-owned steel and coal industries. In 1980 a three-month strike in the steel industry ended in defeat for the trade unions. The miners' strike of 1984 in the coal industry involved violent confrontation between the police force and the strikers. After eleven months of bitter struggle the miners were defeated and returned to work. The number of pits fell sharply and the coal industry was privatized in 1987. The once vast mining industry almost disappeared. Over the course of the 1980s the membership of the National Union of Mineworkers declined from over 250,000 to just under 10,000 (Brown, 2003: 415).

Between 1980 and 1993 a sequence of Conservative Government legislative measures radically changed the legal context in which trade unions operated, making strikes and trade union organization more difficult. The anti-strike legislation narrowed the definition of a lawful strike mainly by banning secondary picketing as well as action that could be considered 'political' (Brown, 2003: 415). It restricted picketing, required union leaders to repudiate unofficial strikes, permitted selective dismissal of strikers and prevented unions from disciplining members who refused to take part in official action. Most importantly, it established a precise balloting procedure, which gave rise to the routine use of strike ballots as a normal part of the bargaining procedure. Other measures were designed to increase accountability and representativeness of trade unions (Brown, 2003: 416). The enforcement of the closed shop was made illegal and employees were given the right to join any union or none. Trade unions' national executives were required to be elected directly by the membership. Ballots had to be held if a union wished the employer to collect union dues or if the union wished to conduct a levy from members for political campaigning. Any member could inspect unions' financial and membership records, and a new commissioner was established to carry out enquiries into abuses of trade union internal authority. The main part of the legislation designed to curb trade union powers was passed during Mrs. Thatcher's government. However, it mostly remained in place under the Labour governments of 1997–2010.

The swathe of legislation made striking more difficult and increased the authority of trade union leadership compared with the grass roots activists. The legislation was of great symbolic significance, although it was not the main factor that contributed to the radical change in the relationship between employers and employees during the era of globalization. The enormous change taking place in the wider economic and business context was much more significant in bringing about the transformation that took place in labour-management relations. Tightening international competition and the break-up of the public sector 'transformed British industrial relations in the 1980s and 1990s' (Brown, 2003: 416). Trade unions increasingly were confined to bargaining within individual enterprises and unions 'became more like company unions' (Brown, 2003: 417). The underlying economic causes of the collapse in industry-level collective bargaining arrangements were independent of the labour market policies of either the Conservative or Labour governments. Trade unions were less able to mount effective industrial action partly due to the fact that their members were aware of the increasingly hostile product markets in which their employers operated. At least as important was the transformation of the nature of the large firm and conditions affecting the international flow of capital. Large firms in the UK, whether foreign firms with big UK operations or UK firms with big international operations, had a drastically reduced interest in the UK economy. For both groups of companies, the UK was a relatively small part of their overall investment calculation. A necessary condition for large global firms, whether UK-based or international, to invest in the UK was a cooperative relationship with their employees. If the relationship was confrontational, employers could shift their investment elsewhere, either in developed or developing countries. These developments drastically weakened employees' bargaining power with their employers. The relationship of small and

medium-sized British firms (SMEs) to their business customers was also transformed by these developments. The threat by their large customers to expand
investment outside Britain weakened the bargaining power of UK-based SMEs.
This in turn weakened the bargaining powers of the workers in British SMEs.

During the era of globalization there was a dramatic decline in trade union
membership and union militancy. Trade union density declined from 53 per
cent of all employees in 1997 to just 27 per cent in 2009 (Brown, 2003: 400 and
2011: 7). In 2009 the density in the public sector stood at 57 per cent, but in the
private sector it had fallen to only 15 per cent (Brown, 2011: 7–8). The average
number of days lost through strikes fell from an annual average of 11.7 million in
1975–9 to 0.5 million in 1995–9 (Brown, 2003: 403). By 2012 the number of days
lost due to strikes had declined to 0.25 million. The number of strikes per million
trade union members fell from 181 in 1975–9 to twenty-seven in 1995–9, and in
2000–9 it was just nineteen per million (Brown, 2003: 403 and 2011: 8).

From its position as the 'workshop of the world', the UK has advanced more
rapidly than any other major country into a post-manufacturing economy. In 1951
the manufacturing sector employed 8.8 million people, amounting to 39 per cent
of the total workforce (Baines, 1981: 54). By 1982 manufacturing employment
had fallen to 5.6 million, amounting to 21.5 per cent of the workforce. In 2014
manufacturing employment was only 2.6 million, amounting to 7.8 per cent of the
total workforce (Rhodes, 2014: 3–4). Between 1997 and 2008 real manufacturing output stagnated at around £151 billion (gross value-added at 2011 prices). In
2009 manufacturing output fell by over 9 per cent and in 2013 stood at £144 billion, still 5 per cent below the level in 2008 (Rhodes, 2014: 3). In the early 1970s
manufacturing output was more than 30 per cent of UK national output. By 2013
its share had fallen to 9.8 per cent (Rhodes, 2014: 3). The service sector today
accounts for 80 per cent of the UK national output. For UK males 68 per cent of
employment is in the service sector and for females the proportion is 91 per cent
(World Bank, 2012).

Across almost every occupation, the drastic decline of trade unions, the
radically increased pressure of competition in product markets and the rapidly
changing nature of work due to the impact of information technology have greatly
increased the degree of employee uncertainty.

The impact of the revolution in information technology has revolutionized the
nature of work and daily life. In almost every sector, from financial services to hospital care, the information technology revolution permits meticulous performance
monitoring in a way that even the futuristic classics such as Zamyatin's *We* and
Huxley's *Brave New World* could not imagine. Old occupational classifications
reveal little about the nature of work. Even in the manufacturing sector, the nature
of work has altered radically in the era of globalization. A large share of manufacturing in the UK today consists of high value-added products, which involve
the application of information technology rather than physical force. A wide array
of routine manual occupations has been replaced by computerization. The most
striking example is the extensive use of robots in car assembly, which is the UK's
largest manufacturing sector. The overall degree of physical arduousness of work

has declined alongside the pervasive impact of information technology and the shift towards an economy based on services.

The fact that the UK economy is comprehensively dominated by service sector employment does not mean that class struggle has disappeared. George Orwell's observation about the class outlook of non-manual workers is even more relevant today:

> [W]e must drop that misleading habit of pretending that the only proletarians are manual labourers. It has got to be brought home to the clerk, the engineer, the commercial traveller, the middle-class man who has 'come down in the world', the village grocer, the lower-grade civil servant and all other doubtful cases that they are the proletariat. Socialism means a fair deal for them as well as for the navvy and the factory-hand.
>
> (Orwell, 1937: 200)

Educational investment, from pre-school to university, is vital in order to face the profound challenges produced by globalization. There is no sector in which the importance of the state is greater in terms both of equity and the ability of the whole society to face the challenges of globalization collectively. The depth of the challenge is comparable to a war in terms of the necessity of a collective response from the whole society. In fact, in the UK globalization has reinforced and deepened class inequality rendering a common response more difficult. There is a massive and expanding gap between the finance-based global elite in London and a shopper in a 'Poundland' store in a provincial city.

The era of globalization in the UK was accompanied by labour market polarization (Goos and Manning, 2003, and Sissons, 2011). The overall effect on the labour market has been likened to an 'hour glass', with contraction in the middle and expansion at the top and bottom. There has been a growth of both 'lousy' jobs (mainly in low-paying service occupations) and 'lovely jobs' (mainly in professional and managerial occupations in finance and business services) alongside a decline in the number of middling jobs (mainly clerical and skilled manual jobs in manufacturing) (Goos and Manning, 2003). In the lower tiers of the labour market, employment in traditional manual employment greatly declined. The biggest job losses have been in those that are highly routinized, and can be more easily replaced by information technology. Between 1979 and 1997 total employment in ten mainly skilled and semi-skilled manual occupations, fell from 380,000 to 60,000 (Goos and Manning, 2003: 37). Alongside this has gone large expansion of unskilled and low-paid 'elementary' jobs (Sissons, 2011). Many jobs in the service sector involve physical labour with a low degree of skill. It is difficult for information technology to replace humans in many of these tasks. Ordinary jobs in a wide array of service activities, including restaurants, cleaning, gardening, garbage collection, childcare, old-people care, hotels, and hospitals, involve manual labour. They are often of an arduous nature with a high degree of pressure from private sector employers under scrutiny from institutional shareholders in large firms or in owner-managers in SMEs. Between 1979 and 1999 the number of 'assistants' in education, personal care and hospital wards increased almost fivefold, from 157,000 to 744,000 (Goos and Manning, 2003: 35). Their average hourly wage in 1979 was £2.3–£2.6 per hour, well below the median national wage of £3.1 per hour. At the same time there was substantial growth in high-skill, high-wage professional and managerial occupations. For example, between 1979 and 1997 the number of software engineers, computer programmers and computer systems managers increased from 153,000 to 654,000, and the number of financial sector managers increased from 145,000 to 443,000 (Goos and Manning, 2003: 35). In 1979 the median hourly earnings of these groups was between £4.5 and £5.1 per hour, 50–60 per cent above the median national hourly wage. If the 'hour glass' characterization is correct, the question arises: to what degree will those at the top of the hour glass be willing to support state-funded social welfare to benefit those at the base of the hour glass?

The radical changes in both product and labour markets strongly affected the distribution of income and wealth in the UK. Inequality of income distribution remained relatively stable between the late 1940s and the 1960s. Thereafter the distribution of income became increasingly unequal.

The Gini coefficient of overall UK pre-tax income distribution increased from 0.33 in 1969 to 0.53 in 2001–2002 (Gazeley, 2014: 174). Although inequality in final income greatly increased, through the impact of direct taxation and benefits in kind, the welfare state helped to contain the extent of final income inequality. Although highly unequal, the post-tax income of the bottom 90 per cent of UK taxpayers is confined within a relatively narrow range, between £7,690 for the bottom percentile to £40,000 for the ninetieth percentile (HM Revenue, 2013). Between 1969 and 2001–2 the Gini coefficient for inequality in final income distribution (including the effect of direct taxation and benefits in kind) increased sharply, from 0.25 to 0.33 (Gazeley, 2014: 174). In part, this was due to a reduction in the 1980s in the highest marginal rate of income tax from 70 per cent to 40 per cent. However, in terms of overall measures of inequality after taking account of taxes and benefits the level of inequality in the UK is still relatively low in historical terms. The welfare state still performs a critically important function in containing income inequality among the main body of the British population.

The biggest changes in inequality in the UK during globalization have taken place at the upper end of the distribution. The share of the top 10 per cent in UK pre-tax personal income fell from 47 per cent in 1910 to 30 per cent in 1950 and remained at roughly this level until the 1970s. Between 1970 and 2010 their share increased from 28 per cent to 42 per cent (Picketty, 2014: 323). The share of the top 1 per cent fell from 22 per cent of total pre-tax income in 1910 to 11 per cent in 1950, and kept falling until the 1980s. Between 1980 and 2010 their share increased from 6 per cent to 15 per cent (Picketty, 2014: 317). The share of the top 0.1 per cent of the population fell from 11 per cent of total pre-tax income in 1910 to 3.2 per cent in 1950 and reached a low point of 1.2 per cent in 1980. By 2010 their share had returned to 5.6 per cent (Picketty, 2014: 319). The issue of the appropriate tax rate on the highest incomes is of great importance for the degree of social cohesion and ensuring a 'community of trust'. The reduction in the highest marginal rate of tax from 70 per cent to 40 per cent was highly symbolic in terms of the nature of UK society. The marginal tax rate on high incomes is especially important in the UK due to the presence of a small segment at the apex of the elite who earn exceptionally large pre-tax incomes. In 2010 the highest rate was raised to 50 per cent, but this is still far below the rate in the 1970s.

After 1945 the impact of inheritance and other taxes on wealth reduced UK wealth inequality. The share of the top 10 per cent fell from over 90 per cent of wealth in 1910 to around 62 per cent in the 1970s. By 2010 the share of the top 10 per cent had returned to 70 per cent. The share of the top 1 per cent increased from 22 per cent in 1970 to 29 per cent in 2010 (Picketty, 2014: 344). After the global financial crisis of 2008–2009 the easy availability of debt at a minimal interest rate helped to stimulate a boom in 'asset' prices, including the stock market, government bonds, and London house prices. This helped to accelerate the increase in wealth inequality in the UK.

A recent large-scale study of social class in Britain (Savage, et al., 2013) divides the population into three broad classes.[11] The lowest class contains 48 per cent of the sample population. It includes three main sub-groups: the 'emergent service workers', with a household income of £21,000; the 'traditional working class', with a household income of £13,000; and the so-called 'precariat', with a household income of £8,000. The 'middle class' contains 46 per cent of the sample population and also includes three main sub-groups: the 'new affluent workers' with a household income of £29,000; the 'technical middle class' with a household income of £37,000; and the 'established middle class' with a household income of £47,000. The 'established middle class' contains a quarter of the population, tends to live away from southeast England, and 'might be seen as the comfortably off bulwark of British society' (Savage, et al., 2013: 16). The 'elite' class contains 6 per cent of the sample population, with a household income of £89,000. The elite group has 'very high economic capital', 'high social capital' and 'very high highbrow cultural capital'. It is an 'exclusive grouping with restricted upward mobility into its ranks'. The elite are disproportionately concentrated in London and southeast England. The survey's findings 'clearly demonstrate the power of a relatively small, socially and spatially exclusive group at the apex of British society, whose economic wealth sets them apart from the great majority of the population' (Savage, et al., 2013: 16).

The rising inequality in income and wealth in the UK during the era of globalization has taken place alongside long-term decline in the rate of growth of output and average earnings. The average annual growth rate of GDP declined from 3.2 per cent in the 1980s, to 2.7 per cent in the 1990s, falling to 1.5 per cent in 2000–2012 (World Bank, 2004 and 2014). The UK's GDP declined absolutely after the global financial crisis and only regained the level of 2008 at the end of 2013. Average real wage growth fell from 2.9 per cent in the 1970s and 1980s, to 1.5 per cent in the 1990s, to 1.2 per cent in the 2000s. Between 2010 and 2013 real wages fell at 2.2 per cent per year (Taylor, et al., 2014).

The UK has a uniquely powerful system for perpetuating class inequalities inter-generationally, namely the private ('public') school system. Only seven per cent of the British school population attend private schools. A small proportion of students are awarded means-tested bursaries, but the vast majority of students pay fees. The total fees for the leading private schools are between £150,000-£175,000 for full cost boarding from the age of 13–18. Entry to top private schools is selective, so investment in high-quality preparatory school education is typically a necessary part of the overall education investment package. Fees for a top preparatory school are around £12,000 per annum. In other words, the total private school education fee package costs around £250,000 per child. For those people who are struggling on the fringe of the upper class the requisite investments can be financially crippling and involve a high degree of risk, in the event that the 'invested child' fails to secure the necessary returns from the educational investment.

The principle reason that the British elite is willing to pay such high fees is the potential return in terms of life-time earnings from the educational investment. Although the share of foreign students at British private schools is still small, it is rising fast. It is quite likely that the share will continue to rise. Equally, given the high rate of return from this investment and the access it provides to the global elite, the real price of education at elite British private schools is likely also to increase. Compared with state schools, private schools have far smaller class sizes, much more homogenous social background of pupils, fewer disruptive pupils and a strong financial incentive for the school to ensure high academic results for their pupils. Having their children at a private school also reinforces the parents' social status as part of the British elite. Attending a private school allows their children to acquire the markers of superior class status, especially language, but includes also cultural markers, such as music and theatre, as well as elite sports skills, such as rowing, cricket, rugby, tennis and golf. However, these social markers are also competitive attributes in many segments of the job market. Investment on such a scale is possible only for a small minority of the population. The biggest single prize, both financially and socially, for the educational investment is gaining entry to Oxbridge. The proportion of state school Oxbridge undergraduates increased from around 44 per cent in 1970 to around 55 per cent today (Bolton, 2014). However, the proportion of private school entrants to Oxbridge is many times greater than their share of the school population, i.e., 45 per cent compared with 7 per cent. In terms of the returns to investment it makes more sense to invest £250,000 in a child's private education than to leave the child £250,000 in a will, which is, moreover, subject to death duties. The level of tuition fees payable by UK students at top UK universities is currently £9,000 per annum, which is a low level compared to the cost of private school education and in relation to the return from the investment in terms of probable lifetime earnings. This constitutes a partial compensation for the elite for their large investment in private school education.

Investment in private school education greatly increases the chances of admission to an elite university, which in its turn greatly increases the chance of admission to the highly-paid occupations within the global elite, within which the British elite occupies a significant place. People who were educated at private schools are greatly over-represented in the upper echelons of the British class structure, including the City of London. Although only 7 per cent of the British population were educated at private schools, they account for 26 per cent of BBC executives, 42 per cent of senior TV, film and media executives, 53 per cent of diplomats, 62 per cent of senior armed forces officers, and 71 per cent of senior judges. Those educated in private schools are still disproportionately important in politics. One-half of members of the House of Lords were educated at private schools. In 2013, 36 per cent of the Cabinet, 55 per cent of junior ministers and one-third of MPs (74 per cent of Conservative MPs and 41 per cent of Labour MPs) were educated at private schools.

The radical decline in manual occupations, combined with the steep decline in trade union membership posed a major challenge for the Labour Party. The trade unions had been the mainstay of Labour Party support since its foundation.[12] The collapse of state ownership and central planning in the countries ruled by communist parties removed an ideological foundation that had sustained the left-wing of the Party since the 1920s. The Labour Party is as bewildered as the Conservative Party by the explosive transformation of information technology that penetrates daily lives in the workplace and in the home, as well as when people move around on foot and in vehicles. The political class as a whole is bewildered by the internationalization of British firms and the deep penetration of international capital into the core of the UK economy and the upper echelons of the UK class structure. Neither political party has developed a philosophy for dealing with the polarization of British society in the face of globalization. The indigenous elite is increasingly penetrated by and is simultaneously penetrating the global elite: the global elite is 'inside our elite' and our elite is 'inside the global elite'. The main body of the working population feels more distant from the global elite even than it was from the national elite prior to globalization. Membership of the Conservative Party declined from around three million in the 1950s to around 1.2 million in the 1970s, falling to 150,000 today. Membership of the Labour Party declined from around one million members in the 1950s to around 700,000 in the 1970s, falling to 190,000 today.

The welfare state and the revolution in information technology are sources of British social stability.

The welfare state has changed the methods it employs in order to deliver its services, including greatly increased use of outsourcing and a revolution in the application of information technology. However, the basic principles are unchanged since the 1940s. The welfare state provides a foundation of security for the main body of the British working population. UK expenditure on social services as a share of UK GDP rose from 20 per cent in 1970 to 25 per cent in 1980 and reached 31 per cent in 2011 (Harris, 2014: 142). Performance of this function was vital during the depth of the global financial crisis. The political consequences of severe erosion of the welfare state can be seen from the example of Greece. The country's social safety net was 'a grand achievement of the post-1974 democratic era that came with the prosperity spurred by EU membership' (Hope and Barber, 2015). Since the onset of the global financial crisis, average incomes in Greece have fallen by one-third and the unemployment rate is nearly 28 per cent of the workforce. Pensions have been reduced by an average of 40 per cent; most unemployment benefits are cut after twelve months; and charges for prescription medicines have risen by around one-third. As a result Greece faces a deep political and social crisis with its social cohesion deeply undermined.

The revolution in information technology provides instantaneous access to knowledge, as well as continuous on-line entertainment, including sports, 'movies', pornography and social networks, at an ever-falling real price. The UK is moving towards the dystopian world prefigured in the novels of Zamyatin, Huxley, Stapledon and Orwell. However, the vast majority of people regard this as tremendous progress in their well-being. It conveys a sense of personal 'empowerment' with the world of 'tweets' and 'blogs' open to all. Conventional measures of real income and welfare are unable to capture the full extent of the impact of the revolution. Up until this point in the high-income countries, including the UK, the 'pacifying' effect of the revolution upon social stability has greatly exceeded its potentially de-stabilizing effect. The information technology revolution has not taken place through national planning by government. Rather, it has taken place through ferocious competition between a small number of global oligopolies, almost all headquartered in the USA, including Microsoft, Google, IBM, Oracle, Facebook, Apple, Qualcomm, Intel, Cisco Systems, HP and Texas Instruments. However, the positive effect on social stability may exceed that of the revolution in 'cheap luxuries' in the 1930s.

The mass of the working population has little desire or capability to engage in overt class struggle in the face of growing inequality in which the indigenous British elite is deeply inter-twined with the global elite and feels decreasing identity with the mass of the working population in the UK. While the global elite is increasingly inter-connected, the mass of working people in the UK have almost no connection with the mass of working people across the world, other than through the consumption of common entertainment in the form of global 'movies', 'music' and sports events. Up until this point 'class struggle' in the UK in the era of globalization has been replaced by political apathy among the main body of the working population, which is reflected in the decline in voter turnout from 75 to 80 per cent for most of the 1970s and 1980s to 60 to 65 per cent in the general elections held since the year 2000. There is no sign of 'class warfare' on the horizon in the UK. The global financial crisis of 2008–2009 saw no outburst of 'class warfare' in the UK, despite great popular anger against 'bankers'. Nor has the period since then seen 'class warfare' despite stagnation in the UK economy and a decline in average real wages. The 'Occupy London' movement from October 2011 to June 2012 was peaceful, relatively short-lived and had minimal impact on the general public or on British politics. However, the nature of class struggle might change in the event of a second global financial crisis. The global financial crisis of 2008–2009 may only have been resolved temporarily through the 'cheap money' policy of Western governments, including that of the UK. There is a high probability that the renewed asset bubble set in motion by these policies will burst at some point. In such a crisis the UK would unavoidably take centre stage due to the importance of its financial sector. Moreover, in common with other high-income countries, the UK has a high level of both personal and government debt, which would make it difficult for the government to manage a second crisis. The way in which this might affect class struggle in the UK is an open question. Is it conceivable that Britain's deep integration into the financial core of the global economy could result in a violent resolution of the class contradictions in the country's service-based, finance-dominated economy? If the welfare state were to be seriously threatened, that possibility would increase. The way in which the different segments of the UK social structure might respond to another financial crisis is an open question: 'when the tide goes out, the rocks appear'.

Conclusion

This chapter has analyzed the long-run evolution of 'class struggle' in Britain from the mid-eighteenth to the early twenty-first century. In each of these four phases attention was drawn to a single author who was especially significant in his analysis of class struggle in Britain, namely, Friedrich Engels, J.S. Mill, George Orwell and R. H. Tawney. There is no comparable figure to whom one can turn for analysis of class struggle in Britain in the era of globalization.

The first era, which lasted from 1750–1867, was characterized by gaping class differences between the elite and the mass of the working population. Engels' *Condition of the English Working Class* remains the most thorough and comprehensive account of life for ordinary workers in the early factory cities. The mass of the working class was denied the vote throughout this period. Workers' 'combinations' were illegal for most of this period. Even after they were made legal, a wide array of legal restrictions limited the actions that workers' in combination could take to achieve their ends. There were innumerable local conflicts, often violent, in which workers clashed with local police and military forces. However, none of these was on a scale that could be termed 'class warfare'. The most violent confrontation by far was in the early part of the period during the Gordon Riots in London. The riots were not stimulated by class warfare. They were a consequence of inchoate mob anger rather than an attempt either to overthrow the system of political rule or to advance workers' rights in the workplace. Even though workers did not have the vote, during the latter part of this period, they and those in the elite who supported them, lobbied MPs to introduce legislation to ameliorate the worst abuses of factory workers. They also lobbied energetically for extension of the franchise beyond a narrow group of property owners. Engels (1845) was convinced that the ameliorative measures were insufficient to prevent open 'class warfare'.

The second phase of class struggle lasted from 1867 until 1914. After a long struggle by workers themselves and by their supporters in the elite, including figures such as J. S. Mill, the franchise was greatly extended, including, by the mid-1880s, the majority of adult males. Political parties needed to consider much more carefully than hitherto the needs and demands of the mass of the voting population. A wide array of social legislation was passed that significantly affected the conditions of both work and daily living for the mass of the working population. During this era the British economy continued to grow strongly. Average living standards of the mass of the population improved significantly, albeit with deep pockets of absolute poverty. The working class increasingly organized itself in trade unions to defend its interests in the struggle with employers over wages and conditions of work. A small number of workers entered Parliament as members of the established political parties. At the turn of the century the trade unions decided to organize their own political party, which was formalized under the name 'Labour Party'. The link between trade unions and the Labour Party remains a key aspect of class struggle in Britain right up until today. There were major confrontations between trade unions and employers during this period. However, the influence of the ultra-left, who wished to use strike action for wider political purposes, remained a small part of the overall tapestry of class struggle. The 'class warfare' that Engels had predicted in 1845 in *The Condition of the Working Class in England* did not come about.

The third phase of class struggle lasted from 1914 until 1945. During this phase the final reforms to the franchise were put into place, so that the right to vote was extended to all adult males and to adult women. Although the number of Labour MPs increased substantially, the Labour Party was unable to command a clear majority in Parliament. It twice formed a minority government during peacetime; however, these were both short-lived, and the Labour Party's policy choices were tightly constrained by its minority position. The 'General Strike' was the largest strike action in British history. Despite the use of troops, the strike was almost entirely peaceful. During the Great Depression the level of industrial conflict was relatively muted. Despite high levels of unemployment during the depth of the Depression, the British economy continued to grow in the inter-war period, and over the whole period, living standards for the mass of the population improved. Continuing pressure from the grass roots of the Labour Party and trade unions helped to sustain continued slow progress in government legislation to improve social welfare for the mass of the population. In both World Wars, and especially in World War II, the Labour Party and the trade unions became deeply involved in the government. The impact of the Great Depression and the sense of community engendered by World War II helped to create a widespread sense across all political parties of the need to extend greatly the welfare state. These hopes were crystallized in the 'Beveridge Report', produced in 1942 under the wartime coalition government. In 1918 the Labour Party introduced 'Clause IV' into its Constitution. Although the clause was ambiguous, it was interpreted by most people inside and outside the Party as committing the Labour Party to comprehensive nationalization of 'the means of production, distribution and exchange'. For many people on the left-wing of British politics nationalization remained a necessary condition of 'Socialism'. The inter-war period saw a growing popular concern in Britain, reinforced by developments in the Soviet Union, of the possibility of 'totalitarian' dictatorship, with central control of the economy and the government system. Even though the Soviet 'planned economy' was a beacon of hope for some people on the left wing of British politics, the main body of working people in Britain showed little inclination to follow a revolutionary path. The British Communist Party only attracted a tiny number of votes in the inter-war years, even during the depth of the Great Depression.

The fourth phase of class struggle covers the period 1945–1979. This phase saw substantial cross-party agreement on the need to construct and maintain a welfare state that ensured equal access for all citizens to public health services and education, and publicly organized unemployment and old age insurance. The philosophical foundations of the welfare state were laid during World War II, but the implementation of the detailed measures took place under the Labour Government between 1945 and 1951. The wide array of legislative measures enacted in this period constituted the core of the post-war political consensus. As well as establishing the welfare state, under the Labour Party a substantial part of the economy was nationalized, including both utilities and key industrial enterprises. Many on the left-wing of the Labour Party regarded these measures as the precursor to much more extensive nationalization and state control under future Labour Governments. They attributed the Labour Party's defeat in 1951 and its failure to become established as the natural party of government to its failure to pledge itself to more comprehensive nationalization. The comprehensive failure of parties to the left of the Labour Party casts doubt on this view. During this era British businesses and workers were substantially protected from global competition due to the fact that communist parties ruled a large part of the global population and the 'planned economies' were isolated from the global economy. In addition, a large part of the non-communist developing world pursued inward-looking import substitution policies that limited their interaction with the global business system. Extensive state ownership and capital controls limited international competition among firms from high-income countries. The level of international merger and acquisition was low. The British economy continued to grow strongly in this period. Trade union strength greatly expanded. On the one hand, trade unions at the national level became ever more deeply enmeshed in the process of government. Organized national-level collective bargaining became the main form of interaction between employees and employers; however, at the same time, under the protected circumstances in which British businesses operated, local-level 'shop-steward' militancy increased. Although rarely resulting in physical violence, the British economy became highly strike prone, culminating in the 'Winter of Discontent' in 1978–79.

The fifth phase of class struggle covers the period 1979–2015. Mrs. Thatcher's government (1979–1990) introduced a wide array of legislation in order to reduce the bargaining power of trade unions. In the early 1980s there were some of the fiercest battles in the history of the British trade union movement, including the miners' strike of 1984. In each case the trade unions were defeated by a determined government. In this era the UK comprehensively privatized state-owned industries and utilities. British firms were acquired by global firms on a large scale and UK firms also acquired firms in other countries on a large scale. Global firms are 'inside us' and British firms are 'inside them'. The comprehensive reform of the command economies laid to rest the left-wing belief that a necessary condition of Socialism was a state-owned economy based on the elimination of market forces. The large parts of the world that were isolated from the global economy opened themselves up to the forces of international competition. These forces radically changed the nature of competition in the UK and greatly weakened the position of organized labour. British trade unions were almost powerless to fight these forces and trade union membership plummeted. The radical decline in trade union membership had large implications for the Labour Party, which had been closely connected to the union movement since its inception. The long decline in the relative importance of the manufacturing sector accelerated. By 2014 the sector produced less than one-tenth of total UK output and employed less than 8 per cent of the UK labour force. The British economy had become almost entirely reliant on services. The financial industry, based mainly in London and surrounding areas, had become the core of the British economy. It is an industry with a global position and London is now the home to a wide array of global financial firms with global employees. The British economy and society has become increasingly bifurcated, with an affluent financial and global economy based in London and a far less prosperous economy across the rest of the country. The distribution of income and wealth has become much more unequal, returning to the levels of inequality in pre-war Britain. Class struggle is moderated by the impact of the welfare state, the availability of mass-produced consumer goods produced in low- and middle-income countries at falling real prices and the revolution in information technology, which provides instant entertainment at a low price for almost the whole population. The British private school system continues to be the main instrument for the inter-generational transmission of class differences. The British university system, especially at the post-graduate level, has become a key instrument in the formation of the global elite. 'Class struggle' has been substantially overtaken by class apathy and political detachment.

The future of class struggle in Britain can only be perceived dimly. Through its global financial functions based in London, the UK is more closely linked than any other advanced economy to the core of the global political economy. The sector through which the link takes place is the most lucrative for those who work in it, but also the most fragile, with the greatest potential dangers. The British elite has chosen to shackle itself and the country to this wild horse, with all the benefits and risks involved. The lives of a large fraction of the mass of ordinary people directly and indirectly depend on this industry. They have little understanding of the Faustian pact that their rulers have made. The decision to make the UK a finance-based economy at the forefront of globalization with all the rich implications that this involves, was not put to the voting public in a general election, let alone a referendum. Can any political party pull together the globalized British elite, with its foundation in financial services in London, in order to work with the mass of the country's non-globalized service sector workers towards a common national purpose to face together the challenges of globalization? Is it conceivable that a 'community of trust' can be established in the face of globalization? Such a solution would be possible only if the nature of the UK's true position within the global political economy and its implications for class struggle within the country was faced squarely and honestly. If this is not done, then the future refrain from the mass of the British working population will be: Why did no one tell us?

The term 'class struggle' is flexible and elastic in both the English and German language. Its meaning can stretch from writing books and pamphlets at one end of the spectrum to violent 'class warfare' between workers and armed forces at the other end of the spectrum. In the British case, 'class struggle' only fleetingly approached the violent end of the spectrum. In those cases where the struggle was violent the confrontation was mostly localized and rarely involved serious injury, let alone death. Class struggle in Britain was mainly conducted peacefully, focused on winning political rights for the working class, ameliorating social conditions through Parliamentary legislation and improving wages and conditions of work through collective bargaining. It is difficult to find a suitable Chinese phrase to convey adequately the flexible and elastic nature of the English phrase 'class struggle' and its German equivalent *'Klassenkampf'*. The Chinese translation *'jieji douzheng'* brings to Chinese people's minds the so-called 'class warfare', which was in reality chaotic and violent factional fighting inspired by Chairman Mao during the Cultural Revolution. The long, complex, evolutionary and unfinished process of 'class struggle' in Britain is quite different in nature.

Notes

1. I am grateful to Dr Zhang Jin, University of Cambridge, for a discussion which stimulated me to write this chapter.
2. The English noun 'struggle' is almost always translated into German as *'Kampf'*, and vice versa.
3. The law was not annulled until 1864.
4. O'Brien and Engerman (1981: 169) estimate that real wages rose by 25 per cent between 1790 and 1840. However, they fell steeply during the Napoleonic Wars and did not increase at all between 1816 and 1840.
5. The first edition was published only in German. It was not published in England until 1892. An American edition was published in 1886, but it was not circulated extensively in England.
6. The death penalty remained in force until the 1960s. Between 1900 and 1949 623 people were executed in Britain. The death penalty for murder was halted temporarily in 1965 and formally abolished in 1969. The death penalty for arson in royal dockyards was abolished in 1971, for espionage in 1981, piracy with violence in 1988 and treason in 1998.
7. i.e., Mill's and Harriet Taylor's ideal.
8. Engels' *Condition of the English Working Class* was published in German in 1845, but was not published in English until 1892. Marx and Engels' *Manifesto of the Communist Party* was published in German in 1848, but was not published in English until 1888. Karl Marx's *Capital Vol. 1* was first published in German in 1867, but not published in English until 1887.
9. Tawney was remarkable for the range of his writing, including *Religion and Rise of Capitalism* (1926), *Land and Labour in China* (1932), and the *Acquisitive Society* (1920), as well as *Equality* (1931).
10. In 2011–12 the bottom 30 per cent of UK taxpayers earned a pre-tax income of between £7,740-£14,700 and the bottom 50 per cent earned less than £20,300 (HM Revenue, 2013). In fact, the number of low-paid workers 'servicing' each of the highest-earning financial sector employees may be even greater than this figure indicates.
11. The study was controversial and attracted much criticism, but it remains the most comprehensive empirical analysis of social class in the UK in recent years.

12. The trade unions retain a key role in the Labour Party. Trade unions affiliated to the Labour Party select 12 of the 32 members of the Labour National Executive Committee and elect one-half of the delegates to the Labour Party Conference. Trade unions affiliated to the Labour Party also participate in the election of the Party leader. Under current rules MPs and MEPs, Labour Party members and 'affiliated members' (principally trade unions), each have a one-third (33.3 per cent) share of the vote for the leader. In the final round of voting in the 2010 leadership election, the two candidates were the brothers David and Ed Miliband. David Miliband was Foreign Secretary from 2009–2010 and Ed Miliband was Secretary of State for Energy and Climate Change from 2008–2010. They held contrasting views about how the Labour Party should face the challenges of globalization. David received 17.8 per cent of the MPs/ MEPs' votes and 18.1 per cent of the Labour Party members' votes, while Ed received 15.5 per cent and 15.2 per cent respectively. However, the 'affiliated members' votes were 19.9 per cent for Ed and 13.4 per cent for David. This allowed Ed Miliband to win the overall contest with 50.65 per cent of the votes compared with 49.35 per cent for David Miliband. In other words, trade union votes had been decisive in determining which leader would take the Labour Party into the second decade of the twenty-first century. Soon after the election of Ed Miliband as Party leader, the rules for electing the leader were changed. Henceforth, the Party would vote for a new leader under a 'one person, one vote' system for the whole Party. However, it was decided that trade union members could join the Party as 'affiliated supporters' with the same voting rights as ordinary members, but without paying the £46 membership fee required of ordinary members. It was thought that trade union 'affiliated members' could outnumber full members in the next election for the Party leader.

Bibliography

Abel-Smith, B. (1992) 'The Beveridge Report: Its Origins and Outcomes', *International Social Security Review*, vol. 45, nos. 1–2: 5–16.

Augur, P. (2000) *The Death of Gentlemanly Capitalism*, London: Penguin Books.

Baines, D. (1981) 'Population, migration and regional development', in Floud and McCloskey, eds, 1981.

Baines, D. (1994) 'Population, migration, and regional development, 1870–1939', in Floud and McCloskey, eds, 1994.

Barnett, C. (2001) *The Audit of War*, London: Pan.

Bernays, E. (1928) *Propaganda*, New York: Ig Publishing Company edition, 2005.

Bolton, P. (2014) 'Oxbridge elitism', London: House of Commons.

Broadberry, S. (2014) 'The rise of the service sector', in Floud et al., 2014.

Brown, W. (2003) 'Industrial relations and the economy, 1939–1999', in Floud and Johnson, eds, 2003.

Brown, W. (2011) 'Industrial relations in Britain under New Labour 1997–2010: a post mortem', Cambridge Working Papers in Economics 1121, Faculty of Economics, University of Cambridge.

Bukharin, N. and E. Preobrazhensky (1922) *The ABC of Communism*, London: Penguin edition, with Foreword by E.H. Carr, 1969.

Carr. E.H. (1950) *The Bolshevik Revolution, 1917–1921, vol. 1*, London: Macmillan.

Carr. E.H. (1952) *The Bolshevik Revolution, 1917–1921, vol. 2*, London: Macmillan.

Chambers, D. (2014) 'The City and the corporate economy since 1870', in Floud, et al., 2014.

Cobban, A. (1963) *A History of Modern France, vol. 1: 1715–1799*, Harmondsworth: Penguin Books.

Communist Party of China, Sixth Plenary Session of the Eleventh Central Committee, 1981 *'Resolution on certain questions in the history of our Party since the founding of the People's Republic of China'*, 27 June, in Major Documents, 1991.

Crafts, N. (2014) 'Economic growth during the long twentieth century', in Floud et al., 2014.

Crosland. A. (1956) *The Future of Socialism,* London: Constable edition with Foreword by Gordon Brown, 2006.

Crouzet, F. (1982) *The Victorian Economy,* London: Methuen.

Engels, F. (2009) *The Condition of the Working Class in England,* London: Penguin edition, originally published 1845 in German and 1892 in English.

Engels, F. (1971) *'Introduction to the Civil War in France'*, in Marx and Engels, 1971.

Fast Track (2014) *Inward Investment Track,* London: PA Consulting and UK Trade and Investment.

Feinstein, C.H. (1981) 'Capital accumulation and the industrial revolution', in Floud and McCloskey, eds, 1981.

Feuer, L.S. (1976) Introduction to Mill, 1879.

Floud, R. and D. McCloskey, eds (1981) *The Economic History of Britain since 1700, vol. 1, 1700–1860,* Cambridge: Cambridge University Press.

Floud, R. and D. McCloskey, eds (1994) *The Economic History of Britain since 1700, vol. 2, 1860–1939,* Cambridge: Cambridge University Press, second edition.

Floud, R. and P.A. Johnson, eds (2003) *The Economic History of Britain since 1700, vol. 3, 1939–1999,* Cambridge: Cambridge University Press.

Floud, R. Humphries, J., and P.A. Johnson, eds (2014) *The Cambridge Economic History of Modern Britain, vol. II, 1870 to the present*, Cambridge: Cambridge University Press.

Foster, J.H. (1974) *Class Struggle and the Industrial Revolution,* London: Methuen.

Gazeley, I. (2014) 'Income and living standards', in Floud et al., 2014.

Glyn, A. (2006) *Capitalism Unleashed,* Oxford: Oxford University Press.

Goos, M. and A. Manning (2003) 'Lousy jobs and lovely jobs', London: Centre for Economic Performance, Working Paper.

Harris, B. (2014) 'Health and welfare', in Floud et al., 2014.

Hill, C. (1969) *Reformation to Industrial Revolution,* Harmondsworth: Pelican Books.

Hilton, B. (2006) *A Mad, Bad and Dangerous People, England 1783–1846,* Oxford: Oxford University Press.

HM Revenue and Customs (2013) Income Tax statistics and distributions, London: HM Revenue and Customs.

Hobsbawm, E.J. (1977) *The Age of Capital: 1848–1875,* London: Abacus.

Hope, K. and T. Barber (2015) 'Grasping for relief', *Financial Times,* 3 January.

Horne, A. (1990) *The Fall of Paris,* London: Papermac.

Lenin, V.I. (1992) *The State and Revolution*, Harmondsworth: Penguin, originally published 1917.

Liebman, M. (1975) *Leninism under Lenin,* London: Jonathan Cape.

Lindert, P.H. and J.G. Williamson (1985) *'English workers' living standards during the Industrial Revolution'*, in Mokyr, ed., 1981.

MacKinnon, M. (1994) 'Living standards, 1870–1914', in Floud and McCloskey, 1994.

Marx, K. (1971) 'Marx to F. Domela-Nieuwenhuis', originally written in 1881, and reproduced in Marx and Engels, 1971.

Marx, K. and F. Engels (1971) *On the Paris Commune,* Moscow: Progress Publishers.

Mayhew, H. (2010) *London Labour and the London Poor,* Oxford: Oxford University Press edition, originally published 1861.

Miliband, R. (1961) *Parliamentary Socialism*, London: Merlin Press.

Mill, J.S. (1994) *Principles of Political Economy*, Oxford: Oxford University Press, seventh edition, originally published 1871.

Mill, J.S. (1976) *On Socialism*, New York: Prometheus Books, originally published 1879.

Millward, R. (2014) 'The growth of the public sector', in Floud *et al.*, 2014.

Milton, D., Milton, N. and F. Schurmann (1974) *People's China,* Harmondsworth: Penguin Books.

Mokyr, J., ed. (1981) *The Economics of the Industrial Revolution,* London: George, Allen and Unwin.

Nee, V. (1973) 'Revolution and Bureaucracy: Shanghai in the Cultural Revolution', in Nee and Peck, eds, 1973.

Nee, V. and J. Peck, eds (1973) *China's Uninterrupted Revolution: From 1840 to the Present*, New York: Random House.

Nolan, P. (1995) *China's Rise, Russia's Fall,* London: Macmillan.

O'Brien, P.K. and S. Engerman (1981) 'Changes in income and its distribution during the industrial revolution', in Floud and McCloskey, eds, 1981.

Orwell, G. (1937) *The Road to Wigan Pier*, London: Penguin Books, 1962 edition.

Orwell, G. (1938) *Homage to Catalonia*, London: Penguin Books, 1966 edition.

Orwell, G. (1940) 'Inside the whale', in Orwell, 1961.

Orwell, G. (1944) Review of *The Road to Serfdom*, by F.A. Hayek, and The Mirror of the Past, by K. Zilliacus, in Orwell, 1968.

Orwell, G. (1947) 'Toward European Unity', in Orwell, 1968.

Orwell, G. (1961) *Collected Essays*, London: Secker and Warburg.

Orwell, G. (1968) The *Collected Essays, Journalism and Letters of George Orwell*, London: Penguin Books.

Pelling, H. (1963) *A History of British Trade Unionism*, Harmondsworth: Penguin Books.

Picketty, T. (2014) *Capital in the Twenty-First Century,* Cambridge, MA: Harvard University Press.

Plumb, J.H. (1963) *England in the Eighteenth Century,* Harmondsworth: Penguin Books.

Polanyi, K. (1957) *The Great Transformation*, Boston: Beacon Hill.

Rhodes, C. (2014) 'Manufacturing: statistics and policy', London: House of Commons.

Riley, J. (1994) Introduction to Mill, 1871.

Rude, G. (1952) *Paris and London in the 18th Century,* London: Collins.

Rude, G. (1962) *Wilkes and Liberty*, Oxford: Oxford University Press.

Savage, M. et al., (2013) 'A new model of social class? Findings from the BBC's Great British class survey', *Sociology,* vol. 47 (2), April: 219–250, online version from soc.sagepub.com.

Shapiro, L. (1970) *The Communist Party of the Soviet Union*, London: Methuen.

Simkin, J. (2014) 'Ralph Miliband', *Spartacus Educational* (online).

Sissons, P. (2011) *The Hourglass and the Escalator*, London: The Work Foundation.

Smith, A. (1976) *The Wealth of Nations*, Chicago: University of Chicago Press edition, originally published 1776.

Stapledon, O. (1930) *Last and First Men,* London: Methuen edition, 1978.

Taffe, P. (1995) 'The Labour Party and the abolition of Clause Four', *Militant International Review*, no. 61, Summer.

Taylor, C., Jowell, A. and M. Hardie (2014) 'An examination of falling real wages, 2010–2013', London: Office for National Statistics.

Tawney, R.H. (1951) *Equality*, London: Faber and Faber, 1964 edition, with Introduction by R. Titmuss.

Titmuss, R. (1964) Introduction, Tawney, 1951, reprinted with Introduction by Titmuss, 1964.

Tranter, N.L. (1981) 'The labour supply, 1780–1860', in Floud and McCloskey, eds, 1981.

Trevelyan, G.M. (1965) *British History in the Nineteenth Century and After: 1782–1919*, Harmondsworth: Penguin Books, originally published 1922.

Trotsky, L. (1967) Rev*olution Betrayed*, New York: New Park Publications, originally published 1937.

Towers Watson (2013) *The World's 500 Largest Asset Managers*, New York: Towers Watson.

UK Trade and Investment (UKTI) (2014) *UK Financial Services Industry, Annual Review, 2013*, London: UKTI.

UNCTAD (1996) *World Investment Report*, Geneva: UNCTAD.

UNCTAD (2014) *World Investment Report*, Geneva: UNCTAD.

Unofficial Reform Committee (1912) *The Miners' Next Step*, Tonypandy: Unofficial Reform Committee.

World Bank (1979) *World Development Report*, Washington, DC: Oxford University Press.

World Bank (1990) *World Development Report*, Washington, DC: Oxford University Press.

World Bank (2004) *World Development Indicators*, Washington, DC: World Bank.

World Bank (2012) *World Development Indicators*, Washington, DC: World Bank.

World Bank (2014) *World Development Indicators*, Washington, DC: World Bank.

Zheng, Zhisi (Cheng, Chih-szu) (1966) 'The great lessons of the Paris Commune – In commemoration of its ninety-fifth anniversary', *Peking Review*, no. 16, 14 April, in Milton *et al.*, 1974. Originally published in *Hong Qi* (Red Flag), no. 4, April, 1966.

Index